second
nature

second nature

HOW PARENTS CAN USE NEUROSCIENCE TO HELP KIDS DEVELOP EMPATHY, CREATIVITY, AND SELF-CONTROL

ERIN CLABOUGH, PhD

SOUNDS TRUE
BOULDER, COLORADO

Sounds True
Boulder, CO 80306

This book is not intended as a substitute for the medical recommendations of physicians, mental health professionals, or other health-care providers. Rather, it is intended to offer information to help the reader cooperate with physicians, mental health professionals, and health-care providers in a mutual quest for optimal well-being. We advise readers to carefully review and understand the ideas presented and to seek the advice of a qualified professional before attempting to use them. Some names and identifying details have been changed to protect the privacy of individuals.

Published 2019

Cover design by Rachael Murray
Book design by Beth Skelley

Illustrations by Shelley Li Wen Chen

Printed in Canada

Library of Congress Cataloging-in-Publication Data
Names: Clabough, Erin.
Title: Second nature : how parents can use neuroscience to help kids develop
   empathy, creativity, and self-control / Erin Clabough, PhD.
Description: Boulder, CO : Sounds True, Inc., [2019] |
   Includes bibliographical references.
Identifiers: LCCN 2018019365 (print) | LCCN 2018027963 (ebook) |
   ISBN 9781683640806 (ebook) | ISBN 9781683640790 (pbk.)
Subjects: LCSH: Empathy in children. | Creative ability in children. |
   Self-control in children. | Child development.
Classification: LCC BF723.E67 (ebook) | LCC BF723.E67 C54 2018 (print) |
   DDC 155.4/1241—dc23
LC record available at https://lccn.loc.gov/2018019365

10 9 8 7 6 5 4 3 2 1

This book is dedicated wholeheartedly to my children. Thank you for sharing your time with me, for your belly laughs, for holding me accountable, for allowing me to not always be the expert, for your commitment to me, and for helping me stay in this nearly impossible balance between skepticism and magic.

For each of your precious souls, the life I want for you is the life you choose for yourself. Grow every day, focus on the positive, understand yourself. Know that everything can be changed at any moment, and you can be the force behind that change. I love you.

Contents

Illustrations

Preface

WHEN MY OLDEST child was 8, he said to me, "Mama, does my brain control me, or do I control my brain?" My 6-year-old asked if alcohol was a kind of poison (as I hid my wineglass). My 4-year-old wanted to know what cheeks are for. And my 2-year-old would gleefully smack me not so gently in the face, laugh, and run away so I'd chase him.

They were each at different stages of discovery. These stages change as children grow and their brains continue to develop on the continuum of maturity. My kids are my real connection to the science I engage in every day. Even as a person trained in molecular biology, I've found the strength of their genetics overwhelming. How could they all share the same gene pool and yet be so unique? Each of them approaches problems differently, struggles with different things, and performs different skills with innate effortlessness. As their mom, it didn't take long before I started to wonder how I could meet each of their individual needs—while parenting all of them at the same time.

I started looking at my own profession for answers to this question. I'm a professor of biology at a small college. In my lab, I do basic research on how our brains develop, how neurons connect, and how the things that we're exposed to can alter who we are as people. What could the neuroscience I was teaching and researching tell me about how to raise my kids?

As I explored this question, I discovered that much of neuroscience applies directly to parenting, including the fundamental facts about how humans learn on a cellular level, how and when certain areas of the brain develop, how brain development is linked to behaviors we see every day, how practice works to make something a habit, and how making decisions has a powerful impact on both parents and kids.

My research also showed me that our society emphasizes some qualities at the expense of others. We say we value things like creativity, empathy, and self-control, but we don't act like we do. Based on what I learned, I now believe that these are the things that kids really need to be successful, and to be good people, throughout their lives. I also figured out that, contrary to popular belief, these qualities are not innate traits or talents, but skills that can be learned. And we, as parents, can help our kids learn them.

Building Specific Brain Connections

To understand how to cultivate creativity, empathy, and self-control in our kids, as well as teach them how to use these skills purposefully (in the act of self-regulation), we need to understand how our parenting is shaping our children's brains. *Synaptic plasticity*, or *neuroplasticity*, is a highly dynamic process in which connections between **neurons** (signaling brain cells) fade away or strengthen depending on how frequently they're used. Everything we do as parents strengthens some neuronal connections in our children's brains while leaving other connections undeveloped or underdeveloped.

If we want our kids to develop creativity, we need to help their brains build the neuronal connections that allow them to be creative. It's the same with empathy, self-control, and self-regulation. And the key to building the neuronal connections for any skill is practice. Neuroscience shows us that just as practice helps our kids learn relatively simple skills like walking, throwing a curveball, or rapping the lyrics to one of the songs in *Hamilton*, practice can also enable them to learn the more complicated skills of being creative, expressing empathy, and maintaining their self-control. There's nothing special about the way we learn these skills; they may be more complicated, but the brain uses the same machinery to incorporate them into who we are as people. (At the same time, we can help our children to *not* practice the behaviors we would love to see disappear so that the neuronal connections underlying those behaviors weaken.)

The beauty of neuroscience is that once we demystify things like creativity and empathy and break them down into teachable components, it becomes clear that our brains all follow the same rules; we're all governed by the neural networks that we activate. Despite the clear and sometimes overwhelming individual differences in the ways we behave, our similarities on a neuroscientific level are staggering. We see that our parenting efforts, particularly early in development, can literally change the architecture of the brain in lasting ways.

Your Road Map

This book explains why the skills of creativity, empathy, and self-control, plus the all-encompassing skill of self-regulation, are so important, and it provides a road map to parenting for these skills. In part 1, I share why I've become convinced that these are essential skills that every kid needs to learn—for both their short- and long-term happiness. I explore the neuroscience behind these skills and the intersections between them. Then I show you how you can bring all of this information together, using parenting techniques that both create space and provide guidance for kids to be able to function independently in ways that make us proud and make them happy.

Then I focus on each of the skills and what we can do as parents to help our kids develop them through practice. Part 2 explores the importance of creativity (both in itself and as a platform for higher-level thinking) and how parents can focus on creativity in a more purposeful way. Part 3 shows you multiple ways of looking at the idea of empathy and the enormous benefits that fostering empathy has for kids. Then it provides activities to help kids practice it.

Part 4 focuses on self-control and how to enhance it, but also discusses the somewhat misguided view that self-control is the *most* important skill needed as kids grow up. While good self-control may keep us out of jail, self-regulation is the key ingredient to a happy and successful life because humans need so much more than simply not being bad. The most fulfilling experiences are not about inaction, but rather they come from being able to manage situations well when we need to put ourselves out there, when we work toward a goal, and when we can manage to get what we want without hurting anyone else. Part 5 provides information about how self-control, empathy, and creativity come together in the brain, theories behind self-regulation, and parenting tactics to keep your kids as motivated as possible and working toward being autonomous.

There are two ways to use this book. To get an overall parenting perspective, it can be read all the way through. For each of the skills, there is at least one quick, rudimentary test to see where your child is in the skill developmental process. You can see which skills your kid has already developed and where some practice would be useful. Alternatively, if you already know what you want to work on with your kids, you can jump to part 2, 3, or 4. Remember that self-regulation is what we're actively working toward, so part 5 will be important for everyone.

Your kids won't need to actively work on all aspects of these qualities because they likely already have some of them; they're part of what we think of as their personalities. You'll see that each skill is broken down into several parts: Creativity is defined as either self-expression or as innovative problem solving (applied creativity), and both definitions are important. Empathy is divided into emotional, cognitive, and applied empathy, all of which are valuable, though applied empathy is what we're talking about when we mention a compassionate kid. Self-control is an essential step on the way toward great self-regulation. These skills all come together in the ability to be a resilient problem solver, and that's what we're ideally working toward.

Finding your own children among these definitions will help you get to know their character better, and it helps you figure out how to best parent each child. For example, one of my daughters is highly expressive with her creativity and is very emotionally empathetic. During conflicts, she will have hurt feelings and can get frozen, so we actively work on applied creativity and cognitive empathy as problem-solving techniques. In contrast, one of my sons can solve any problem using creativity and has high levels of cognitive empathy, but he has little emotional empathy. Every day, he and I talk about the impact of actions on others, and we work on self-control so that he doesn't plow right through conflict situations. The skills my kids were born with are different, but the values we work on are the same.

Short-Term Gains and Long-Term Goals

Although it's important to be long-sighted when parenting, it's not just about the endgame. Parents deal with daily crises. If you commit to working on creativity, empathy, and self-control and self-regulation with your kids, you will be resolving the immediate threats to family harmony: those tantrums, the lying, and the bickering. Why? Because nearly all behavior problems kids have are associated with these skills—or an underdevelopment of them.

But beyond that, developing these skills in your children means you are fostering their default way of thinking about any given situation. You are providing a platform for their perspective. Just as important are the actions they will be able to take because of that perspective. The ability to think critically and then make decisions plays a vitally important role in a person living the life they choose. You can feel creative or empathetic all you want, but if you don't act on your creativity and empathy, then those things will never make an impact. If you don't interact with the world, no one will ever know what you think inside.

So, when we parent to cultivate these three specific skills, we're not just putting out parenting fires, we're also laying the neural groundwork for our kids to become happy, successful, emotionally resilient adults. It benefits them (and us) not only in the short-term, but also in the long-term. In other words, using neuroscience to inform our parenting can determine not only how our kids behave now, but also what kind of adults they will become.

Every parent reading this book is reading it because of love. We're trying to fit together all the ways we know to love someone well into a parenting push that might launch our child's boat in the best direction.

We all come with certain starting material. But that's all it is—a starting place. Parenting works by supporting or not supporting certain connections within our child's brain. That's the internal map we're crafting and the literal mind-set that our child will navigate by. Despite all our best intentions, we can't tell our kids how to live; we have to show them, and they have to experience it. Just as we can't expect a child to start running without practicing walking first, we can't expect her to be creative, be empathetic, or exercise self-control without practice.

Neuroscience tells us that neuronal pathways that are used frequently while we're young are more likely to be used in the future. It's our job as parents to help this connective process along, making sure that certain behaviors in our kids become *second nature*. They may not have been born with these characteristics, but you'd never know it when you're talking to them as adults. It will become their default way of being—the platform from which they approach the world—and developing these pathways is what this book is all about.

part 1

SECOND NATURE
PARENTING

1

Creativity, Empathy, and Self-Control

Why These Are the Skills Kids Need

WE LIVE IN A WORLD where we can Google any fact, where voice recognition software will make spelling accuracy irrelevant, where computers can read books to us. This means that as parents, we should rethink the skills that we're placing emphasis on. Of course, we want to raise kind people, but it's also true that we want our kids to have relevant skills and a valued place in society when they grow up. We need to keep our kids from being replaceable or outsourced. To prepare our kids for future lives in a computer-dominated world, we need to hone skills in our kids that are vastly different from the things that computers can do so easily. We have to incorporate things like flexibility, rulemaking, and problem-solving into our school curricula and our homes. We have to deemphasize procedure and facts. And we need to give our kids practice—tons of practice—doing the uniquely human things that still elude computers, like the capacities to surprise, to empathize, to create, and to love.

We Aren't Computers

Our society has a love affair with computers. We admire them, but we've started to view our own skill sets through the eyes of technology and to think about human memory and learning differently because of it. We relate to computers, compare our brains to them, and identify with them in ways that are contrary to the principles of neuroscience, such as thinking about our brains as being hardwired for certain skills or having a limited amount of memory space.

As computers have changed the landscape of our collective ability, we have shaped our lives around the benefits that technology provides. Our value system has changed, and as a result, we're parenting differently. We're cultivating the skills of a computer in our kids, such as multitasking, quick computation, and fact memorization, sometimes at the expense of the things that make us truly human. (We forget that the brain can't turn off like a computer. Our brains are always learning something, always working, even during sleep.) As a result of cultivating the wrong skills, we're setting up our kids for failure and frustration because they won't be prepared for the jobs of the future—jobs that we may not be thinking about yet, human jobs that no computer can do.

Humans and computers approach problems in fundamentally different ways. Computers require two things to work: (1) information coming in and (2) a set of rules to process that information. Computers execute those rules, and they do it rapidly, whereas humans process incoming information in a more flexible way. Computers specialize in tasks that need to be done quickly, while humans are better at finding solutions to messy situations. Compared to computers, humans are exceptionally good at leadership, social collaboration, goal setting, teaching, coaching, encouraging, and selling things. Humans can also more easily decide what is relevant when working with new information.

These differences mean that humans are better than computers at certain types of jobs. These jobs include roles with no strict sets of rules to follow, such as a designer writing a new web application or a doctor diagnosing someone with highly unusual symptoms. They include jobs where you need to easily decide what is relevant when working with new information, such as underwater exploration or convincing your manager that a new type of human resource management system will serve the company better than the current one.

In addition, jobs that require a "human touch," like counseling, customer service, and delivering medical diagnoses, will always be preferentially given to humans.

Humans retain more flexibility than computers because of *synaptic plasticity*—the way our nervous system can pivot and adapt to change (we'll discuss this in chapter 2). Computer memory grows by adding more computer chips. Human memories grow by strengthening the connections between neurons—no chips or more storage needed. Constant modification and refinement of these connections is what allows us to learn, remember, and hold an unlimited amount of information. We are constantly adapting, and doing so in a way that computers cannot, by choosing which of our brain's neuronal pathways get activated and then honing how those circuits are used, using an adaptive flexibility that is never exhausted.

If future humans will need to solve problems and clean up everything messy in ways that computers cannot, then we're going to need creativity, empathy, and self-control—three qualities that make us uniquely human—and we're going to need a lot of them.

Creativity

Creativity is key to competitiveness in a global economy. In a competitive workplace, applied imagination may mean the next big thing happens at your company. According to a 2013 *Time* magazine poll about the role of creativity in the American workplace, schools, and government, more than 8 in 10 people surveyed thought America should be considered a global leader in creativity, and many of those who said America is *not* a global leader in creativity felt that American schools are not building creativity in students (31%) or that the American government is not doing enough to support creativity (30%).[1]

Creativity is associated with genius in tangible ways. Albert Einstein was able to imagine the theory of relativity, Leonardo da Vinci was able to think up a helicopter in the 1500s, Alexander Bell was a prolific inventor, and Mozart's lasting musical works are surely hallmarks of creative genius. We know genius runs in families. Sir Francis Galton proposed a genetic basis for genius back in 1869 in his book *Hereditary Genius*. However, if you consider that the majority of inventions come from unknown inventors, we see that creativity is the rule, not the exception, in humans.[2]

There are business journals dedicated entirely to finding creative talent and effectively managing it. Finding creative people takes time and money; it's hard because they are rare. When we encounter a creative adult, it's like sighting a unicorn because so few of us make it through our school gauntlet with our creativity and imagination unscathed. We wonder how those creative people still have that spark as adults. We often conclude that they must have just been born creative. We think of creativity more as a talent than a skill, and we certainly don't teach or cultivate it. But there's a disconnect here between what we are taught and what we need: the majority of the 2,040 adults polled by *Time* (62%) say that creativity is more important to success in the workplace than they anticipated when they were in school.[3]

Building creativity in your child from the ground up serves two purposes: First, creativity will give your child a career boost—not just for jobs with an artistic slant, but also in business, entrepreneurship, engineering, teaching, law, and medicine. But creativity is also essential for effectively solving problems, which will make your child more successful at life, regardless of career choice. Imagination, a natural bridge between empathy and self-regulation, is intimately associated with decision-making. For our children to have confidence in diverse situations and to be effective leaders, we need to teach them to think creatively about problems and then act on their ideas. We won't be always there to point out to our kids all the possible decision routes that are available during a conflict, so they'll have to take the creative lead in conflict resolution themselves. To do this, they'll need to develop creative pathways. Creativity is not a bonus or the finishing touch in our children's development; it should be part of their core curriculum.

CREATIVITY DEFINED

There's a fundamental difference between ideas about creativity in Western and Eastern cultures, and both views contain important concepts.

Western culture sees creativity as divergent thinking—thoughts that take the road less traveled. Western culture values creativity in terms of innovation and the act of harnessing these insights for a specific purpose.[4] Creativity is defined by the presence of two components: originality and effectiveness. America, it seems, wants to know your ideas *and* what you can *do* with your ideas.

The Eastern definition of creativity, on the other hand, describes a sense of self-fulfillment or self-realization. The Eastern tradition involves an awareness of the truth about yourself, an event, or an object: it's more about finding a new point of view rather than breaking from tradition. We're perhaps not as familiar with this view, but we shouldn't be quick to dismiss it. Practices such as yoga and mindfulness/meditation can help cultivate self-regulation (as we'll discuss in chapter 10).

Not surprisingly, parents also have very different ideas about what creativity means. Sometimes we think about creativity in a Western way, like Doug, who defines creativity as "making thought visible in a tangible product," or Catherine, who describes creativity as "being able to solve problems by taking what you know, adding new knowledge, and coming up with solutions. Then picking the best solutions and trying them out. Then adjusting them, if necessary." These definitions reflect a way of thinking about creativity as unique thought with a purpose. In his 1993 textbook *Human Motivation*, Robert Franken defines creativity as "the tendency to generate or recognize ideas, alternatives, or possibilities that may be useful in solving problems, communicating with others, entertaining ourselves and others."[5] His Western definition taps into other human aspects, like critical thinking, keen perception, empathy, and honed social skills.

Other parents see creativity in a more Eastern way: When Brit says, "Creativity is self-expression on every level," she's identifying more with the Eastern tradition; she's seeing messy paints and unique outfits. She's joined by Kevin, who says that creativity is the "ability to express oneself artistically, verbally, in writing in ways that are from one's heart," and by Rachel, who thinks of creativity as "being artsy—having the ability to create beauty out of anything." And Katie says creativity is "the ability to express yourself as a child in various ways/modes and be free-form and unstructured in these explorations." This is self-expression based on knowing yourself, the idea that we should let our kids become who they want to be.

Parents who define creativity as self-expression may feel that creativity is like dessert after a healthy dinner: it's a plus, but you'll be fine without it. Some parents may see finding your own truth as paramount to foster in kids, while other parents might place cultivating creative self-expression at the bottom of a long list of parenting to-dos.

Different definitions lead to differences in how we talk about creativity and how much we value it, ultimately leading to either prioritizing or marginalizing creativity in our lives. For example, when parents define creativity as a purposeful process, as active problem-solving, then it often pops to the forefront of parenting attention. Doug, because of his wholly Western definition of creativity, probably sees creativity as extremely important to foster in his own parenting style. But because Brit sees creativity as simple self-expression, she doesn't work creativity into her parenting choices. She feels no need to self-express while parenting.

No matter how we define it, creativity is worth cultivating. The Eastern and Western traditions are two sides of the same coin, and one can build on the other. Creativity is truth with utility that can take many forms.

CREATIVITY IS A BIOLOGICAL QUALITY

Creativity involves innovation, which is why computers aren't so great at it. Repurposing by finding new uses for old things and problem-solving by making connections between seemingly disparate items necessitate an attitude toward rules that eludes computers. It requires both a bending of the rules and an understanding of why the rules are there to begin with.

Is it possible for computers to be creative? There are computers that can generate works of art: They have no visual system but can be programmed to work with hues and saturation. They can be programmed to do what a human artist would do in a given situation. But in the end, the pictures that the computer creates are actually created by the computer's programmer, right? Unless the computer has a sense of self, its creativity is limited.

CREATIVITY IS THE FOUNDATION
FOR EMPATHY AND SELF-CONTROL

Imagination is intricately linked to both empathy and self-awareness.[6, 7] There are several types of neurons involved in these processes, including the mirror neurons (in empathy) and von Economo neurons (in self-awareness), and they likely play a role in imagination as well.[8] Individuals with autism have a greatly diminished capacity for imagination, and they also show alterations in both of these types of neurons.[9–12]

Imagination seeps over into empathy, as we can actively imagine what others must be feeling or experiencing, and this empathy often happens during the creative process.[13] If you are more creative, you can easily see things from a different point of view, which is the definition of empathy. And the inverse is also true: if you have an ill-defined sense of empathy, you are less likely to be creative.

Creativity and empathy are so linked that it can be hard to tease them apart, but it's easy to tap into both simultaneously. In one study, when 126 undergraduate students were asked to draw a neuron, all but three reproduced a standard version of a neuron they had learned about in a textbook. However, when undergrads did exercises first that made them see or act like a neuron—like fanning out in the classroom in a way that mimicked the fanlike growth of a neuron—then their drawings were better and more varied.[14] Having empathy for a neuron by imagining the neuron's perspective enhanced their creativity. Teaching in this creative way makes variation okay, makes play acceptable, opens assessment up so that there are multiple "right" answers, and increases the students' ownership of learning, and so enhances conceptual understanding.

Creativity is equally important for self-control since it's much easier to have good self-control if you can generate more solutions to a problem (we'll see this in chapter 4). And it's easier to regulate your own behavior if you can entertain yourself with thoughts instead of fixating on the one thing you're not supposed to be doing, like getting out of your seat, for example. Clearly imagining both the causes and consequences of behavior is a creative act that can motivate you to control yourself. Imagining causes and outcomes is also a fundamental part of self-regulation: taking action to make your life the way you want it to be.

Empathy

Most parents say empathy is being able to take another person's perspective and understanding what someone else is feeling. More empathy will build trust between people, which will lead to a better future and world peace, right?

Yup, that's an excellent pageant answer. But when my son whacks his sister—again—it's pretty tough to convince him that being empathetic and kind to others is worthwhile. After all, "It's not going to make me rich or anything," he says. (To my 11-year-old, the best imaginable adult outcome is to be rich.)

However, research clearly shows that empathetic people will be more successful at navigating social situations in the long-term. They have better interpersonal relationships, and they stay married.[15, 16] They end up being better bosses and more effective leaders, and they make better life decisions because they can better predict the future.[17, 18] They *may* even be richer. And happier. Empathy turns out to have many hidden benefits:

> **It makes kids safer.** An empathetic child may be safer in life both physically and emotionally. Empathy gives your child a superpower: the ability to predict someone's behavior, and thus the future, in very real ways. Empathetic people are better at reading faces and emotional cues to figure out how people are feeling, and that's important for survival in a basic, back-alley way. When dealing with others, it helps them know when to stay still, when to fight, and when to take flight. If your child can anticipate that his playmate will respond angrily when his toy gets broken, your child

can plan ahead, share his own toy, move away, and be ready. Empathy also reduces bullying in older kids; higher levels of empathy mean better conflict resolution and a willingness to come to the defense of a bullied peer.[19, 20]

It turns kids into leaders. Empathy-enriched children often turn out to be leaders since they're more socially competent.[21] Why? They have an enhanced ability to manage other people's perspectives and expectations, which is a skill that transcends age. Leaders on the playground become company leaders, where empathy can increase employee motivation, job commitment, and productivity.[22]

It makes kids happy. As an added reward for good behavior, benevolent acts make us feel good inside. Giving gifts to another person makes us feel happier than giving gifts to ourselves. Researchers gave people cash and instructed half the participants to spend the money on themselves, while the other half was instructed to spend the money on someone else. The people who were instructed to spend the money on someone else reported being happier over the course of the day, regardless of the amount of money they spent.[23]

It makes us feel rich. When we give money away, our sense of abundance and wealth increases.[24] When we act in empathetic ways, our sense of time expands. It is actually the *perception* of having things, like time and money, that matters more than the actual measured amount. That enriched perception makes us happier.

It's healthy for us. Empathetic grown-ups have healthier and more satisfying relationships, and they're more likely to stay married.[25–30] After an injury or surgery, they heal more quickly.[31] Research has shown that compassion may even lengthen our life spans, possibly due to decreased inflammation and a tempered stress response in those who help others.[32, 33] Older people who are happy have a 35% lower risk of dying than their unhappy counterparts, and so if having empathy makes us happy, maybe we'll live longer, happier lives.[34, 35]

Although empathy brings safety, happiness, leadership skills, abundance, and wealth, studies have shown that self-reported empathy has been declining for the last 30 years. Research shows that empathy, concern for others, and the ability to take other people's perspectives have sharply declined in American college students, particularly since 2000.[36] Why? We can blame it on smartphones and on the social isolation propagated by our vast number of virtual Facebook friendships compared to our shrinking number of deep friendships. We can say that perhaps it's the increase in violent media that numbs the empathetic response. But maybe it's even simpler than that: maybe our children just don't practice it.

Lucky for us, empathy isn't just an innate trait but also a teachable skill. There are programs designed to teach empathy, and they work. Many research studies have found that mindfulness/meditation and service learning/community partnerships are proven, simple ways to enhance empathy. Specific evidence-based programs target empathy, social learning, and conflict resolution, including Roots of Empathy (K–8), Positive Action (K–12), Responsive Classroom (K–5), and Second Step (Pre-K–8).[37]

Teachers are figuring out that if kids don't come into the classroom with empathy, it's worth taking the time to teach it to them. Not only will empathetic kids not disrupt the class for other students, but research has also shown that empathetic individuals are better learners. An analysis of 213 social- and emotional-learning programs involving over 270,000 kindergarten through high school students showed that interventions increased academic performance by 11%, as well as decreased aggression/emotional distress and increased helping behavior in students.[38] Empathy training results in higher student GPAs, better reading comprehension, and more developed critical thinking skills.[39–41] In the absence of one of these school programs, parents can teach kids empathy simply by making time to do it.

EMPATHY DEFINED

For some, it's hard to see empathy as an adaptation that nature would select for. In fact, we tend to think of empathy as a skill specific to the more sensitive types—or even as a weakness. And yet empathy is a human quality conserved by evolution. Why is empathy so important? The human relationship with empathy is a complicated issue, and it hinges on our personal definition of empathy.

The concept of empathy evolved from a theory of art appreciation, invented only about 150 years ago. (The word *empathy* comes from the Greek *en*, meaning "in," and *pathos*, meaning "feeling.") The idea was that to fully appreciate a work of art, you have to project your own self into the art. And the art could make you feel. Psychology stole the word *empathy* from the art world and turned it into a thinking verb: *empathize*. To empathize, you need to understand someone else's point of view and put yourself into that person's world. You must be able to imagine what your friend is feeling, imagine what might make her feel better.

But even if you are great at feeling sad for others, and you can see things from the sad person's point of view, for empathy to truly be useful to the human condition, empathy must lead to compassion, or applied empathy. There's how we *think* about emotions, there's how we *feel* emotions, and there's what we *do* about the emotional content in the world around us (that is, express compassion). Recognizing these different types of empathy is the first step in helping our kids become doers of good things in the world around them.

EMPATHY IS A BIOLOGICAL QUALITY

Empathy is another quality that sets us apart from computers. Computers can't do compassion. Computers could be programmed to follow the rules for cognitive empathy and say the appropriate thing to a grieving person or to offer a discount on the next order to a disgruntled customer, but taking another's perspective requires imagination. Compassion involves encouragement, good communication, social collaboration, and often, personal sacrifice to solve someone else's personal problem.

Have you ever picked out the perfect birthday present for someone and couldn't wait for them to open it? If so, you can probably understand why giving money to charity activates the same pleasure centers in the brain as receiving money yourself, and why empathy is a great contributor to personal happiness.[42] This means that when both parents and children choose to regard caring for others as important, happiness will come along too.

EMPATHY REQUIRES SELF-CONTROL AND CREATIVITY

Acting compassionately, based on empathetic thoughts or feelings, takes both self-control and creativity. Self-control is required to stop yourself from acting on your gut impulses, like not hitting when someone takes your ball away. And then you need to have creativity to process the situation—to try to figure out the "why" of it. It takes creative thinking to realize, for example, that there is only one ball for twelve kids to share, and the kid who took it away from you was playing with it before he left it to run to the bathroom. At its root, empathizing is an active, creative exercise—a kind of subtle art form. You have to imagine someone else's experience. As such, empathy increases creativity, and creativity increases empathy.

Self-Control

Researchers say that the most important skill you can help your child to develop is self-control. A study of 1,000 children showed that the amount of self-control that a child has predicts health, wealth, and crime rates by age 32, and self-control can predict those things better than intelligence or social class can.[43] Self-control can predict grade performance better than IQ scores can.[44] People with high self-control are more emotionally stable, are rated as better bosses, and are in better relationships.[45, 46] They are happier people.[47]

The authors of the 1,000-children study defined self-control as the ability to "delay gratification, control impulses, and modulate emotional expression."[48] Most parents would define it in a similar way: self-control is the ability to not do the things you shouldn't be doing.

Good self-control means that you can override seemingly automatic urges that interfere with your own goal-directed behavior. Good self-control means *you* won't get in the way of *yourself.*

And on the other hand, self-control failure means you experience interpersonal conflict, lower intellectual achievement, irrepressible appetites, addictions, and many other adverse outcomes.[49, 50]

It sure seems like if we can give our child adequate self-control, we will be giving him the gift of control over his own life—the freedom to become anything he wants to be—and that we will be saving him from self-destructive behaviors. So, as parents, we work on it nearly constantly with our kids. And research clearly shows that development of self-control is a very long process, reaching far past the elementary school years. One mom, Jenn, told me, "One of our daughters has insane self-control, but the other has none. Her impulse to hit or pinch her sister instead of telling her why she's upset is a huge problem. We are trying to actively work on it, through everything from consequences to thinking through scenarios with her to model how she could use her words rather than resort to physical aggression. No success yet!"

We know that some kids just naturally need more help with self-control than others. Studies show that between 50% and 90% of self-control is dictated by genetics, but we also know that self-control is tied to the structure and function of the brain's prefrontal cortex.[51] The formation of the prefrontal cortex is set in motion by genetics, but it is also susceptible to environmental influences. That means that the part of self-control that's not genetically regulated is learned through experience. Parents can be the environmental influence, and parents can direct experience.

SELF-CONTROL IS A BIOLOGICAL QUALITY

Self-control is always about an urge, followed by a choice not to act. Computers obviously can't choose not to do something they want to do; they simply execute rules. The struggle and balance between what we want and what is in our best interests never happens in a computer. A computer never has multiple impulses competing for its attention, nor does it ever need to battle its own impulses. There's never a moment of indecision within a computer. The type of self-listening required to weigh the best option happens when brain circuits are firing and signals are being summed up. The split second when a person is deciding whether to follow a base instinct is a remarkably human moment. And, as we'll see, the moment that comes next—the moment of self-regulation—is even more important.

SELF-CONTROL REQUIRES CREATIVITY
OR EMPATHY (OR BOTH)

The actual act of self-control has nothing to do with creativity or empathy, but the decision to have self-control absolutely does. In fact, there are only two reasons someone can have good self-control. One is if she can see the impact that the behavior will have on other people. (She has enough empathy to understand how others will feel.) The other reason is if she can see a better way of getting what she wants. (She can imagine the consequences of behavior, and she has enough creativity to see a different path to achieve her goal.) Both of these reasons have us pulling ourselves up out of the current situation, and both require us to think bigger than ourselves.

Building One Skill Also Builds the Others

The skills of creativity, empathy, and self-control are interconnected. One always bleeds over into the others. Neuroscience shows that the circuits that govern each of these are so deeply connected that to separate them from each other is virtually impossible. Building ability in one area can translate to greater ability in the other two. If you cultivate any one of these skills, you are also bolstering the other two, as well as many more traits that tap into these skills (see figure 1.1).

Self-Regulation Is the Culmination of
Creativity, Empathy, and Self-Control

Creativity, empathy, and self-control culminate in effective self-regulation, which is the process of weighing the past, present, and future and making a single decision to act. Self-regulation means acting in a way that is contrary to your natural instincts in order to solve a problem or be compassionate. By itself, self-control is a straight "no." There's no personal reward for not doing something you want to do or not having something you want to have. So really, there's no intrinsic motivation to have self-control.

By contrast, self-regulation says, "You can't do or have what you want in this way, but let's figure out another way to do it or get it." Self-regulation is a complicated skill, mostly because it taps into so many other skills. It's a tightrope walk that's just as hard for the wall-flowers as it is for the class clowns. But practicing self-regulation is so

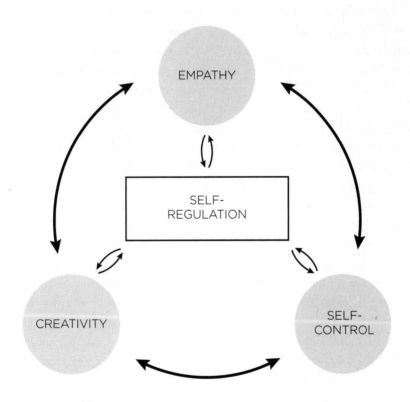

Figure 1.1 The skills of creativity, empathy, and self-control are interconnected. If you cultivate any one of these skills, you are also bolstering the other two.

important to defining the person that your child becomes, for instilling the kernels of confidence to both know the right thing and to choose the right thing, and for teaching kids how to claim personal happiness in a way that builds others up in the short-term and the long-term. In fact, it's really the end skill that we're trying to cultivate in our children and worth every second of effort that we can put into it.

Use Neuroscience to Raise an Awesome Person — Starting Now

We should not wait until we feel that our kids have attained a certain level of development to begin teaching them creativity, empathy, and self-control.

Traditional psychological theory holds that abstract reasoning isn't developed until adolescence; consequently, early education has not pursued the development of building abstract connections. In fact, it is a widely held belief that until a certain developmental stage, young kids can't begin to connect abstract ideas. When my son was in second grade, his soccer coach told me that his team could finally start executing plays because they were just starting to think abstractly.

But studies show that infants can detect metaphors and that preschoolers commonly use metaphors in their own speech.[52, 53] A metaphor—a descriptive term applied to something it wasn't originally meant to describe, but instead captures aspects of the meaning—is the embodiment of abstract thought. And *babies* understand them.

Neuroscience tells us that there are elements of self-control, empathy, and creativity that even very young children can learn. The brain is always developing; connections between neurons are always being refined. So, when we practice these skills, we build the connections for them in our kids, regardless of their ages. This simply requires a refocusing of the parental lens, starting with an agreement that these skills are important. In 1890, William James observed that "my experience is what I agree to attend to."[54] This is true for our kids as well: they will pay attention to the things that we as parents require them to experience and, eventually, to the things that they habitually notice.

Focused attention is rare and unbelievably important because what parents pay attention to are the things that families end up valuing the most, whether intentionally or not. If we as parents focus on empathy, creativity, and self-control in an environment that allows for autonomy in personal decision-making, then we will raise creative thinkers who get things done in a way that benefits others as well as themselves. In a kid, these skills come together in the form of self-regulation and ownership. If life is presented as a problem that you figure out, then you accept the conclusions you come to, and you accept responsibility for not just your thoughts and actions, but also your own learning.

By-products of developing these skills are increases in grit, critical thinking, social responsibility, resilience, and personal accountability—all those missing ingredients that we're trying to instill in our kids, so they are not weak reeds in a windy world. We're not here to raise bystanders. Instead, let's raise a generation of people predisposed toward kindness and proficient at being uniquely human.

2

Practical Neuroscience
for Parents

Key Facts and Processes

IT IS IMPORTANT for parents to have a basic understanding of how
the brain and its neurons work. An awareness of the nuts and bolts of
brain connectivity allows us to see how our parenting is shaping our
children's brains—specifically, how connections between neurons are
forming in the short-term. From there, we can see how to use that
information to reach our long-term parenting goals.

If you think I'm going to suggest that you learn all the parts
of the brain, don't worry—I'm not. You don't need to know tons of
anatomy to understand how the brain works. You only need to
learn how individual neurons and neuronal connections are formed.
Which neuronal connections survive and strengthen, and which
ones fade away, depends on how much each is used. And we parents
are perfectly placed to influence which connections in our children's
brains get used the most. We can modify our child's experiences
to refine her brain, define it, and encourage the development of
certain aspects of it. This refinement is possible on both a cellular
level and on a circuit level. If you *are* interested in delving further
into brain anatomy, I've included a crash course in appendix 1,
"Commonsense Neuroanatomy."

Meet the Neuron

Most things in biology follow the "structure dictates function" rule. If you had never seen a chair before, you could probably deduce what it's for simply by looking at its shape. Neurons follow this rule too: they're perfectly shaped to communicate. These special cells in the brain can receive and transmit signals over long distances through their long, fragile cell extensions called **axons**.

Although you've probably never seen an actual neuron, you may already be familiar with its structure. Neurons look like trees (see figure 2.1). Information comes in at the uppermost dendrite branches and gets transmitted down the axon trunk, and then the roots pass the information on to the next neuron. The signal can only go in one direction down the axon, like lightning hitting the tree from the sky. Information is never sent back up to the branches.

The neurons connect with each other to make pathways (see figure 2.2), and the pathways can go in multiple directions, like roadways, to form circuits (see figure 2.3).

Brainpower isn't centered in a neuron or even a group of neurons. The number of neurons we have doesn't matter as much as the amount of interconnectivity between them.

Timing Is Everything: The Stages of Brain Development

It is well-documented that early childhood experience is vitally important in determining adult competence, health, and overall well-being.[1] But when does our parenting make the most impact on our kids' brain development? A lifetime of brain development can be broken down into three stages (see figure 2.4):

> **Stage 1:** When the first neurons are made and migrate to the places they will occupy in the body (neuron birth and migration)

> **Stage 2:** When connections between neurons form and unform (synaptogenesis)

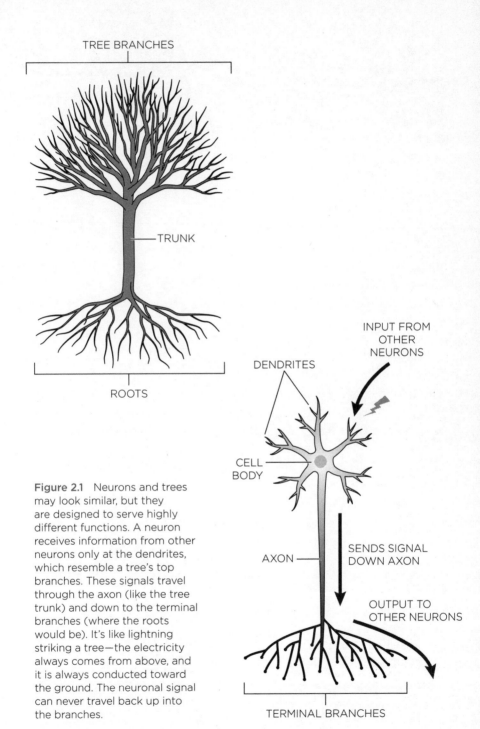

TREE BRANCHES

TRUNK

ROOTS

INPUT FROM
OTHER
NEURONS

DENDRITES

CELL
BODY

AXON

SENDS SIGNAL
DOWN AXON

OUTPUT TO
OTHER NEURONS

TERMINAL BRANCHES

Figure 2.1 Neurons and trees may look similar, but they are designed to serve highly different functions. A neuron receives information from other neurons only at the dendrites, which resemble a tree's top branches. These signals travel through the axon (like the tree trunk) and down to the terminal branches (where the roots would be). It's like lightning striking a tree—the electricity always comes from above, and it is always conducted toward the ground. The neuronal signal can never travel back up into the branches.

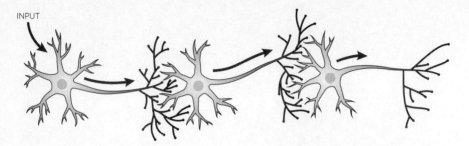

Figure 2.2 Neurons line up in pathways, primed for communication.

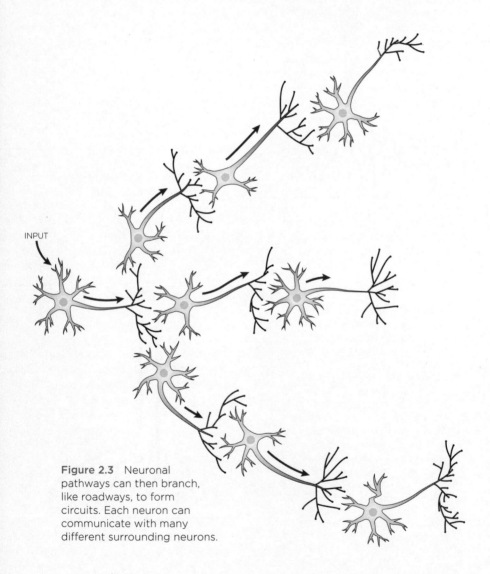

Figure 2.3 Neuronal pathways can then branch, like roadways, to form circuits. Each neuron can communicate with many different surrounding neurons.

Stage 3: When information traveling through neuronal pathways can speed up (myelination)

Stage 1 of brain development is pretty much hands-off, but parents can make a big impact during stages 2 and 3 of neurodevelopment, which—not coincidentally—occur mostly after you finally get to meet your baby. And even after brain development is technically over at the age of 25 or so, our brains are constantly changing in little ways as we interact with our environment, even as adults.

The two brain stages that continue after birth are when the brain is more responsive to outside stimulation, so during these stages, the way parents act can change the way the neurons work. This timing makes sense from an evolutionary point of view, but it's also a completely amazing opportunity for parenting: when we're around to make an impact, our child's brain is primed to respond to our parenting.

Neuronal connections are formed at an astounding rate during the early years in response to early experiences. As the brain matures, the developmental focus shifts to pruning away the connections that are not needed, while supporting essential connections and forming new ones.[2]

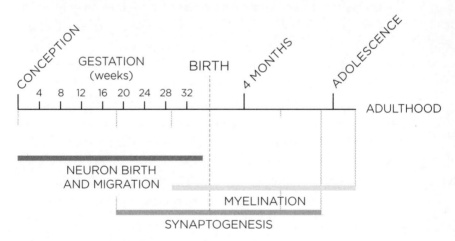

Figure 2.4 Brain development can be broken down into three stages: (1) neuron birth and migration, (2) synaptogenesis (the process of forming the first neuronal connections), and (3) myelination (when neurons become faster). Though it's not depicted on this timeline, synaptic plasticity, or the ability to change synaptic connections in response to the environment, never stops.

The three stages are genetically predetermined to happen, but *experience* always allows for neural modification throughout every stage of development.

STAGE 1   THE FIRST NEURONS ARE MADE AND MOVE INTO PLACE

The first part of this stage, called neurulation, is completed during the first few weeks of pregnancy, so by the time you find out you're going to have a baby, it's probably already happened. This is when the embryo sets aside the cells that will become the brain. The body is actively making neurons during this small early pregnancy window, and the neurons that are formed during this period of development are pretty much all you're going to get.

Then the neurons migrate to their correct places, and the process of eliminating unneeded neurons begins. Neurons have found their way to the positions they will occupy in the mature brain by the sixth prenatal month, but only the neurons that make healthy connections will survive.

As a parent, can you change the processes of neurulation or neuronal migration in your child? Only slightly, because they're mostly dictated by genes. Parents aren't in charge of where a neuron ends up sitting in their child's brain. We want to let nature take its course here because the default pattern of organization is the most efficient. This stage will happen completely during pregnancy and, in the absence of genetic problems, will occur like clockwork, without parental awareness. Our job as parents during this first brain development stage is to avoid exposing our babies to substances that are known to alter these processes, such as outside toxins or alcohol. We can also get regular prenatal care, pay careful attention to our diet, and take our prenatal vitamins.

STAGE 2   NEURONAL CONNECTIONS FORM AND UNFORM

After neural migration, neurons mostly remain anchored in their same places, but each neuron eventually makes thousands of

Neurodevelopment Is a Continuum

Throughout history, scientists have argued about whether babies were simply mini-adults, or whether (equally wrong) a baby's brain started to form at birth. But with the invention of neuroimaging techniques, we can see a lot more of what is going on inside the young brain, how exquisitely formed the baby's brain is at birth, and how vastly different the landscape looks from an adult's brain.

Your child's brain is *not* a blank slate at birth. Fetal behavior begins as reflex movements and it gradually expands into behavior that is distinct and responsive as the birth date nears. Even during the birth process, he is already collecting sensory information, evaluating his environment, using sophisticated neural machinery, and—perhaps most impressive—constantly remodeling his brain in response to what he senses. Neurodevelopment is a continuum. There is no magical neural event that occurs at birth. Instead, the baby can use the pathways he's been laying down for months in preparation for life in air instead of in liquid.

connections with other neurons. An adult brain contains *trillions* of connections in each square centimeter of the cortex, and young children have even more.[3]

Neurons are electrical cells. Neurons don't touch at their connections; they are separated from each other by a tiny space called a synaptic cleft that is only about 20 nanometers (billionths of a meter) wide. If neurons physically touched at each connection, the electricity could spread through all connected neurons unchecked, resulting in symptoms much like a seizure. Instead, the body has developed an amazing way of tightly controlling how neurons talk to each other through the use of neurotransmitters, which are chemical signals that traverse these tiny spaces between the neurons (see figure 2.5).

An activated neuron sends a very mild electric current, called an **action potential**, down to the **synapse**, where it is turned into a

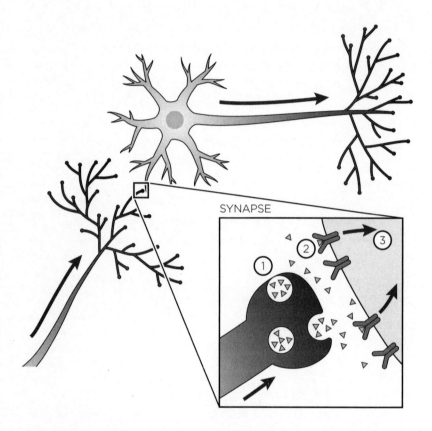

SYNAPSE

Figure 2.5 Synapses are connection sites between neurons that can be strengthened with repeated use. Every synapse has a giving and receiving neuron, separated by a small space. (1) An activated neuron sends an electrical signal down its axon toward another neuron. (2) Rather than passing that electricity directly to the next neuron, when the signal reaches the end of the neuron, it's converted into chemical neurotransmitters that must traverse the tiny synaptic gap between the two neurons. Once on the other side, the neurotransmitters can bind to the other receptors there. (3) If the neurotransmitters are *excitatory*, then the second neuron will turn that chemical signal back into electricity and send an action potential down the next neuron. If the neurotransmitters are *inhibitory*, then the second neuron won't fire.

chemical signal that is then received by the next neuron and turned back into an electrical signal. So one message will be electrical, then chemical, then electrical again as it goes from neuron to neuron. Sometimes the next neuron will be asked to fire, and sometimes the next neuron will be inhibited. This extra layer of control shows the power of using a neurotransmitter system instead of simple electricity, which would always be a "go" signal. A synapse, then, refers to the end of one neuron, the synaptic cleft, and the beginning of the next neuron, and there are many, many ways we can change neuronal communication at the synapse.

Synapses are the basic units of all brain functioning, and the process of forming synapses is called synaptogenesis. The peak period of synapse formation occurs from about 34 weeks after conception through the initial newborn stages. During this peak period, new synapses are being formed at a staggering rate, with *each* synapse eventually retaining about 7,000 synaptic connection.[4] These synaptic connections organize neurons into circuits, columns, and functional areas, which allow the brain to do things like remember a street sign, recognize the smell of bread baking, fear a snake, and love a favorite blanket.

Crafting Who We Are

Some brain systems, such as the visual system, need only a minimal amount of stimulation to form properly. But other systems require experience-dependent synapse formation (also known as activity-dependent synapse formation). This means that synapses may be refined, strengthened, or lost based on what we experience and the neurons that activate when we experience it. Connections can be shaped by experience in a powerful way. These experience-dependent brain changes end up being highly individualized, depending on what experiences a person is exposed to.

Proper brain development also includes synapse elimination, or pruning. We initially create more neuronal connections than we need in our brains, and then much of the rest of our development is spent getting rid of the ones we don't need. By the time your child is a teenager, about half of her synapses may have been discarded in a normal process, and the landscape of her brain will continue to shift and change in minute ways for the rest of her life. We keep what we need. We keep what we use.

Can parenting change synapse formation? Yes. We have an invaluable opportunity to help this process because the connections between neurons remain highly dynamic. Neurons get better or worse at talking to each other, and these processes are both experience and activity dependent. This means that *what* you are exposed to matters, and *how many times* you are exposed to it matters.

You can actively change your own brain simply by paying attention to different things, practicing different skills, or choosing to act in a different way. And you can influence your children's brains by encouraging them to do the same things. The pathways your kids use will be strengthened, and over time, their brains will eliminate the connections that have been ignored. This is especially true during the period of synaptic refinement that occurs during early childhood. Kids have the most synapses in the cortex at about 8 to 9 months; after that, they experience the natural pruning of synapses that are not needed, until stabilization occurs at about 11 years of age.[5] During this refinement period, the neurons can change which other neurons they talk to. Whole axons can be pruned away, or synapses can simply be eliminated. If we strengthen the right synapses, then we keep the desired neurons and the desired connections.

Parenting the Synapse

In my own research, I spend a lot of time figuring out what synapses do when something bad happens to them—like when a baby's brain is exposed to prenatal alcohol, for example. But the flip side of synaptic plasticity can be equally powerful: our parenting can also positively change synapses through the processes of gene regulation.

This is the fundamental way that neurons learn: Every time your child learns something, gene expression changes to support the strengthening of a new synapse and long-term memory. Genes make proteins, and proteins make nearly everything in your cells. (This is explained in more detail in appendix 2, "Epigenetics.") You can't create something

Brain Development Facts

Ever heard that you only use 10% of your brain? It's not true. The human body is very streamlined, particularly when it comes to doling out resources. If a cell was not needed in the body, it would not be there. *Every* neuron will be used, so the brain will carefully choose which ones survive.

The number of neurons in the brain reaches its highest peak 28 weeks after fertilization—long before birth. Adults have nearly 100 billion neurons, and every child is born with most of his neurons already in place. The inner layers of the brain form first, followed by the outermost layers. That's why attention and maturity—which are regulated in the outer cortex—take so long to develop in our kids!

But brain development is different from the development of all other body parts. Neurons don't usually divide or make more neurons. They're not like skin cells or muscle cells that are constantly turning over. New neurons are rarely formed in an adult. That's why the periods of prenatal and childhood brain development are crucial. They set the road map for life interactions.

from nothing. Genes must turn on because learning requires that the neuron makes some functional and/or structural changes.

Neurons respond to experience by changing their actual structure. Synapses are concentrated in highly dynamic structures called spines, found at the interface between neurons. Typically, the more spines that are present, the more connections a neuron makes—a single neuron may have hundreds or thousands of spines. The spines look like leaves on a tree branch, but they come and go in response to activity levels.

Sometimes this can happen in a way that appears to be almost spontaneous, and sometimes it happens in response to stimuli or the lack of stimuli.

There's a lot we don't know about spines, but there are some key points that parents need to know:

- Reinforcement spines are sent to the synapses that we need, and the ones we don't need are not maintained. Once a spine is there, changes in activity can lead to spine enlargement or shrinkage.

- Spines are much more dynamic in kids than in adults. Right after birth, spines can come and go in under a minute, and as neurons get older, there are less-dynamic spine changes.

- Animal studies have shown that environmental enrichment leads to increases in spine density.

- Skill training leads to the formation of new spines, while also destabilizing old spines. In other words, you're remodeling the neural circuits at work as you learn. You can literally see synaptic spines developing or shrinking under a high-powered microscope (see figure 2.6). Spine changes have been observed within hours after learning something new (for example, when a songbird learns to sing a new song or when a young mouse is trained to reach for and grab a seed).[6, 7]

Importantly, even though spines can be fickle structures, repeated training on a task will make the spines get bigger, become mature, and be more likely to stick around. Research shows that the process of forming and stabilizing spines means that behavior associated with those spine changes also gets stronger. Prolonged use of these brain pathways will make lasting, presumably permanent, memories.[8]

STAGE 3 MYELINATION—SPEEDING UP THE MESSAGE

If synapses are key to connections within the brain, then **myelin**, a white matter covering that forms around a neuron's axon, is the key to the brain's efficiency. When neurons start to become myelinated, they can pass messages to each other faster.[9] Myelination is a simple process, but it's very important to the way our brains work. Brain support cells, called **oligodendrocytes**, wrap around the axon of a neighboring neuron to provide insulation (which is important for conducting electricity; see figure 2.7). This myelin insulation speeds up how fast a neuron passes an action potential by a factor of 10.[10, 11]

The development of myelin is a maturity indicator. In fact, the timing of the appearance of this white matter is so precise that the age of a baby in the womb can be calculated based simply on which neuronal pathways have been myelinated. Myelination starts about halfway through pregnancy, and this developmental stage lasts a long time—continuing into the fourth and fifth decades of life.[12, 13]

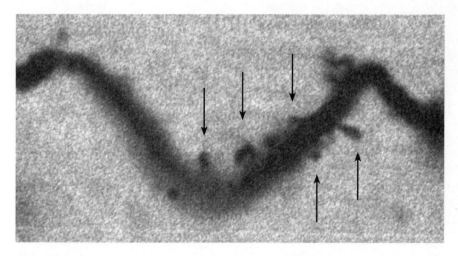

Figure 2.6 Human neurons are virtually indistinguishable from mouse neurons. This is a photograph of a dendrite from a neuron in the striatum of a mouse brain, magnified 1,000 times. I filled this individual neuron with a dark dye so we can see its structure, while the surrounding neurons remain invisible. This dye combined with high magnification allows us to see spines protruding from this dendrite (black arrows). These spines are dynamic structures and are able to come and go to support changes in neuronal activity.

Huge increases in myelination have been reported across the brain from ages 5 to 12 years, but not all axons get myelinated at the same time or rate.[14, 15] Instead, myelination occurs in waves, moving across different functional areas. Areas among the last to develop myelination include the reticular formation (responsible for wakefulness), parts of the cerebellum (which controls fine-motor coordination), and the

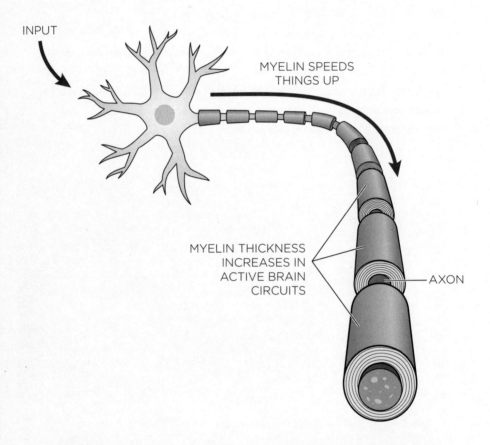

INPUT

MYELIN SPEEDS
THINGS UP

MYELIN THICKNESS
INCREASES IN
ACTIVE BRAIN
CIRCUITS

AXON

Figure 2.7 Neuronal axons transmit signals very quickly, but myelinated neuronal axons are even faster. Myelin wraps around the axon to provide electrical insulation for a traveling action potential. This speeds things up. This process happens normally as our brains mature, but myelination can also be enhanced by activity so that frequently used neurons can swiftly communicate.

association cortexes (which help us make sense out of all the signals coming in).

As a parent, it probably won't surprise you to know that the last areas to be myelinated are in the frontal lobes—those responsible for mature judgment, impulse control, and decision-making. Neurodevelopment is still incomplete in these areas when kids turn 18, the age of legally required grown-up decision-making, and it's still incomplete in our college-aged kids when they start navigating the world on their own.

Although myelination is obviously a highly regulated, normal developmental event, recent studies have proposed that myelination can also be influenced by functional interaction with the environment, and *this* is where parenting can make a difference. Just as there is activity-dependent synapse formation, there's also such a thing as activity-dependent myelination: activity based on experience can encourage myelination of axons. This happens particularly during early development, but it also continues into old age.[16]

Human neuroimaging studies have shown that practicing skills, including things like practicing playing the piano, can change the amount of brain white matter present.[17–19] As we learn skills, new neurons can be myelinated, the myelin can get thicker on neurons in the circuit that is active, and new oligodendrocytes can be made in order to support this process. Importantly, the brain circuit that is getting used is the pathway that gets more myelin and becomes faster.[20] This is a directed, focused process, not a global phenomenon, so parents have to pick and choose what is important to practice.

We know that myelination can profoundly affect how incoming signals are integrated by the neuron, and therefore it can change how we process information. But myelination is also a sign that the neurons in the brain are highly connected, and parents can help foster that interconnectivity by encouraging children to practice the skills that activate those connections. Using neuronal pathways to change white matter is a less known (but equally important) way that we can encourage our children's brains to change and learn.

Myelination Can Alter Synaptic Plasticity

Speeding up neurons by changing myelination can alter synaptic plasticity, too. Neuronal connections also can be altered depending on when signals arrive at the next neuron to cause that neuron to fire an action potential and pass the signal on. When a message arrives right before or exactly when firing occurs, that synapse will be strengthened. But if a signal arrives even a few milliseconds afterward, the synapse is actually weakened.[21]

Using Brain Plasticity to Parent Better

Your parenting choices have the power to dramatically shape the neuronal connections that survive in your child's brain as it develops. Neuronal activity determines what connections she keeps, and therefore it determines who she becomes. These connections will then determine what she should expect from the world around her and how she should interact with others and will ultimately shape her own parenting skills.[22] So we as parents need to start thinking about experience as a parenting tool that can actually change our child's physiology. We know that to keep our kids healthy we need to feed them right and encourage them to exercise. It's the same with the experiences our kids practice. We should select experiences for them as carefully as we choose foods for them to eat.

BRAIN PLASTICITY DEPENDS ON PRACTICE

Malcolm Gladwell's book *Outliers: The Story of Success* puts forth the idea that you need 10,000 hours of deliberate practice to become a world-class expert in any field.[23] His idea that practice makes perfect—that anyone can become an expert at anything if they only practice enough—has since been debunked by other studies, but neuroscience backs up the claim that if we practice something, we get better at it.[24] Why? It's because practicing an activity or skill supports the development of the neurons and pathways needed to perform it with increasing ease.

When we activate brain circuits between neurons via practice, our brains adapt to that experience using a process called activity-dependent plasticity (see figure 2.8). Activity governs the way neurons connect with a few simple rules:

- The connection between two neurons gets stronger if the pathway between the neurons is used frequently.

- When a pathway is used repeatedly, changes happen at the synapse, and after lots of activity, new synapses can be formed there.

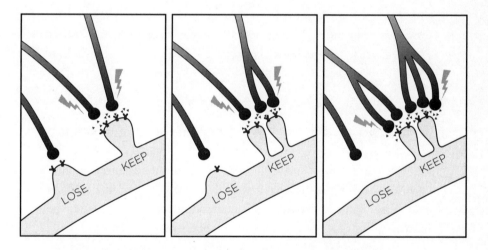

Figure 2.8 Spine dynamics are at the heart of the "use it or lose it" neuroscience principle. Neuronal spines are very changeable structures, particularly in young children. Spines usually are found on the receiving end of excitatory synapses. When a neuronal connection is activated repeatedly (as in the spine shown on the right in each panel), the synapse adapts in an amazing way. It builds up the connection by recruiting more neurotransmitters or receptors, and it can make more spines to receive all the incoming information. But when a connection isn't being used (as in the spine shown on the left in each panel), the spine will retract, making it less likely to keep that neuronal connection in the future.[25]

- With disuse, previously formed synapses can wither and disappear.

- Pathway use can increase myelination of frequently used neurons, which will make the circuit work faster.

PRACTICE CHANGES THE WAY GENES ARE USED

Neuroscience tells us that deliberate practice will change the way the neurons fire and connect. We know that restimulating the same brain circuit results in increased synaptic strength, and we know that practice works best when it's not intermittent. But even if a year goes by between the first and second time a pathway is used, the response to the second use will still be stronger than the first. Practice is a precise controller of gene regulation, of how loud or quiet genes are. Practice allows the genes that dictate learning to be turned up, new protein to be made by these genes to support the enhanced connection, and new synapses to be formed (see appendix 2, "Epigenetics," for more details on this process). This means that practice leads to progress no matter how old the brain is.

PRACTICE MAKES HABITS

What we practice becomes habit. A habit is a series of actions that were, at one time, actively initiated by a person, but have since become automatized. If you set up your child to practice a skill often enough, eventually it will become a habit with an anatomical neurological basis to it. First, habitual activity enhances synaptic strength. Second, the behavioral skill becomes easier due to enhanced information flowing through this behavioral circuit. And third, the ease of flow predisposes the circuit to being used in the same way in the future.[26]

Parents have this miraculous opportunity to push certain neurons down paths, and neuroscience shows us that once a neuron has activated a particular pathway, it's more likely to fire that way again. There's not only a physical strengthening at the synapse through the dedication of neuronal components to support that connection, but the neuron also has a heightened response to being stimulated.

Presumably, habits form simply so we can avoid the stressful process of deliberate decision-making for situations where a rational decision has already been made. Habits are essentially the same as instinct, but they are acquired behaviors rather than innate behaviors. Once a habit has formed, brain activity is highest when the habitual activity starts; it quiets down as the habitual activity continues, and starts up again when the task is finished. During the habitual activity itself, the brain does not have to think about what it's doing—such is the nature of a habit. For example, getting up daily at 6:00 a.m. to exercise before work can become habitual behavior. At first it requires some effort, but soon it take less, until eventually getting up at that time becomes relatively effortless. Every habit was once a goal-directed behavior. Once it's nailed down, it becomes second nature.

Neuroscience defines habits not as automatic behaviors that we repeat, but instead as a stable predisposition to act in a certain way. Habits do not necessarily make us rigid automatons. We want to craft a stable brain structure that is organized in a flexible manner. This flexibility is the actual habit, and new actions can arise out of that. It's your usual way of accomplishing something.[27]

There are two sorts of habits: The first, called routine-habits, emphasize a routine way of doing things and, not surprisingly, increase rigidity and decrease flexibility. These routine-habits, although they are an old parenting trick effective for entraining behavior, aren't really the sort of thing we want for our kids. We don't want robots that follow rigid instructions. Instead, we're trying for thoughtful people who remain adaptable.

As parents, we want to cultivate the other kind of habit, called learning-habits. Learning-habits increase our cognitive control over our own actions and allow us to be more flexible.[28] This happens when we have the general conventions under control so that we don't have to think twice about them. Good behavior is important, but only in that we want our kids to have their approach down pat so that they can move on to the next thing, which is the creative process or the harder task of thinking about the impact of behavior on others.

Learning-habits make the basic start of a behavior separate from conscious control, freeing up your brain's real estate for higher and deeper engagement with the situation. For example, if you know how to both read musical notes and find those notes accurately on the keyboard when you play the piano, you have room to pay attention to playing the instrument in an expressive way, or even possibly improvise. The difference between a piano player and a virtuoso is being able to master the rules and then go beyond the rules with creativity, to work on not just synaptic plasticity, but to show *behavioral* plasticity or adaptation.

PARENTS CAN INFLUENCE BRAIN CIRCUITS

We prioritize some brain circuits over others simply by using them more than others. In many ways, people choose who they become by what they choose to do—and the neurons they choose to fire as a result of doing specific activities. When our kids are young, parents have the privilege of choosing which activities they do and, therefore, which initial circuits get developed in their brains. Gradually, our kids will start to prioritize some circuits over others and so form values by priming certain circuits for easier use. Our kids will form value habits. This process of value formation can be modulated by two things: (1) the way our children think about things, using their higher order processing, and (2) by the experiences they have.

Parenting is the business of shaping people. People are shaped by what they practice, practice changes neural connections, and neural connections make us who we are. So, determining what our kids practice is the most important part of parenting, and we do this by setting specific experiences in the direct path of our children.

Remember that every thought and every action strengthens some synapses and not others, and this neural refinement is constantly happening, even during sleep. Therefore, every thought ends up being a developmental process. When we think in a certain way, we are strengthening certain synapses. As parents, we're in a place to help determine what our kids' automatic behavior looks like because we can participate in habit formation. This is all about using the brain pathways we want strengthened.

Our children have about 25,000 waking hours over a 5-year period, taking into account 10 hours of sleep per night. We get to have about

5,000 hours of potential interaction time with our child each year, or we get to place them in situations where they can practice the skills that we want them to develop and maintain. If we, as parents, focus our attention on helping our kids practice going to sleep, as so many of us do, then they'll eventually sleep without us. If we drill in the multiplication tables, the brain will learn them. If we focus our time and attention on creativity, on empathy, on self-control, those skills will blossom.

Debunking the Left-Brain/Right-Brain Myth

As a parent, you need to cultivate the whole brain. Throw out the idea of the right brain being the creative side of the brain and the left side being the logic side, because it's completely inaccurate. Trying to teach something to only the left brain and ignoring the right brain is about as effective as yelling into the left ear and hoping the right ear can't hear it. If a teacher designs lesson plans targeting only the left brain, he's wasting his time.

When we're drawing conclusions for parenting, it's important to understand much of what we assume about lateralization in the brain isn't founded in real science. Somehow the science got misrepresented. The truth is that human brains *are* slightly asymmetric, but those differences vary from person to person. These universal left-brain/right-brain ideas are probably a result of the misapplication of studies that looked at brain lateralization (meaning an event is preferentially localized on one side), which concluded that in *extremely right-handed* subjects, language processing is localized in the left side of the brain, and emotional content/graphic information is processed in the right. However, even in these extreme cases, language processing occurs on the right side of the brain as well. Language areas like Broca's and Wernicke's are typically found on the left (95%–99% of right-handers and 70% of left-handers), but a large portion of the population actually are right-brained for language.[29]

Investigation shows that people don't have stronger neural networks across either the right or left side of their brain but instead use both halves of their brain.[30] Creative thought favors neither hemisphere.

Unfortunately, popular culture is replete with myths about how the brain works, and it is often difficult to sort out fact from fiction. See appendix 3, "Neuromyths Versus Neurofacts," to learn how to make your way through the maze of often-confusing claims so that you can identify information that is based on solid science rather than popular misconceptions.

3

Second Nature Parenting

Methods for Developing the Three Skills

EXPERIENCE IS A DRUG that can shape the brain—not just by having the right experiences, but also by avoiding the wrong ones. These experiences change our neuronal architecture and make us who we are. Our kids will naturally get some experience-based knowledge through living, but there are other skills that may never fully develop if we don't focus on them.

As parents, part of our responsibility is to help our kids develop the brain pathways that make second nature the skills we find to be most important, and to allow brain pathways for qualities that we don't want our kids to have to go unused, like the inclination to put self first, the tendency to minimize cooperative effort, or a comfort with conflict avoidance. So how do we get our kids to use the synapses that we want them to keep? The key is practice.

If giving our kids the right kinds of experiences is the parenting goal, then we need some tools to get our kids to practice those experiences. (I'm not talking about forced practice, like "I'm going to set a timer for 45 minutes, and you had better practice the cello for the entire time, because I'm listening in the next room.") Instead, we have to teach kids the utility of creativity, empathy, and self-control so that they believe as much as we do that these skills are worth practicing. We need buy-in from our kids, or our tactics won't give us long-term results.

The only way to get experience is to, well, experience it. Here's a game plan for turning our purpose into practice:

Step 1: Have a plan.

Step 2: Create space for your plan to work.

Step 3: Give your child guidance.

Step 4: Give your child some more space.

STEP 1   Have a Plan

Once we know that both activity and inactivity are constantly shaping specific brain circuits, parenting seems quite weighty. Good parenting means acting with full consciousness of the nature of what we're doing and the effects that it will have on brain development. There's this idea that we have to be "on" all the time and that we can't miss a moment. But we can parent effectively without deliberate action 24 hours a day. In fact, sometimes you purposefully want to step out of the way of what's happening with your kids. Instead, simply having a plan about what to practice is enough. Keep these three things in mind as you parent your child's experience:

- Make creativity, empathy, and self-control your parenting priorities. Share these priorities with your kids. Explain why these skills are important.

- Once a day, using the tools in this chapter, set up an experience in your children's world that allows them to practice creativity, empathy, or self-control. These experiences don't have to be daylong adventures; 10 seconds is enough to pull something into your kids' awareness. Some of these will be actual experiences, while some will be simply framing normal experiences differently.

- When things aren't going right, be consistent and remember the big three skills you're aiming for. This might mean not acting on your gut response to a child's behavior, but instead pivoting the situation toward practicing one of the skills. It means being proactive instead of reactive to our children.

STEP 2 Create Space for Your Plan to Work

Space comes in a lot of forms: It could be some thinking space or some alone time. It could be disconnecting from our normal routine, a time-out, getting off social media, enforcing silence, taking a walk in the woods, yoga, some space without someone else telling us what to do. Regardless of how we get it, space is essential, and it seems there's never enough of it. You'll need to carve it out for both yourself and your kids. This space can be created by allowing free play, providing your kids with decision-making opportunities, helping them experience both power and powerlessness, and/or encouraging reflection and mindfulness.

ALLOW FREE PLAY

I once heard an elementary school teacher say, "I love 10-minute recesses. There's not enough time for anyone to get into trouble." It's true. Extended playtime gives time for conflict to happen. But it also gives kids time to figure out what to do about the conflict and to resolve it.

We shouldn't be surprised that our schools are squeezing the playtime out of preschool and kindergarten. It's simply a reflection of the way most families currently raise their children. We keep them busy. We enrich them with extracurricular activities. But the things we give them to occupy their time are always adult-guided. Being in ballet class or playing soccer or learning violin after school steals time from our kids—time to play by the rules they make up themselves and time to practice regulating their own behavior.

Unstructured playtime is a magic space where kids learn to make decisions, to resolve conflict, and to self-regulate; it's where a thousand life lessons can be learned. It's the ultimate "how-to" for the adult world that is coming—the basis for how to eat dinner by yourself at a restaurant, how to deal with not getting the job you worked so hard for, how to avoid a catty coworker, how to get back into the game when you're failing or when you have to be "it." And play is only available for a limited time in your children's lives.

Jean-Jacques Rousseau, an eighteenth-century Swiss philosopher, believed in learning by doing and thought that knowledge acquired through direct experience is more permanent. According to Rousseau, children should be educated by carefully placing various experiences in their life paths in order to develop a strong moral character. The end result of these natural consequences will be—ta-da!—a self-governing adult. Though this type of child-centered education is not neuroscience-based, it does capture a way of parenting in which children take responsibility for their own learning and that rightly puts the emphasis on the experiences that a child gets to have.

PROVIDE DECISION-MAKING OPPORTUNITIES

There's little unstructured space in our children's lives for independent decision-making. If a kid is shuttled to school, adheres to rules all day, goes straight to afterschool baseball practice, comes home, eats dinner, does homework, and watches TV or plays a video game before going to bed, that's an entire day where she has made no decisions for herself except whether to follow the rules or not.

Grown-ups helicopter over kids, around them, and between them, and at the same time grown-ups expect kids to act like they're adults who cannot drive yet. As a result, decision-making skills are not being strengthened in our children. After 18 years of being told what to do, of letting mom and dad and teacher and coach decide things for them, our kids have weak and spindly decision-making pathways. We expect them to magically problem solve and self-regulate when they leave our houses simply because they're old enough now, and we think their brains are done developing. But our children got good at what they practiced—they are now fine young adults who can make the decisions we've told them to.

The lack of unstructured playtime means our kids don't truly experience personal consequence. They're not learning resiliency or problem-solving skills. They're not experiencing what it feels like to be powerful or powerless when a grown-up is always keeping things fair. We're expecting them to use high levels of self-control at every step of the way without helping them practice the two essential skills that make self-control efforts effective: empathy and creativity.

If we want our children to grow up to be good decision makers, we need to let them make decisions (see figure 3.1) and give them the tools they need to make good ones. Decisions are an executive function balancing act of all the things you have learned and your current emotional state, so making decisions is an extremely complicated process that depends on many levels of neural operation. It involves not just the ability to pay attention, but also the ability to suppress

Figure 3.1 There are many practical benefits to enhancing decision-making skills in our kids and in ourselves. Parents can help by allowing autonomous decision-making whenever possible, by encouraging mindfulness and reflection, and by providing play opportunities and practice.

irrelevant information, keep all the pieces of a situation in your head, and have enough impulse control. These cognitive pieces are also components of executive functioning.[1, 2] You don't just walk in a room and juggle those balls well without hours of practice.

There's a lot of interconnection between the different executive functioning skills. These are not just traits that people are born with, but they can change in an experience-dependent way through—you guessed it—synaptic plasticity. Evidence shows that training in one area can influence other similar executive functioning processes, though the transfer may be narrow, and we're still figuring out where the overlaps are.[3, 4] For instance, we know that working memory, which is the amount of short-term information you can hold on to while you're in the process of making a decision or a judgment, is really important for learning and for reasoning. Working memory training may lead to an increase in working memory capacity, which then may cause an increase in overall processing efficiency, which can result in the ability to pay greater attention.[5-7] However, working memory training may not enhance things like self-control or processing speed.

Once we become aware of how our children's daily activities are designed without opportunity for choice, we can work to modify them in small ways to allow true decision autonomy. It may start with a child simply "choosing" whether to sort magnetic letters, play with pattern blocks, or complete a handwriting worksheet during free time at school. But eventually this approach requires kids to experience true choice. It's the difference between a kid picking his own flavor at the ice cream shop or actually making the ice cream himself. Kids need more than just the illusion of choice to fully develop true self-regulation skills. Sometimes major creativity will be required on our part to make opportunities for decision-making to happen, but we need to set up these opportunities for our kids, let them make decisions, and then step back so that they can implement the decisions they make.

Choose Your Own Parenting Adventure: Decision-Making
Parenting for the three skills doesn't mean you have to be a superparent who is always "on." Not only is that impossible, but it will drive

your kids crazy and will leave you feeling guilty and exhausted. Instead, recognize that if you're clearly steering the ship, it only takes a few minutes each day to practice the skills you want your kids to build. The easiest way to do this is to simply change your parenting approach to normal situations.

Everyday life with our kids can be like those "choose your own adventure" books many of us checked out from the library in grade school. At critical points in the plot, the reader is asked to choose what the characters should do next. You'd choose one option, and then you'd turn to a certain page of the book to see the consequences of that choice for the characters. Make a different choice, and the plot would go a different direction. The same thing happens in real life as we're interacting with our kids. We're constantly being asked to choose our own parenting adventure by deciding how to respond to our kids' actions.

Here's a common parenting scenario: It's 6:00 in the morning. You are in bed, soundly sleeping. Your 3-year-old son calls out to you. "Come get in bed with me for a few more minutes," you call back, and you feel a warm body crawl in beside you. It's quiet for a minute. Then you hear: "I need a toy." You grope beside the bed, coming up with a library book and passing it over. "Here, have this," you say. You hear pages turning in the barely lit room. Then, from the other side of the bed, you hear your 6-year-old daughter say loudly, "That's *my* book." You feel her standing there. And as your son starts to cry, you know your daughter is pulling on the book, and he is clutching it tightly.

What do you do? You have several options to choose from, and each option will take the scene in a different direction.

You could just decide the ownership of the book. But, ah, the ownership of library books is a tricky one. If you think your son should have it, you'll sternly tell your daughter, "It's a library book. It's not actually yours. He can read it too." Your daughter will loudly protest, wait until you close your eyes, and twist her brother's arm as she pulls the book out of his hands and leaves the room with it. He'll start to scream. Now you're awake and have to deal with her misbehavior.

On the other hand, if you think your daughter should have the book, you'll make your son give it back to her. "Sorry, it's her library book," you'll say. Your daughter will leave the room with the book. Your son will cry and throw the next book that you hand him—along with anything else you thrust his way—on the floor.

Or you may just take the book away from both kids. "If you fight over the book, no one gets the book," you could say, and put the book under your pillow. Your daughter will cry. Your son will cry. You will kind of feel like crying. During breakfast, your son will scream because you served his sister some juice in his cup, and you'll have to deal with this conflict all over again.

But maybe you would like them to share the book. You could say to your daughter: "It's a library book, honey. It doesn't actually belong to you, and you can have it in 5 minutes." She'll protest loudly. "Fine, then you can read it with him now," you can say. Your daughter will climb into bed with you, too, and they'll fight over who should hold the book until the book pops you in the head, hard. Not a wonderful way to wake up!

Sometimes, no matter how creative or fair your solutions are, you just can't make two kids happy. You could help your daughter solve the situation herself. If you can get her to come up with options herself, it may work better, since she not only makes a choice, but she picks the choice. Ask her: "How can you make this situation better? Is there a way you can both be happy?"

If she comes up empty, you can offer suggestions. You could say to her, "Sure, it's yours, honey. But if you'd like to read it right now, can you go get him another book instead? I bet there's a book he'd like even better, and then you can read your book all by yourself." Your daughter may look puzzled and then go get her brother a tractor book. She'll climb back in your bed, and they might switch books. You get to doze for 5 more minutes to the sound of flipping pages.

But maybe your daughter refuses to get her brother another book, or maybe her brother says he doesn't want the new book. Don't give up on this. This is your first look at "scaffolding" an emotional situation for your kids and giving them tools to do it on their own. (Scaffolding is a method parents can use to provide a framework or template to help their children practice skills or behaviors.)

Of course, you might need coffee first for this scenario, but it won't always be this hard. The first few times you do it will be new for all of you, but it will become both quicker and easier each time.

ST330

Dear Sounds True friend,

Since 1985, Sounds True has been sharing spiritual wisdom and resources to help people live more genuine, loving, and fulfilling lives. We hope that our programs inspire and uplift you, enabling you to bring forth your unique voice and talents for the benefit of us all.

We would like to invite you to become part of our growing online community by giving you three downloadable programs—an introduction to the treasure of authors and artists available at Sounds True! To receive these gifts, just flip this card over for details, then visit us at **SoundsTrue.com/Free** and enter your email for instant access.

With love on the journey,

TAMI SIMON Founder and Publisher, Sounds True

 **SOUNDS TRUE**
many voices, one journey   800.333.9185

With repeated practice, children will eventually come up with their own ideas. And when you give them some space to think about the scenario, even if your daughter says nothing in the moment that you wait, she is practicing. Responding to conflict is becoming more familiar for her; it has a structure to it and has a potential solution that can be tackled head-on.

ALLOW ROOM FOR POWER SHIFTS

Respect makes us feel powerful, as does the perception of control, which makes us more likely to act and interact with things in our environment.[8] Making space to recognize and feel these power shifts can help us make better decisions because we achieve a more complete understanding of a situation. Power is a strategic advantage that comes in many forms. It can be power of place, financial power, social power, the power of knowledge, the power of experience. In every social situation, somebody is a little bit more in charge. A loss of power—which can be as simple as being in the minority, such as being the only female in a business meeting or being a new student trying to find a seat in the cafeteria on the first day at a new high school—puts someone at a disadvantage.

Ideally, all of us would get to practice being in both the power positions and the weaker positions. This makes for a relatively balanced life perspective. But sometimes we are dealt a stacked hand in life, with an imbalance of privilege or of disadvantage. When you've been in a position of privileged power for a long period of time, typically your empathy levels are lower, and you have to work even harder to see things from someone else's point of view.

But when you're always the underdog, the effects of constant disadvantage will impact you in other ways. Constant power disadvantage is present in normal living situations. It's worth taking note of because power can change decision-making, and as we make different decisions, we change activity levels in different neural circuits, strengthening some and weakening others.

Unless we point out power differentials to our children, they will experience these transient power shifts simply as changes in their level of comfort in different situations. We want our kids to feel powerful, but we also want them to understand what it's like to not have power. So we need to have them practice in both spaces.

As we know, some types of power can be fleeting. In every new social scenario, the power is up for grabs. The easiest way to give a kid power is to let him decide between two choices. This might make for happier children during free choice kindergarten activity time, but it's not enough to grow kids who can think for themselves.

The *best* way to give power is to allow a child to both pick the choices and then make a decision. Kids need structure and guidance to do this well, but with practice you can set up a situation where your daughter can mediate her own conflict with her brother the next time they fight over a library book at 6:00 a.m. (even while you're still asleep).

Power can explain a lot about family dynamics—like birth order effects. Take my 6-year-old son, Bryant, for example, who is the youngest of four siblings. Since he was born, Bryant has been living a power imbalance in both age and experience: He never gets to sit in the front seat, he never gets to know it all, and he's always being corrected. Being the last of four kids comes with vast benefits as well: extra love, extra social connections, and extra role models. But as a parent, I give him opportunities to boost his power whenever I see a way to even out the playing field.

What does boosting power look like? I let him dole out the cookies when it's time for dessert. I choose him to go first when we all talk about our days at the dinner table. I ask him to teach us all how to do the finger knitting he learned in kindergarten. And in doing so, I can momentarily "deal him an ace," so he feels what it's like to be on top.

To keep everything balanced, sometimes I purposefully decrease my oldest child's power. I remind him that it's not playing favorites—it's evening things up. My firstborn got to go first at everything for several years of his life before he had siblings. I do this because I worry most about those kids who have always been on top, who have always come in first, whose parents have always gone in and fixed things with the teachers. I worry for their empathy skills, their problem-solving ability, and their ability to make good decisions. From a neuroscience perspective, I mourn the loss of the sheer beauty of what the brain does when it's making synaptic connections to figure out how not to be the underdog anymore. With a lack of practice, these skills will remain stagnant.

Parents, I urge you to let your kids fail—in a balanced way. Not always, but perhaps failure every fourth time a kid gets in a difficult situation is the ideal recipe for raising an empowered kid. Failure relinquishes power. And then the problem-solving and creativity can begin.

Choose Your Own Parenting Adventure: Power

How might you respond to the following parenting scenario?

Three-year-old Ellie is feeling left out of a card game that her older brother, Paul, and sister, Katie, are playing. You've just finished making lunch, and as you call them all in to eat, you hear Paul say, "So, Ellie, what's 2 plus 2? See, she doesn't even know." Ellie enters the kitchen crying, the older kids trailing behind.

As the parent, you may choose to intervene in this situation:

> **You could send Paul into time-out.** And you'll probably watch Paul protest loudly and then brush hard against Ellie when he finally leaves the kitchen, making her cry again. "That's 5 extra minutes!" you'll yell after him.

> **You could make Paul apologize.** Lunch will go on without incident. Afterward, the kids go outside to play, and in 10 minutes, Ellie will probably come in crying again from a new insult.

> **You could try to talk it through with Paul.** You might say, "She's little. Of course she doesn't know 2 plus 2 yet. Look at her crying. How do you think it makes Ellie feel when you leave her out like that?" Paul might mumble, "It makes her feel sad." That's a start. But then you might ask him to tell Ellie that and to come up with a card game that Ellie can play. After a minute, Paul might decide she could play war, but refuse to play himself. If you offer to

play war with Ellie after lunch, you might find that Paul eats his lunch quietly, but as soon as he's done, maybe he'll say he's ready to play war. Hopefully you'll hear him orchestrating a fair card game in the living room as you clean up the lunch dishes.

You may also choose not to intervene in this situation. But you'll probably have to get involved later anyway. During lunch, Paul might ask Katie if she will play cards with him again in his room after lunch. She agrees, while Paul pointedly ignores Ellie asking to join in until she's crying again.

There are ways of intervening in this situation that are not overt, though. You could tell Paul he needs to teach Ellie how to add 2 plus 2, as well as 1 plus 2 and 1 plus 1. There will be a quiz before dessert, and she has to get 100% correct. Lunchtime may become a game, with Katie pitching in as well to get Ellie to say the right answers. After Ellie passes the test with flying colors, lunch will be over, and the kids might decide to play outside together.

Or you could simply hand Ellie a box of cookies, hoping to even the playing field. She will instantly stop crying, and Paul will start protesting, "Hey, that's not fair! Why does she get all those cookies? Just because she's crying?" You can ignore Paul and say, "When you're done with your sandwich, Ellie, you can hand out dessert." Placing Ellie in the important role of cookie-keeper means that the power balance has been temporarily flipped. "How many can I have?" Paul will ask. "It's up to Ellie," you say. After she gets to be generous with her siblings, you might finally hear Paul orchestrating an inclusive card game in the living room.

ENCOURAGE MINDFUL REFLECTION

We are all refining synapses with every experience. Parents do it as they parent, teachers do it as they teach, and children do it as they learn to become who they are. Psychologists and experiential learning teachers consider mindful reflection a fundamental part of that learning experience. When we critically reflect on an experience, we stop to assimilate information, we evaluate which elements are important and which we need to let go, and we see how it connects to where we've been and where we're going. Finally—and most importantly—we decide how we want to respond.

Mindful reflection permits many complex neurological processes to happen by fostering interconnection, both in ideas around you in the world and in your actual brain circuits. Mindful reflection goes hand in hand with feeling power in a situation, which in turn gives the decision maker control and increases ownership over personal decisions. If you are rushed or forced to do something, you're less likely to act in a deliberate way and less likely to take responsibility for your actions. I'm constantly telling my kids (particularly when I hear tattling), "The only person you're in charge of is yourself." When we give our kids a mindful moment, we're giving them space to self-regulate, which is a skill they desperately need to practice. And when we allow them to make their own decisions, embedded in that is the idea that they can deliberately hold themselves accountable for the outcome of those decisions, even when we are not standing right next to them.

Mindful reflection is something we can teach and something we can practice. Mindfulness training taps into three ingredients of self-control: (1) what we pay attention to, (2) how we regulate the emotions we feel, and (3) self-awareness. Remarkably, the brain gets better at all three of these things when we practice mindful reflection. We're still figuring out the functional impact that mindfulness has on the brain: brain imaging studies find it's probable that mindfulness changes synaptic functioning and myelination, but it may also decrease the stress response and boost the immune system.[9] Mindfulness causes rapid changes in gene expression, including decreasing expression of stress-related genes, such as genes associated with disease-causing inflammation.[10] Practicing mindfulness is an easy, researched way to change how our brains work.

Mindfulness is a deliberate awareness of *now*, in the absence of what it means. Mindfulness keeps attention right here for just a moment. The processing of *now* in the context of what's already happened and what is to come—termed *reflection*—can happen in the next minute. But they are both important because you can't properly process without having a clear understanding of the current situation. Mindful reflection is the awareness together with the processing.

We need to start in our own homes, but mindfulness can have a big impact even in larger-scale classroom situations. At Visitacion Valley Middle School in San Francisco, the introduction of an optional 15-minute quiet time at both the beginning and end of the school day decreased suspensions and truancies in students that attend this "tough" school. The students were happier and doing better academically, despite the neighborhood proximity to drugs and gang violence.[11] That's it: a simple, optional quiet time.

As parents, we can easily insert moments for reflection into our kids' lives as a way of allowing them to process events. Sometimes this means putting a child in a purposeful time-out where release will require a conversation. Sometimes, it simply means not intervening in a situation. Sometimes, it means respecting a child's decision even when you disagree with it. Sometimes it means talking through a bad decision and helping your child decide to do it better, based on the impact on the people involved. In these mindful moments, we're practicing self-regulation for our kids and with our kids. (For more on how to incorporate mindfulness and reflection into our kids' everyday lives, see "Guided Mindfulness" on page 57.)

And, importantly, we can use mindful reflection ourselves to keep our parenting goals in mind, since the benefits extend to us as well. We desperately need those quiet moments when we can, first, breathe all the way in, and, second, consider, "Is this the direction I want to go in? How will this affect those around me?" It's rare that we take those moments in the middle of go-go-go and shuttle-me-here and where's-my-shoe-mornings. But mindful reflection is good for children, and it's good for the adults in charge of them. In fact, the introduction of that quiet time at Visitacion Valley Middle School also increased faculty retention there.

When we intentionally place mindful moments in the paths of our kids, the result will be kids who act with intention. If we practice mindful reflection with our kids enough, it will become second nature to them.

STEP 3   Give Your Child Guidance

Your child will need your guidance to deal with the issues that inevitably come up as he experiences the consequences of his decisions. Importantly, you want to teach him how to do it better next time, to make sure you're strengthening the brain connections you want to retain. You can provide guidance through modeling, guided mindfulness, scaffolding, or discipline (which is discussed further in chapter 11).

MODELING

The best way to invest in the three skills and to keep them a priority is to adopt them yourself. To actually model good self-regulation as a parent, you have to first work on creativity, empathy, and self-control in the ways that you interact with your child and in the ways you deal with the world around you. Try to cultivate one of these skills in yourself every day. Periodically take time for reflection. Make sure your approach is working. If not, make changes to ensure you're heading in the right direction.

GUIDED MINDFULNESS

Guided mindfulness provides a bit of a structure to the mindful reflection process, and it can be a good place to start with your kids, rather than just allowing unmonitored space where bad decisions can snowball or putting them in time-out and shutting the door. Guided mindfulness can be as simple as doing these two things:

1. Ask your child to *observe* what she sees and what she notices about the situation. At first, you can provide an example, focusing on what you think is important about the situation.

2. Ask your child to *reflect* on how those observations apply to herself, to others, to the world, and to the actions that could possibly come next.

Encourage children to take a mindful moment when conflict arises, when they feel confused, or when they feel sad. These moments let kids check in with themselves, allow them to pivot if needed, and allow them to make a decision and claim a direction.

Eventually, you want your child organically taking this space for herself. The time investment required to start is minimal compared to the giant gains your kids will make in independent thought and personal accountability. A mindful moment doesn't have to be a whole minute—it may not be more than your child being quiet for a few seconds. It may take a few times of practice, but you're working toward autonomy in your child. If your child doesn't take a mindful moment on her own, step in and offer it, discussing how you feel, how your child feels, or how others may feel.

PARENTAL SCAFFOLDING

Sometimes our kids will do the right thing simply by thinking through all the options. But sometimes they'll need a push in the right direction. Parental scaffolding is key to changing how a child thinks about a situation and what the child sees as important in any given scenario. Scaffolding is where parents provide children with a framework or template for understanding situations, particularly social scenarios or conflict resolutions. This structure could be only verbal, parents could model the behavior, or it could be just plain pointed practice that the parent sets up. The point is to get a child's brain processing the situation enough times that it becomes second nature to him, to do it over and over in thought and in action until it becomes part of who he is.

Parents can verbally scaffold things for a child, for example, by talking through an event while it's happening with the child or by elaborating on their recounting of the event after the fact. This verbal scaffolding affects the way a child talks about the event later since what you highlight is what they will remember better, and it helps connect the event to more things in the child's head.[12, 13] Our explanations make a difference.

Verbal scaffolding works for traumatic situations, such as providing a framework for me to discuss with my kids the Nazi demonstrations that happened in our hometown of Charlottesville, Virginia, in 2017. But it also works for more ordinary experiences, like our family outing to the local Dogwood Festival where we went on the carnival rides, and where, unfortunately, one ride made the kid in the neighboring compartment so dizzy that he vomited, and his mother yelled at him.

In the same way that you can talk through things that happen to or around your child, behavioral choices can be scaffolded and reinforced so that a child can be primed for the right habits. A hands-on approach is needed at the beginning, but a hands-off approach is needed by the end, when your child leaves the house to start an independent life. Once the construction is done on a building, you remove the scaffolding around the structure as soon as possible. It obstructs the view. As a parent, you have to know when it's time to step away from your child. You're working on an oceanfront mansion here!

Let's say we're at that same Dogwood Festival, and another kid takes the stuffed animal that your 9-year-old daughter won playing Skee-Ball and throws it up on the roof of the bathroom. Of course, she'll come crying to you. You need to give her a framework to deal with the situation as independently as she is ready for. The younger she is, the more you should model for her—for example, the first time you try this with her, demonstrate or talk through what she should do in this situation. (See "Conflict Resolution Tool #1: Teach Your Child to Communicate Very Clearly" in chapter 7.) Have her go with you as you talk to the other child. If the other child is gone, just practice with her what to say next time.

After you have helped scaffold an event like this for her two or three times, she should be able to talk through a similar event herself. And when the next time comes, whether it's the next day waiting in line to check out groceries or at the next visit to the Dogwood Festival, encourage your child to try scaffolding for herself and help her make sense of the outcome. If your child is the one who threw the stuffed animal on the roof, you can still scaffold, but you'll need to be practicing something different (see "The OUT Framework" in chapter 7).

We remember things that we don't know we remember. A stunning example of this is given to us by Henry Molaison, who had an operation to control his seizures in 1953.[14] The physicians removed brain areas where the seizures were originating, including parts of his temporal lobes that contain the **hippocampus**. As a result, Henry's seizures went away, but he could no longer form new memories once he recovered from surgery. He couldn't remember the doctors who cared for him daily, and as time when on, he didn't know what year it was or who the president was.

This is, unfortunately, the way we pinned down that the hippocampus is responsible for making short-term memories. But Henry was still intelligent because memories aren't stored in just one place. Instead, they are held in multiple brain regions, and superior IQ can be retained even in people who have had large portions of their brain surgically removed.[15] Henry was also able to show us a lot about how memory works in other ways. Henry was asked to draw a five-pointed star without looking at the paper, using only the reflection in a mirror to guide his work. Each day he had no memory of doing the task, and yet over a 10-day period he got better and better at it. There are additional brain areas being activated while these procedural memories form, and an awareness of learning wasn't a requirement for his learning.

It's the same with our kids. They may not have overt memories of our instructions, but they are learning every time they experience something, every time they practice, every time we orient them to an issue by asking a question, even if that question hangs in the air unanswered. We need to figure out how we can more frequently activate the neural pathways that control those behaviors we want to see, and we need to figure out what to do if our kids act in the exact opposite way from what we want to see. To do this, we need to (1) give our kids specific practice and (2) hold them accountable for practicing learning-habits in the right way (see page 39).

Why It's Important to Scaffold Experience

If repeated, an experience can eventually change the way a child's brain works through synaptic plasticity. That's the neurological definition of habit formation: the neuronal landscape will change in response to consequences, irrespective of whether those consequences are natural or artificially crafted.

If you skimp on the scaffolding, you won't provide enough early direction to make the impact on neurological habits, even if your own life is an excellent example or model. It's not enough for kids to simply watch you. Parts of their brains and characters will unfold without your parental intervention, but not all skills are present from the beginning in all children, and they will instead require work in order to develop. Neuroscience tells us that action is crafting the synapses, and so we must use scaffolding to make sure our kids aren't practicing actions that are the opposite of the creativity, empathy, self-control, and self-regulation skills we want them to develop.

The Kind of Practice Is Important

If kids naturally handled social interaction in the best way, parents would be out of a job. We have to be involved in order for kids to practice things in the right way, and that parental focus during the initial practice ensures that our kids will keep activating the neural circuits we want them to keep. Practice works well enough that we have to carefully choose what we spend our time doing. For example, research has shown that classical musical training can enhance myelination and restructure the area of the brain that controls finger movements but that it is not associated with enhanced connectivity between creative brain areas.[16]

But another study showed that adults who have more musical improvisation practice have more connectivity within the area of the brain that interprets and processes connections between diverse concepts (called the association cortex), which provides good evidence that creative behaviors can be automated by training.[17] The differences here are subtle, but important: Both of the studies involve musical training, and both show that the musical training changes the brain. But the way people are trained in music is important. Are they practicing rote musical routines, or are they practicing improvising new melodies? The first study demonstrates routine-habits while the second study shows learning-habits.

Can you imagine your son spending his piano practice time just playing whatever comes to mind? It would be hard to resist the temptation to make him practice specific songs—to become proficient at music someone else has written. The idea that novel responses can become automatic for a person is an interesting one, but it does fit with the way that brain development occurs. Remember, if you use a pathway, it become stronger. So, if you have forged multiple pathways of brain connectivity and use them often, it's easier to come up with divergent thoughts using those pathways. It's like running on well-worn trails versus making a new path through the woods. Strengthen the pathways between cortical association areas now, and you have a lifelong creative thinker. This is the difference between fostering kids who have routine-habits and kids who thrive with learning-habits—you want to make autonomous, creative thought processes a matter of course.

Scaffolded Practice Can Help in Three Ways

We can orchestrate situations for our kids to practice skills we want to foster, like teaching an only child how to react to a cousin's playful but slightly mean teasing. Or we can kindly force our kids to walk through situations for their own self-development when they're in the wrong—like requiring your child to go through the right way to make amends for practicing a soccer slide tackle on a little brother in the dining room. ("I should have asked him to put the batteries down instead of tackling him and grabbing them out of his hands.") Forced or not, practice changes the way the brain works.

There are three ways we can use scaffolded practice with our children: to boost skills that aren't so strong, to deal with small things, and to change bad habits.

Boosting skills that aren't so strong. My daughter Katherine hates making people sad and hurting their feelings. This is a lovely way to be, and her kindness is awe-inspiring to me sometimes. But her dad and I worry that there may be a blurry line between being accommodating and saying no when a no should be said. We want her to stay true to what she thinks is right, even if it might make someone sad or mad. So periodically, we set her up in the kitchen and act out scenarios in which she needs to say no. We pretend to be kids in her fifth-grade class. ("Hey BFF, will you tell my mom that I'm at your house if she calls? I'm really riding my bike to 7-Eleven to buy a ton of candy by myself.") Or we pretend we're workers at Dairy Queen. ("I'm so tired from scratching off all these lottery tickets I bought because I'm trying to win the big jackpot, so would you mind cleaning off all those tables for me over by the window when you're done with your ice cream?") And sometimes we act like we're random strangers. ("Hey, I've just been struck by lightning. Will you come inside my van and help me find a Band-Aid?") Katherine practices saying no. Even though acting out these scenes are borderline ridiculous, she learns that telling people, "No, I can't help you," is sometimes the right thing to do. And because the practice is done in a fun way, we are on the same team as Katherine. We work on saying no before it ever becomes an issue.

You know your children better than anyone else. You know where they're great and where they need a boost to be balanced and well-rounded. Taking literally 2 minutes a day to focus on a skill that needs a boost will give you results faster than you ever dreamed. If, for example, every day for 7 days you have a conversation with your child in which you explore how someone feels, you can bet they will become more aware of people's feelings and the impact of their actions on those feelings. Your actions will bring that to the forefront of the way they look at the world.

Dealing with the small things. The next three parts of the book will show you how to use practice to help your kids get better at self-control, have more empathy, and be more creative. This book focuses on big skills, but neuroscience principles don't discriminate. You can practice anything. Want your child to get in the car on time every morning? Start positive: make it a race, leave a new library book hidden in the car for him, or let him pick the music played in the car if he's strapped in on time. The point is to get him doing it. Get those neural pathways working. Let him have the experience of setting his own little timer and getting himself out to the car, irrespective of his motivation to do so. Let him figure out how to get it done. This will strengthen the pathways that underlie getting to the car on time.

Then, after a few days of success, abandon the incentives and focus on the central issues if the good behavior stops. Each time you drive away together from the house on the mornings that he's late, ask him to own what he did, and give him the words to articulate if he gets it wrong. Ask about the impact his behavior has on others and explain better if he gets it wrong. Ask him to come up with several ways to get in the car on time, make him commit to one way for the future, and then work to make that way easy for him to accomplish. Eventually, that conversation will be relatively self-guided by your son.

To set up a practicing scaffold, you simply have to get your kid into the situation you want to work on. Sometimes this will happen naturally over the course of a day, like a kid who's consistently late to things. Sometimes you may have to introduce fake scenarios and talk through them, like my husband and I did with Katherine. These interactions must be deliberate verbal scaffolding of an event, as simple as posing a few well-placed questions, even if you don't get an answer back. Or they can be behavioral practice (which, in my opinion, is one of the most fun and rewarding parts about parenting because you are playing the game of life together with your kid).

For example, when my son had his first middle school dance, I had a brief moment of panic. I had a flashback of my own painfully awkward first dance and thought, "How will my son know what to do?" He needed to practice approaching others and asking them to dance and receiving rejection gracefully. So, I turned on some loud music in our living room, arranged his little sisters around me in a corner cluster, and instructed him to come and ask me to dance in a few minutes. I told him what to do if I said no. He gave me a look, but he waited a few minutes and then walked over and shouted over the blaring music, "Would you like to dance with me?" I laughed and said, "I don't think so." And he said, "Okay, let me know if you change your mind," and walked away.

Think of each skill that you want to cultivate like a new board game that you're playing with younger children. You have to read the rules out loud and teach them how to play. Then that first game takes a while. There will be confusion and complaining. It might not be much fun for you. But the second time you play, your kids will know what's coming, and by the fourth time you won't have to join them. You could even go read a book on your own. In fact, kids will come up with their own game-winning strategies, now that the objective of the game is clear to them. It's the same with the skills of being creative, being empathetic, and maintaining self-control.

Changing bad habits. If actions are good ones, they don't need to change. But habits aren't always good, and sometimes behavior needs to change. The neural circuits involved in habit formation are under active scientific investigation, and, luckily, there's not a firm critical period of time in which to change behavior through practice.[18] Synapses can always change. An old dog can still learn new tricks. We just might be out of practice.

Thomas Aquinas pointed out that "before the habits of virtue are completely formed, they exist in us in certain natural inclinations, which are the beginnings of the virtues. But afterwards, through practice in their actions, they are brought to their proper completion."[19] This statement holds true, but the inclination doesn't need to be "natural," which implies that it's only nature and not nurture that matters.

As a parent, you don't have to wait for the long process of random mutation and natural selection to occur to change genes. Your behavior makes a difference now. No matter your child's age, it's not too late. Experience can change the way our genes are used, and researchers are showing that epigenetic patterns can be reversed (see appendix 2, "Epigenetics"). Gene regulation is happening at every second in every neuron. Your kids will strengthen some pathways and weaken others as they grow up; let's make that a purposeful process.

Obviously, kids don't always listen to us or do what we say. We need to respect the decisions our children make even if we don't 100% *agree* with the decisions they make. Just planting the idea that they are the only one in charge of their own decisions is the first step toward letting your children be accountable for their own actions. And it's true: the only behavior you can control is your own. Repeat this after me because that applies to parents as well: *the only behavior you can control is your own.*

However, by design, bad decisions will be unwanted practice of negative skills, and we don't want the default reaction pathway to be these undesirable activations of brain circuits. Good practice means practicing positive skills in the right way. Being purposeful in your parenting by choosing the right things to focus on is a great start, but it's not enough. To become proficient at something, your kids need to learn how to do it correctly. If they don't practice a skill correctly, they're choosing to keep the wrong circuitry in their brains.

Decisions, good or bad, are crafting synapses. So, we can't just sit back, let our kids make decisions, hope they feel the consequences of any bad behavior, and then cross our fingers hoping they decide better the next time. Our role as parents is to let them decide and then follow up by helping our kids activate the neuronal circuits we want to see them using. When our kids make a bad decision, we need to walk them through a way to make a better decision using scaffolded practice and give them as much choice along the way as possible. Scaffolded practice to change bad habits should always tap into the three most important skills a kid can have: How does it make people feel (empathy), how could you do it differently (creativity), and what will you do next time (self-control/self-regulation)?

This follow-up is important, because if a child practices making bad decisions, she will eventually become an adult who makes bad decisions. Letting kids practice making decisions and then having an adult help them work through a better way to have acted in that situation sets up our children for success the next time they encounter a similar decision. It's all about the redo. When we practice, we redo it until we get it right.

STEP 4   Give Some More Space

Lastly, you need to give space again. Then give guidance again, and then space again—you see where I'm going with this. Eventually, you won't need to give the guidance anymore, and your children will have all the space of a life ahead of them to work with.

Our true jobs as parents are to allow our children to experience making as many decisions as we can while they're under our roofs, while at the same time purposefully placing our kids in situations where they will have to make decisions that practice using neuronal pathways we want to keep around and that foster the skills we think will be most important to their life success. It's not enough just to model great values and allow independent decision-making. We need to be following up on those decisions with our kids and asking for active practice as well as encouraging space for reflection and mindful behavior.

part 2

RAISING CREATORS

4

The Neuroscience
of Creativity

IF WE WANT to cultivate something, we need to not only define it
and perhaps measure it, but we also need to understand it as much as
possible. A creator is thought to pass through four steps during the
creative process: (1) preparation, which is basically just thinking about
the task at hand, (2) the incubation of the idea, which may take some
time, (3) an illumination, which is the "aha" moment, and (4) verification, where the idea is carried to fruition.[1] This step-wise definition is
simple enough, but the neural basis for creativity taps into some more
complicated human brain functions.

In neuroimaging studies, it's nearly impossible to capture the
moment of creation, since measuring brain activity in someone who
is *trying* to be creative in a lab setting is vastly different from catching
someone actually in the middle of a creative illumination. So how do
we know what's happening during the creative process?

One of the more persistent and untrue theories about creativity
is that creativity lives in the right side of the brain. As mentioned
earlier, this long-held, popular theory that the left hemisphere of the
brain is rational and logical, while the right hemisphere is the source
of all creativity, is completely untrue![2] This single-hemisphere model
just doesn't hold up in the face of modern neuroscience. There's a
lot of evidence against it. There's zero evidence that creative people
can more easily access the right-brain hemisphere, and if you damage

the right half of the brain, it doesn't eliminate creativity.[3] In fact, for every study that shows creativity lives in the right hemisphere, there's another study right behind it finding left hemisphere involvement.

Neuroimaging studies show that the creative process appears to tap into both halves of the brain, and evidence suggests that creativity depends on the interaction between the **temporal lobes**, the **frontal lobes**, and the **limbic system**.[4]

The cortex contains those temporal and frontal lobes and functions as an umbrella of reason over the lower areas of the brain. The creative drive comes up from a lower area called the limbic system and then activates the association cortexes—areas that are involved in creativity—in both the prefrontal and temporal areas. This lower limbic system generally sends emotion-tinged content to the cortex. The role of the prefrontal cortex umbrella of reason is to filter and temper those signals to keep your actions socially appropriate but still in your own best interests. It's a battle that plays out with every decision we make as humans, and in the case of creativity, it determines what innovative ideas make it to the next stage of the creative process.

So how are the brains of "creative people" different from noncreative people's brains? The simple answer is that their brains are more interconnected. The most essential feature of a creative brain is the degree of connectivity it has, both between the brain hemispheres and within them. This creative connectivity is something that shows up on neuroimaging scans: creative brains show activation in many, sometimes distant, brain areas, though researchers have yet to figure out why.[5] Interestingly, the creative process appears to also tap into areas where previous studies have shown that **theory of mind**—the ability to see things from someone else's point of view—resides.[6,7] Creative people (in both science and the arts) are likely to experience vivid imagery, have a high ability to sense what others may be thinking or feeling, and feel things more deeply.[8]

Neuroimaging can loosely measure the amount of "connectedness" in a person by looking at the grey and white components of the brain: neuronal cell bodies appear grey, and white indicates the presence of myelinated axons. The myelination stage is the final stage of normal brain development, continuing into the third and fourth

How Did the Left-Brain/ Right-Brain Idea Originate?

There is an actual physical space, or split, between the left and right sides of the brain's cortex; that dividing line is called the longitudinal fissure. But underneath that split, there are massive communication tracts—the **corpus callosum** and the smaller anterior commissure—that connect brain areas on the left and right sides. Some people are born without a corpus callosum, and you'd never even know it, but if those connections are severed *after* brain development is completed, problems can result.

In 1981, Roger Sperry won a Nobel Prize for his studies on split-brain patients who underwent cutting of the corpus callosum to stop seizures from spreading across the brain. When communication is stopped between hemispheres, these split-brain patients could process information coming in on the left and right sides differently and could even arrive at different conclusions or decisions in each hemisphere.

These experiments gave rise to the idea that creativity is contained in the right hemisphere, but research on normally functioning individuals shows that creativity is housed on both sides of the brain. It's not the right hemisphere that accounts for creativity, but the amount of connectedness within both hemispheres.

decades of life. Normally, the association cortexes are the last brain areas to finish myelination.

Why do we care so much about myelination? Recall from our earlier discussion that although myelination is a highly regulated, normal developmental event, recent studies have proposed that myelination can also be influenced by brain activity and by functional interaction with the environment. The more a neuron fires, the more it becomes myelinated.[9] If you use a neuron, it will change gene expression—not just in the neuron, but even in the support cells surrounding the neuron in order to myelinate the axon.

Axons tend to bundle together and form pathways, or tracts, that travel together through the brain, and are similar to fiber-optic cables. Creative people have better integrated white matter tracts, particularly in the association cortexes and corpus callosum, which are the main connections between the right and left hemispheres.[10]

Practicing a skill can myelinate the axons involved, make those neurons faster, and enhance the skill, whatever it is.[11] We need to take advantage of the open developmental window in our children and take heart in the fact that once an axon becomes myelinated, that neuron stays myelinated for life.[12] Neuronal changes we encourage in our children are long-lasting.

Are There Genes for Imagination?

The DNA of different people has different versions (called **alleles**) of genes that make cellular components, but some alleles may work more optimally than others. We know there's a central role for neurotransmitter systems in creative innovation, including the naturally occurring **excitatory neurotransmitters dopamine**, serotonin, and **norepinephrine**.[13] But different DNA means that all the components of these neurotransmitter systems also vary slightly from person to person, and that can change how efficiently the neurotransmitter transporters or receptors work. If we want our kids to be creative, it has to feel good for them to do it, and some kids are just born with that inclination.

Researchers have shown that novelty is rewarding in and of itself, and exploring novelty can activate the dopamine-reward system.[14] Dopamine is a neurotransmitter that influences creative drive and novelty-seeking behavior, making both naturally more rewarding for some people than for others. But dopamine must be only part of the creativity story since it doesn't appear that dopamine is involved in cognitive flexibility (which is also an important part of creativity and, coincidentally, is part of executive functioning and self-regulation). We do know that the norepinephrine system is involved in cognitive flexibility: less epinephrine is better for being able to think in a flexible way.[15]

We can't change the genes that our kids are born with, but we may be able to change how these genes are used. Perhaps creativity, or imagination, even if held in the genes, may also have an epigenetic component to it (that is, the ability to be changed through experience), possibly through how the dopamine system is regulated.[16] (See appendix 2, "Epigenetics," for more information on this process.) We know that the dopamine transporter gene is sensitive to epigenetic mechanisms and that environmental forces can impact the role the dopamine plays in our bodies, possibly leading to variants of neurological disorders like attention deficit hyperactivity disorder (ADHD).[17, 18] The first step toward controlling this process more effectively is simply trying to understand it.

Neurotransmitter systems are delicate. You don't want to just flood synapses with extra dopamine. In fact, that's exactly what happens when you take methamphetamines or cocaine, which make you feel alert and feel good but also have huge potential abuse and addiction consequences. Addictive drugs involve the dopamine system because that reward feels good. Researchers have found that lots of things besides drugs can activate dopamine pathways, including social interactions. A study in monkeys showed that monkeys who were lower on the social ladder were more likely to become addicted to cocaine than the monkeys who were socially on top. This decreased susceptibility in the dominant monkeys happened because they began to express more dopamine receptors, since being in charge of a social situation is rewarding. As those dopaminergic neuron pathways are activated more frequently, the body adapts to support the activity and strengthens those connections. Over time, the dopamine systems in dominant monkeys adapted to their personal situation by producing more receptors on the receiving neurons. Their dominant social situation already met their dopamine needs, so they didn't need as much stimulation from a dopamine-activating drug.[19]

We all know that our behavior can change based on the environment we're in, but now we have a clear neuroscience explanation for *why* and *how* this change is occurring. Those who aren't feeling any reward will find it elsewhere, which has big implications for potential addictive behavior. Our brains are wired for reward, and we'll seek it out, whether

Dopamine Rewards the Brain

Dopamine is involved in motivation and reward. Dopamine-reward pathways connect different important parts of our brains together in circuits.

For example, if you eat chocolate, and that experience is pleasurable, then the reward pathways will try to make sure that you eat chocolate whenever you get the opportunity. They will connect back to brain areas involved in learning, reinforcing the memory that chocolate is good. The dopamine-reward pathways will also connect to sensory areas (to reinforce the recognition of chocolate) and to motor areas (to strengthen the ease of physically picking it up and eating it), all of which make it more likely that you'll repeat the behavior. And because specific neuronal connections get stronger every time they're used, every time you eat chocolate, these particular reward pathways are strengthened. As a result, chocolate-eating behavior gets strengthened too.

This same dopamine-rewards connection system can be used to strengthen creativity too. If the creative process is rewarded by activation of the dopamine system, a person is more likely to use imaginative processes, in which divergent thinking promotes connectivity through the development of new synapses.[20] This means that if your children consistently experience creativity as rewarding, their dopamine pathways will be primed for activation during creativity later in life.

it's social reward, the reward that comes from doing compassionate acts, or the reward we get from solving a creative problem. The more we as parents can make these "good" things personally rewarding, the less likely our kids are to seek that reward in ways that are potentially negative. Exposure to experiences that shape dopamine pathways while our brains are still developing has a lasting impact on the way that these circuits form and will impact the things that are rewarding to us as adults.

Measuring Creativity

It's hard to put "out-of-the-box" thinking into a standardized box, but some relatively good neuropsychological tests have been developed to assess creativity. Creativity tests are by design subjective. Most of our assessments, such as multiple choice tests and even IQ tests, measure *convergent* thinking—the ability to arrive at a single correct answer.[21] And yet, this isn't the way real life works. Instead, we'll spend most of our lives trying to become more comfortable with *divergent* thinking in a world full of many possible correct answers. We may keep wondering when convergent thinking—the thing we've been trained at—will come in handy.

The most common creativity assessment method measures divergent thinking. Divergent thinking focuses on producing inventive solutions to open-ended questions.[22] The Torrance Tests of Creative Thinking (TTCT) have many components. These tests may have open-ended question prompts, such as "What would happen if we no longer needed sleep?" or may ask the test-taker to describe what would happen in a given situation, for example, "What would happen if people could transport themselves from place to place with the blink of an eye?"

There are also incomplete drawings to finish, and what people draw can indicate how creative they are. If you turn an open triangle shape into a shark or a hat, you'd lose creativity points because those are very common ways of finishing these half-drawn pictures. But points go to you for literally drawing outside the box, inserting humor or motion into your drawings, giving your drawings detailed titles, telling a story, connecting seemingly irrelevant things together, or looking at things from a different angle.[23, 24]

Psychologists like to measure creativity by idea generation—not just how original your idea is, but also how many ideas you can come up with. For example, take 1 minute to name as many uses you can think of for a brick. You get points for (1) fluency (high number of answers) and (2) originality (answers that few others come up with). Together, fluency and originality give you a creativity score.[25]

Yet we shouldn't completely discount convergent thinking. There are also creativity tests that measure convergent thinking, such as the Remote Associates Test (RAT), which asks a person to come up with a single solution to a problem. Three words are provided, and the person must correctly name the word that connects all three words together. For example, the correct answer for the words *falling*, *actor*, and *dust* is the word *star*. For convergent tests, accuracy is most important.[26]

High-level creative thought will require both convergent and divergent thinking. The idea-generation stage will be divergent thinking by its nature. But the verification stage, where we explore how our ideas can be implemented, is by definition convergent thinking, as we guide our thought process back to solving the problem at hand and organizing our ideas.[27] If we only foster divergent thinking, we will spin out so much that our ideas aren't useful. If we only foster convergent thinking (as our schools tend to do), we discount the value of ideas and lose both the desire and the ability to effectively generate them.

Why Creativity Is Hard to Teach

Most of today's parenting practices cultivate creativity only as an aside. I did an informal survey of 59 local parents and found that only 47% had recently worked on creativity with their children. School efforts ignore creativity completely in many cases, or, at the very least, we can agree that the current structure of our schools fails our most creative children—and has done so for some time. Famous British comedian Lenny Henry was told to stop cracking jokes in school. Scientist Sir Harry Kroto was told by teachers to stop doodling, yet it was his drawing ability that helped him visually represent the atom structure of carbon that won a 1996 Nobel Prize.[28]

Creativity can be easily smooshed by goals that are imposed by others, which makes it hard to incorporate into formal education. A bit of wandering is good for the creative spirit. Sometimes, it is only after naturally creative people have exited the formal schooling system that they begin to recover—to assume their true shape that has been crammed into a narrow chasm for too long. Some people never recapture their creative impulses at all, having skirted around them for so many years.[29]

This marginalization of the creative spirit is multifaceted and often unintentional, but why is creativity marginalized? Our current education system has difficulty fostering creativity for the following reasons: (1) Creativity is work for many of us. By definition, everyone is creative in different ways. The rules aren't firm, so it's hard to teach. (2) Creativity requires a lot of personal space, which is difficult to do if the space isn't used with proper empathy and self-control. (3) Creativity means the parents/teachers must relinquish control to the child, which is challenging for us to do sometimes. (4) In addition, teachers may see creativity as counteractive to classroom management. It's difficult to supervise well when each student has an individual goal in a large class of 20 to 25 kids. (5) Our focus is often on teaching other skills, and creativity gets what's left of the time, energy, and money resources, even if we say we value it. (6) Creativity, by its very nature, doesn't fit into the box, so it's hard to assess it, and training funding sources can be hard to come by without meaningful outcomes.

And yet it *is* possible to teach something so individual, and creativity can be taught in a way that folds in nicely to other school subjects. It's not a stand-alone class, but instead it's a way of approaching topics, activities, and problems. A creative mind-set is gained by repeated practice. Remember that we're strengthening interconnectivity, and this will have the most impact if we've already started teaching this way in preschool and elementary school.

Creativity can be overtly used as a teaching tool, and so it can perhaps have a quite natural fit in our schools, despite an institutional emphasis on test scores. We can do this by changing not so much the content that we teach, but the *way* that we teach. Creativity activates dopamine pathways, and when you tap into the dopamine system, it enhances learning. Evidence shows that pathways modulated by dopamine are important for synaptic plasticity and modulation of learning.[30] Fostering student creativity goes hand in hand with optimal teaching methods. Creativity makes learning rewarding. And reward increases student buy-in for their own education.

As a modern parent, the burden of cultivating a creative spirit in your child falls directly in your lap. You can not only deliberately foster an imaginative spirit in your child and create a creativity oasis in your own home, but you can also be a voice for change in our education system. Even with good intentions, we must be careful that we are injecting true creative practice into our curriculum. Fine arts classes are typically viewed as a "creative outlet," but even here actual creativity can still be excluded: if students are all expected to produce the same kind of cookie-cutter art, or if students are only taught to read musical notes instead of to create their own music, we are still teaching them only rote skills, not having them practice creativity.

While it is true that art and music classes in our school system can focus on creativity skills, there's no reason we can't also do this within the academic curriculum—for example, by using inquiry-based science labs with no known answer . . . yet. We want our kids to view creativity as a process that makes everything easier and more interesting, as a skill worth having in every task, as a life approach.

5

How to Raise a
Creative Child

AS A SOCIETY, we think about creativity as something that naturally occurs in children and gets weeded out and strangled as they grow up. This is true to a certain extent: our children are primed and ready to think in nontraditional ways from a very young age.

When kids do better on creativity tests than adults, it makes sense from a neuroscience perspective. When adults name things with wheels, they might tap into a memory list of all the types of vehicles they can think of, and they kind of get stuck there. They may not remember the wheelchair, the rolling desk, or the Ferris wheel.

The principles of neuroplasticity apply to creativity: remember that the most frequently activated pathways are more likely to be activated again, and if we don't use a pathway, we'll lose it. And our kids *are* losing creativity. It's been shown that until a certain point in the schooling system, children are open-minded and are likely to give unique responses to questions; however, due to the conformity promoted at schools and at home, many lose the ability to come up with inventive ideas. Overall analysis of the Torrance Tests of Creative Thinking (TTCT) Abstractness of Titles subtest scores shows a score decrease starting in 1998, indicating a decrease in the creativity and critical thinking processes of children.[1] We're losing creativity by what we reinforce as parents and as a society.

We can reinforce creativity in our kids with just a bit of practice. Take, for example, a study where subjects were asked to design a new tool.

People formally trained in design showed differences in brain organization during the creativity task compared to people who were novice designers. This shows that design training resulted in brain reorganization, specifically causing more right prefrontal cortex activation (a brain area involved in creative program solving) in the design experts.[2]

You may be surprised to learn that creativity training courses have been using a cognitive approach for nearly half a century now. That is, they are trying to make people more creative by educating them about the creative thought process, emphasizing the four steps a person takes throughout the cognitive process (preparation, incubation, illumination, and verification). This type of metacognition, or thinking about your thinking, helps enhance creativity. But learning about neuroscience is even more effective. An 8-week creativity training program at business schools in Denmark and Canada that also taught students about the underlying neuroscience principles of creativity led to greater student creative gains than training courses without the neuroscience content, and especially increased fluency in divergent thinking.[3]

We can do this as parents too. Some children will always be naturally more creative than others, but creativity can also be trained in a number of proven ways. To make your house a creativity haven, work toward doing the following throughout your life: be open, share knowledge, and scaffold practice for creativity.

Be Open

We never know which of our talents will end up being the ones that define us: it's our job as parents to let our kids explore many aspects of their creativity.[4] But our society has no idea what to do with polycreativity—creativity as an approach that permeates many areas of life and work. The idea of a Renaissance man, or competence in many fields, is a thing of the past. Take Ben Franklin, for example. A gifted politician, prolific inventor, orator, and writer, he was creative in many ways. Our culture no longer produces Ben Franklins.

We funnel, and we shape, and we require labels that prohibit creativity across multiple fields. If you're a surgeon, be a surgeon, and we'll expect to find you sleeping at the hospital. If you are a poet, write poetry, and we expect you to get a job teaching at a college somewhere. We give strange glances to surgeons who write poetry, and we wonder if they are working hard enough at their first job.

It's fallacy to think that creativity comes in one form for each person: that a creative spark will fan into a single flame. Once you've been taught creative thinking and understand that it's an okay—and even desirable—way to be, once you know that it's not a have or have-not situation, once you stop looking over at Becky's creative, artsy son with jealousy and instead start actually working on creativity as a skill with your own kids, once you practice it enough, then creative thinking will take over as your default. You don't need to have an "artist" daughter or a "math-oriented" son. They can be both. Your daughter may forget the capital of Hungary, but using creativity as a tool, as an approach to tackling problems, whether in social conflicts or engineering dilemmas, will become who she is by force of habit. Our kids won't undo brain interconnectivity—myelin sticks around; reinforced synapses are relatively permanent—because it is a way of living, developed simply through practice.

FOSTER OPENNESS IN YOUR KIDS

Parents can make a home environment open to creative thought. To do this, we must value novelty, we must allow failure, and we must not judge worth.

Encourage your children to come up with lots of ideas about everything. Ask them to be prolific. And then keep a notebook. Creative ideas can be fleeting, so write things down. You can do this, or your kids can: they can draw pictures of their ideas even before they can write about them. If they build something, take pictures. Time lines can help young kids envision how a project will come together or provide a planning structure for older kids. Make concept maps—a tool to show relationships by drawing lines between words—to capture and organize everything that is even remotely associated with their ideas: it's the interconnectivity that matters.

Highly creative people actually have a subtle frontal lobe dysfunction—an inhibition of inhibition—where the frontal cortex allows an uninterrupted flow of creative thought processing from the lower brain areas.[5] This may be a product of our experiences: sometime the frontal lobes decrease idea generation, in part, because the brain has been taught to evaluate an idea's worth before it comes to conscious fruition.[6]

So, once those ideas spring up from kids, don't comment on their worth. If you judge your child's ideas tinged with negativity, they will learn to more tightly regulate their ideas. When my family went crabbing, my 5-year-old daughter said, "Can we cook it (the crab), make it red, and turn it into a tiny jewelry box?" Of course we can. If you judge other people in front of your children, it can have the same effect. You will teach your children to activate those brain prefrontal cortex areas that are involved in clamping down on divergent ideas.

When we discriminate against certain ideas based on our past experience, it hampers creativity. The one aspect of creativity that computers are quite good at is the ability to see one thing as something else. In human terms, we get trained to see an oil stain as a mess that needs to be cleaned up and not as a face, for example. Machines have no such predisposition. So, in that way, machines have more free will than humans do. This is an area that can handicap us when it comes to creativity, and this is where a perspective of openness can help. Remember, based on the principles of neuroscience, the pathways that we use the most are the most likely to fire again. Humans become wired to see things using the brain path most traveled.

GIVE EXPERIENCES

Russian psychologist Lev Vygotsky maintained that every act of imagination has a long history, or incubation period. He theorized that a child's prior experience provides tools for creativity and that the more a child hears, sees, and knows, the richer that child's imagination will be.[7] Experiential learning has been shown to increase creativity in school settings, and it works at home too.[8–10]

Every new thing a child experiences will become a tool in his creativity bucket. Now we need to get our children those experiences. Think about experience as a way to alter how our DNA is used and to potentially modify who a person is. Choose to give your child experiences instead of stuff for birthdays. The more open to new experience he is, the more he'll get out of it.

ENRICH YOUR CHILD'S CULTURAL LANDSCAPE

Though we are marching toward a more global society, various ethnic groups traditionally do things quite differently, and the fresh perspective is valuable in creating an open child. Extensive multicultural experience makes kids more creative (measured by how many ideas they can come up with and by association skills) and allows them to capture unconventional ideas from other cultures to expand on their own ideas.

As a parent, you should expose your children to other cultures as often as possible. If you can, travel with your child to other countries; live there if possible. If neither is feasible, there are tons of things you can do at home, such as exploring local festivals, borrowing library books about other cultures, cooking foods from a different culture at your house once a month, interviewing someone you know who is from a different country, watching a TV show online from a different country, and practicing words in a different language.

Bilingual children grow up knowing that there are two very correct names for a car, for a bookshelf, for family. Bilingual brains have connections that are wired differently from a very early age, creating parallel pathways to the same concept or destination. Overwhelming research shows that bilingual individuals are more creative than monolinguals.[11] They can more easily come up with new and unique ideas, and they are more willing to bend category rules a bit.[12] Makes sense doesn't it? They've been reaching the same conclusions through divergent ways for years.

With your younger children, you can look at the different side of the street that people drive on in Britain compared to America, the popularity of different sports in other countries, the people who traditionally make up the family unit in different cultures, how Americans and Mexican attitudes differ toward death (think Day of the Dead), or the stark difference in attitudes toward dogs in the American versus Islamic cultures. Teach your child another language if possible;

simply exploring the differences between languages is valuable. There are countless ways that people say hello to each other every morning across the globe, and no way is more correct than any other.

If your child is open to the multicultural experience in the first place, she'll get a lot more out of that exposure.[13] You can encourage an open attitude both toward the current culture in foreign countries and cultures from long ago by modeling that openness yourself. Any cross-cultural experience is fertile ground for creative thinking and can produce interesting conversations as you both observe and then reflect on what you experience. A neutral investigation of how different people explore the same ideas will show your children that one approach is not backward or wrong, but, instead, that views can just be different.

My husband and I prioritize travel as an experience that develops many things in our brains, including creativity and empathy. When we've scraped together enough money, or have enough room on the credit card to put six airline tickets on it, we go on vacation. We've never been to Walt Disney World, never done an "all inclusive" resort, never crammed into a cruise ship cabin. Instead, we pack rash guards, flip-flops, and a first-aid kit, and we hightail it down to Costa Rica to take up residence there with our four small children. The places we stay are not fine or fancy. We always go to the same area—a tiny town lined with dusty shacks, with a mountainous jungle rising steeply on one side and the roar of the ocean behind a thin veil of vegetation on the other. We all stay in one room, with the kids' cots propped up off the floor to avoid the scorpions.

We bring our family to Central America not because we thrive on difficulty or danger, but because we're searching for a space that values creativity. Our kids see our Central American friends (heavily populated by ex-pats we've met over the years) running a small bakery, teaching yoga, starting a surf school, making jewelry, having babies without husbands. They see motorcycles pass between a frenzy of trucks on unpaved, dusty roads. They hide our food in outdoor kitchen cabinets from the monkeys, and they gather hermit crabs as friends. We dive down as deep as we can into this alternate world in the limited time we have there.

Another parent I know, Margriet, a Canadian artist, is raising her 3-year-old daughter in Costa Rica. She believes that creativity naturally springs up from all children, and it's her job to channel it, encourage it, and steep her daughter in it. She hopes that moving there as a single woman and opening an art café, as a place to both make a living and sell her art, will one day serve as a clear sign to her daughter that all paths are open to her.

To make real use of these quiet spaces to get creatively connected, the brain needs to use the pathways between creativity brain regions repeatedly. As a neuroscientist, I know that the value of my family's multicultural immersions far outweighs the negative aspects that come packaged with it. The influence of parents on creativity cannot be understated. If we truly value creativity, then our children will also value it.

The Duncker Candle Problem

The Duncker candle problem is a classic test of creative insight. First, you are given some tools (a candle, a pack of matches, and a box of tacks), all placed on a table next to a cardboard wall. Then you are given a task: you must attach the candle to the wall so that when the candle burns, it doesn't drip wax on the table or the floor. The solution involves the ability to envision a different use for the objects at hand. Several studies have shown that the longer people had spent living abroad, the more likely they were to come up with the creative solution, particularly if they still maintained ties with their original culture.[14, 15]

Did you come up with the correct solution? You need to empty the box of tacks and then tack it to the wall to hold the candle—a candleholder is a valid use for the box, but it's not the original use.[16]

Share Knowledge

Experiences, and what we do with them, become knowledge that we can use as a tool for the creative process. Giving our kids experiences is a powerful way to give them knowledge and to teach, but there are other ways too.

READ A LOT

Travel isn't the only way to visit someplace else. Reading is a great (and cheap) way to expose your child to new ideas, fantasy worlds, and other cultures, as well as to explore the nuts and bolts behind lots of interesting processes in how-things-work books. Reading not only taps into the reader's imagination, but as your child assimilates someone else's social or historical experience into her own understanding of the world, it also adds to her own creative palate.

MODEL CREATIVITY

Modeling creativity helps a kid become an expert. Observation has a potent effect on creativity. The simple act of watching someone be creative enhances your imagination, even if the creative process you watch has nothing to do with your own work. One study allowed children to watch a video *demonstrating* creative behavior, watch a video *talking* about creative behavior, or read a book designed to promote creative ideas. Children who watched the actual creative behavior scored higher than the other groups on creativity tests afterward.[17] Sometimes you just need to see the process at work. This means you should participate in the creative activity with your child or expose them to other creators.

Victoria is a British-born designer who captures beach and animal scenes in watercolor images. As an artist, she lived in New York City for years designing dinnerware and towels for Crate and Barrel, Williams Sonoma, and Pier 1. She now has her own textile line based in North Carolina called A Good Catch. She tells about how her father had demonstrated artistic principles for her when she was young. "My dad went to Japan, and he came back and brought watercolor brushes and watercolors for the first time," she said. "He taught me how to paint a shark. You know how a shark goes from dark grey to light underneath? It was a really nice way to demonstrate the dark to the light. It was a shark coming towards you, with the tail coming out the side. It was neat. I remember it vividly, so clearly, him showing me that."

A study that asked subjects to draw aliens to inhabit an Earthlike planet showed that exposure to examples early on during the creative process enhances creativity and the quality of the drawing, maybe because the first step in the creative process involves recall, or bringing things to mind that can be used in the process.[18] But showing examples later in the process may increase conformity. So, consider showing your children examples of famous buildings way before you show them how to construct a tower with frozen peas and toothpicks.

ALLOW YOUR CHILD TO BECOME AN EXPERT IN SOMETHING

Teaching things creates opportunity as well. Your son could spend his piano practice time just playing whatever comes to mind, but a bit of instruction would make that music easier to hear. Exploration makes sense for a very young child, but once he's old enough to read music, it would be perhaps more useful to make him practice specific songs—to become proficient at music someone else has written before he tackles making up his own music. That's where knowledge as a creative foundation comes in.

If your children are interested in a topic, encourage it. Allow them to wallow in it and learn all about it. Creativity can come once you have all the basics down and you know the ins and outs of your craft. Especially in advanced fields, where invention builds on prior knowledge, you can't defend bending the rules until you know the rules. I think about this in my own profession as a scientist. It's impossible to think differently about the impact of a toxin on cellular pathways, for example, unless you are first familiar with those pathways. You must have foundational knowledge to be creative in an advanced field. The mind of an expert works differently from that of a novice: experts have a well-organized knowledge base and so can deal more effectively with new information that may paralyze a novice.[19] Understanding your field allows you to evaluate the utility of new information to solve a problem, as well as to understand how older information may be applicable to new situations.

Give Space

Understand that enhancing creativity takes both passive and active parental support. Both are important to the creative process. Remember that the creator prepares with knowledge and then thinks about the idea for a bit before having the illumination and fruition of the idea. That part takes time. Your job is to help your child make connections between as many things as possible. Make the space to let that happen.

In our social networking worlds, we are focused on the best way to do absolutely everything—posting perfect kids' birthday party pictures to Pinterest and posting photos of our kids holding up their college acceptance letters on Instagram. And although Americans value unique, alternative ways of being proficient at something, we tend to value only the ideas, not the thing that generates the ideas—namely, the quiet space that leads to creativity. But creativity is not about the best, or most proficient, way to do something. Creativity is a source of innovation and of new ways of thinking. It allows the mind to play. It allows society to advance, to branch, to illuminate.

One of the reasons we see creativity draining from the pool of our next generation is the willingness of parents to step in and help. Don't fix it for them. Remember that necessity is the mother of invention. Why would our kids need to problem solve if that's done for them? The answer here is to make space in every way for creative thought to become a habit.

We are always stepping in to prevent our kids from being bored, to keep them happy. It is not your job as a parent to entertain your children. In fact, it is *no one's* job to entertain your children. Finding things to engage with in the world is a life skill that can take practice for some people. Having "nothing to do" allows for reflection time. Being disengaged—or even bored—can lead to creative inspiration.

DON'T FORCE CREATIVITY

If the first rule of innovation is pleasure, we have to remember that pleasure typically doesn't come with something you're forced to do, so creativity can't be bribed. The idea of bribes works great for enhancing self-control (as we'll see in chapter 11), but for creativity it may backfire. These are pathways that need openness, free reign, and no social expectations on what they produce. That's why an open attitude must come first. You want to show interest, make space for it, and then get out of the way.

Kids should know you value creativity, but requiring it can squash it. It's funny how a child's motivation to perform a creative task, such as creating a short cartoon graphic novel, for example, may be crushed when a teacher offers to give extra credit for it. It's far easier to crush intrinsic motivation than to instill it in someone, so if you see your daughter working with gusto on a project that makes her happy, stay well enough away!

Creativity as an Emotional Outlet

Do you create more when you're in a good mood? While that makes sense because the dopamine system is involved in creativity and mood, studies show that not being in a good mood can enhance creativity.[20] Last week, I put my daughter in a time-out on the porch to calm down after an altercation with her sister. After she came out a few minutes later, I noticed an intricate pattern of clothespins and seashells carefully arranged on the porch railing. She'll create while reflecting on how she feels. She'll create when she feels upset. Creativity can be a healthy outlet for channeling how we feel. There's conflicting evidence about whether being in a good mood or a bad mood is more likely to yield creative output; it may be dependent on the particular person. As a parent, you can teach your children how to use creativity as an emotional outlet, regardless of their mood.

MAKE TIME FOR CREATIVITY

To be creative, you have to make creativity a priority. To be creative, you have to *do it*. Set time aside for it. Keep working at it. Don't accept the first solution. Generate multiple solutions. You can't choose the best one if you only have one. The first solution that pops up is rarely the one that is different and outside the box.

You can't force creativity, but you can practice it—not in the same way that you make someone practice the piano, though. Practicing creativity can mean purposefully setting up a situation that will permit creativity and then stepping out of the way as a parent. You simply need to make space for creativity in your value system: by the moments you set apart for it, in the way you encourage your kids to deal with conflict, and by how you allow your children to make space within your parenting.

ENCOURAGE FREE PLAY

Free play should be a huge part of your child's life. It contributes to cognitive, physical, social, and emotional development, but importantly for this conversation, self-directed play increases creativity.[21] A study of 5- and 6-year-olds showed that preschoolers who participated in a simple 75-minute play session per week had higher verbal and graphic creativity scores at the end of the school year than peers who didn't, and they also had better-developed creative personality traits and behaviors.[22]

Not only is play related to greater creativity and imagination, but also to higher reading levels and IQ scores.[23] Based on the evidence, the equation consistently comes out as Play = Learning. In 1974, scientist Art Fry dreamed up the idea of Post-it Notes during a nontraditional work setup at the 3M company. 3M's 15 percent program, launched in 1948 and extended to every employee on the technical team, allows 3M employees to take a chunk of their own workday to follow whatever they are interested in. Google and Hewlett-Packard also offer personal creative time. These methods seem most effective in a creative culture, where employees can present their work to each other and aim to impress.[24]

At the 3M company, the 15 percent program translates to a daily adult free-play session. Since free play is the natural way that children explore the world, the time children devote to daily creative play should be much, much higher. Along these same lines, don't over-schedule your children. If every moment is spent in a directed activity, there's no time to simply free play, no time to try things on their own terms, no time to make their own new neural connections.

CONSIDER MAKING A PHYSICAL CREATION SPACE

Creating physical space for kids can be somewhat dependent on the type of creativity, but your children should know that there's a place set aside where they can be nothing but inventive. I have found no published evidence that setting aside physical space to be creative enhances creativity, but there is certainly a long historical precedence for writers who have a dedicated writing space or visual artists who maintain a studio. There are no specific requirements for the space that you pick, and it will be somewhat dependent on your living arrangements. It can be as small as a table or as large as a room. If you identify an interest within your child, you should run with it. I established a Lego corner for my son—a building fanatic—a designated space with no parental complaining about pieces on the floor and where completed projects could live indefinitely.

This summer, I set aside a corner of our admittedly run-down garage to be dedicated to art. I bought mistinted gallon paint cans for a few dollars at our local hardware store and put them in various bottles. I let my kids pour, smear, and push the paint around real canvases or gessoed cardboard. The kids got filthy, I hosed them off, and those works of art took weeks to dry. I contacted a local coffee shop, which graciously allowed my kids to hang their works of art on the walls, and we had a tiny art show opening event. What did my kids learn from that? Hopefully, their brains learned that art for the sake of art is valuable, that it's okay to get messy (and I mean *messy*), that they can be proud of their creative projects, and that creativity is satisfying.

GIVE YOUR CHILD ENOUGH SLEEP

Sleep and the creative process are intimately related. First, sleep allows memories with important emotional or motivational value to be better incorporated into our brains, and activation of these circuits during dreaming can enhance memory, allow us to better regulate our emotions in social situations, and improve creativity.[25] Intact REM sleep, which typically happens in intermittent periods throughout the night, appears to be particularly important for creative problem-solving.[26]

It's interesting to me that patterns of brain activation are the same during REM sleep and during the creative process when we're awake. Take the example of jazz improvisation in musicians, which is a spontaneous creative activity. While making music, the musician's dorsolateral part of the prefrontal cortex, which consciously controls performance, is turned off, and the medial prefrontal cortex, which is involved in internally motivated behaviors, is activated.[27] You see those same high and low activation patterns during REM sleep, showing similarities between sleep and the awake creative process.[28]

The second reason to make sure your child gets enough rest is that there's also a potential link between dreaming—particularly lucid dreaming—and creativity. Some historically monumental ideas had their origin in dreams, including the discovery of the structure of the benzene molecule by the organic chemist August Kekulé; the idea for the frog heart experiment that won Otto Loewi a Nobel Prize; the invention of the sewing machine by Elias Howe; and the rather dreamlike creation of Robert Louis Stevenson's novella, *The Strange Case of Dr. Jekyll and Mr. Hyde.*

DISCONNECT FROM DEVICES TO MAKE MENTAL SPACE

Call it what you will: meditation, reflection, mindfulness. Research shows that creativity increases as you step away from your electronic devices and immerse yourself in nature for a few days—if you can make it through the disconnection syndrome, that is.[29]

Maria, filmmaker and creative director of a production company, and Paul, CEO of a large corporation in Europe, are a German couple who go to Costa Rica each December for several weeks. They view their holiday with an intense clarity of purpose: it allows them to be more efficient and more creative when they return home. The unapologetic way they discuss their trip rationale is both refreshing and thought-provoking: the yearly multicultural disconnection is an absolute requirement for their work productivity.

When we're in Costa Rica, we disconnect our children from electronics, from their normal life patterns, and from their comfortable ways of living so that they have the space they need to create. We want our children bored stiff, reading books for adults they find in a friend's art café. We want them desperate enough for TV that they watch whatever few cartoons they encounter in an unknown language with no complaints.

But it's not always the most popular tactic. I have a friend who traveled with her 15-year-old daughter to Costa Rica last year. While hiking near a remote waterfall, her daughter stood at the bottom, tears streaming down her face. "It's so beautiful, isn't it?" my friend said to her. "No," her daughter said, "I don't have my phone." Did she want to post a picture of it on Snapchat? Did she want to tweet about it to her friends? The *why* doesn't matter; she was unable to be in the waterfall moment without that social framework. And this presents a very big problem for our brains.

Welcome to the new sense of social connection. We currently experience our life moments through singular internet photographs and counting our "likes." We perhaps are connected not so deeply, but we have many more points to hang from. We bat around things that are already on the internet, look for affirmation, and ride waves of popular opinion looking for the next thing that has a finger on the pulse of the nation. The change from veritable relationships to virtual connections seems not like a change at all for our children. This is the way it's always been for them. But this swift change in social interactions is unprecedented in our evolutionary history, and I'm not so sure that the human brain is ready for it.

Perhaps even more problematic for my friend's daughter is the instant deflection and volley of the moment to a social media platform. If she had had her phone, her immediate reflection about the waterfall moment would have consisted of sharing it on social media. I like to share a nice waterfall picture too, but we need to preserve the space for our kids to be mindful about things first—and allow social media second.

I'm reminded of the internet video I watched yesterday of a giant alligator in a South Carolina neighborhood, and though I know I was supposed to be awestruck by its slow but hefty amble across the residential street, I was distracted by the man literally getting out of his car next to the gator in order to get good video footage. It's not good to get out of a car next to an alligator.

It will be good for our children and everyone around them if they can experience the amazing things that spring from just being present for a minute, mentally disconnected from social media. Kids may not miss personal mindful moments, especially if they've never experienced them, but parents can see the utility of these moments and enforce some level of media detachment for them. We need our children to put themselves first, process things, and then share what they've found with the rest of the world.

The first part of disconnection can be painful—the second part deeply rewarding. Being connected all the time means that we're not getting quiet space to think and reflect and create and be deliberate. There's someone always "with" us. Sometimes we can easily dismiss the Eastern tradition of creativity as a sense of self-fulfillment or realization because we wonder where the value is in "doing nothing." But there is absolute value in that nothing. Leonardo da Vinci recommended gazing at stains on a wall or similar random marks as a stimulus to creative fantasy. A game where you see something in nothing is creativity.

When we marginalize the Eastern perspective of creativity, we essentially eliminate the spaces where the Western ideas of creativity can take root. In reality, the true nature of creativity pulls both from self-reflection and purpose. It's the marriage of both thinking inwardly and thinking outwardly into an expression of something another person can appreciate.

Scaffold Practice for Creativity

We can raise creative kids if we generate opportunities to be creative, and so make creativity a habit. To change neuronal development and brain connections in a long-lasting way, your children need time to create. They need to practice the skill of being imaginative daily. But it can happen in small ways. Scaffolded creativity practice can occur by smuggling in some creative time. And creative practice doesn't have to all be hands-on, either. Remember, you are encouraging a way of thinking, not a concrete talent in studio art or architectural design.

We can "teach to the test" at home by planting some scaffolded practice. Sometimes you need to start your kids off by modeling creativity. Your kids might struggle with the idea of free play at first. They'll pop up right beside you and ask for direction. Get them set up. Get them started. Arrange a game with race cars or set up a stuffed animal tea party. Spend 5 minutes, create a scenario, and then leave them alone. Do it more than once; try it daily for a week before deciding it doesn't work.

You can try an overt idea-generation session. If you incorporate 5 minutes per day into your life for your child to be creative, that's 150 minutes a month. By the end of a year, you will have given your child 30 hours of practice in divergent thinking! Ask the creativity test question: How many uses can you think of for a paperclip? Name things that are round, things that have wheels. You become what you practice. These activities are easy to do in the car, while you're making dinner, or as a daily bedtime exercise. You may be surprised at how connected you feel to your child afterward!

Try to keep your child engaged with a question or task for 5 minutes, and help your child to follow a train of thought to its conclusion. If your child stalls, you can offer some ideas of your own to jumpstart the process (remember that presenting examples can spark the creative process early on). Some of the following activities are modeled after the standard tests of creativity used by neuropsychologists, but in this case teaching to the test is a good thing:

> **Possible choices.** Pause a movie right after the conflict
> and ask about all the options that the main character has.
> Which will she pick? Do this during a board book, a sitcom,
> an issue you run into at the drive-thru.

Alternative uses. Give your child a tool they've never seen before and ask them to describe potential uses for it. Pick up anything that's nearby and ask your child what it could be used for (other than the original intention).

Idea generation. Have a round-robin story session where you pass a story around, taking turns adding details to it as you go. You can even have recurring characters, like mean ol' Randy who does marginally inappropriate things.

Product improvement. Hand your child a stuffed animal in the cart at Target and ask him what he'd do to improve it.

Possible consequences. Present a hypothetical or real situation and ask your child to name all the possible consequences of the action.

"Suppose" questions. Ask what would happen if people didn't have to sleep. Maybe your kids will tell you there'd be no need for pajamas anymore or that work productivity will increase, that vampires would have to change their night habits, that the birth rate would decrease. You never know until you ask.

Asking questions. Show your child an ambiguous picture and have her ask as many questions as she can about it. Ask a sibling to answer her questions. Resist the urge to explain anything.

Guessing causes. Give a hypothetical or real action and ask why someone would choose to act in that way. Last week, an angry driver in the car next to us chucked the McDonald's burger she was eating through our SUV's window. It hit my 13-year-old in the face. We played this backstory "game" when he got home as a way to understand the event: Why would she have thrown that food at a car with a child in it? With her own kids in the car? What happened to her that morning? Where did she grow up? What is her occupation? What did she get for Christmas this year? Does she celebrate Christmas?

Playing games. Catherine, a neuroscientist who cofounded a company called Catlilli Games, suggests that parents encourage their children to play certain games, such as Mad Libs, Scattergories, Dixit, or Story Cubes. These games are fun to play, but they also incorporate ideas from creativity tests and allow us to practice making unusual connections. Games that solve puzzles, idea-generating games, and games where the goal is to figure out something (even old standards like Pictionary or charades) are fantastic ways to generate creativity.

Pictorial creativity. Draw a squiggle line and ask your child to turn it into a work of art. My kids love this drawing game and beg to do it instead of a bedtime story, so in the last few weeks we've done it a handful of times. Their pictures are always so much better than mine (see figure 5.1).

You may think that these exercises are simply a fun diversion, but don't underestimate the power of these experiences. My son found me today in the kitchen and laid out an array of smooth creek rocks on the table. He had used a marking pen to draw a picture of a drone on one, with an accompanying small rock remote control. He created the *Titanic* on a rock and turned another into the iceberg that it hit (these rocks were to scale). These small practices are allowing him to connect disparate thoughts in his brain and are strengthening his creative process. I can't wait until this translates into the way he approaches a tough legal case or allows him to negotiate a peace treaty with a difficult nation as a grown-up one day.

Sometimes we play an alphabetical game at dinner based on a theme. We go around the table and offer an idea that fits our assigned letter. For example: "What does our dog do at home while we're away

Figure 5.1 Draw a shape on a piece of paper and take 2 or 3 minutes to see what drawing your child can come up with. Panel A shows the abstract figure prompt (a squiggle). The other drawings were done by my kids: panel B is a PAC-MAN video game, panel C is a squid superhero being eaten by a fish, and panel D is a young girl.

all day?" She *p*lays video games, *q*uietly eats ice cream, *r*earranges the furniture, *s*wings in the hammock, *t*inkles in the toilet. . . ." It's funny and surprising. Their minds are amazing.

Ideally, you'd also have a larger project at least once a month, like dragging the paints out to a scenic location or building a double-decker train track that lives in the living room all weekend. A longer creative session allows your children to be totally immersed in the creative activity and lets them experience all four stages of creativity (preparation, incubation, illumination, and verification). Importantly, spending more time working on a project may make it more likely for the last stages of illumination and verification to occur.

When we practice creativity, our family's not always playing idea-generation games or painting outside. We're often just lining things up so that it's more likely that creativity will happen.

Creativity and Honesty

Studies show that creative people can be more likely to lie or cheat and more likely to justify it afterward than people who score lower on creativity assessments.[30] That might result from a creative tendency to view rules not as concrete, but instead as something to navigate through or around. If you notice your child bending the truth, refer to part 3, "Fostering Compassion," and part 4, "Cultivating Self-Control" for parenting tips.

part 3

FOSTERING
COMPASSION

6

The Neuroscience
of Empathy

IN AN INFORMAL SURVEY I did with 59 parents, all stated that fostering empathy in their own children is either extremely important (78%) or very important (22%) to them. But wishing to be more compassionate will do you about as much good as wishing for a million dollars. We know how to work toward being a millionaire: get a job, work hard, invest your money, save your earnings. But as a society, we are missing tools to become more empathetic, so no matter how much we prize empathy, we aren't getting there. We shrug and say, "She just wasn't born with much empathy."

Self-reported empathy has been declining for the last 30 years.[1] Though this empathy plummet is major cause for concern, neuroscience says that the fix is an easy one: we just have to practice empathy. The fact that empathy levels can change so quickly means that empathy is more fluid than perhaps previously thought—changing and responsive to our everyday life experiences.

Empathy is a skill that develops over a lifetime and is regulated by both nature and nurture. Twin studies of identical and fraternal twins show us that nature (heritability or genetic makeup) controls 33% to 50% of a 2-year-old's empathy, meaning that 50% to 67% of the empathetic response is dependent on the environment that a child is raised in.[2] Half or less of your child's empathetic behavior is already wired into her brain. The rest of it you're already teaching—or not teaching.

It's impossible for dramatic DNA changes to occur within just one generation, so these empathy changes *must* be environmental. If life choices can drive it down, then making different choices through practice can bump it back up again.

Your child is always practicing something every single minute. One of the most staggering moments in parenting is when you realize the impact you can have through simple repetition—not just waiting for opportunities to arise, but actively creating them.

You don't need to wait until your children are older to start working on empathy. Start now. Younger children show more gains in empathy than older children after empathy training, and the lower the initial score, the higher the gains following the training.[3, 4] Boys can be trained to empathize in the same way that girls can.[5-7] The richness of neuronal connections is constantly being crafted in our kids, and, in fact, social connections are being formed even more so in preteens and high school kids. Empathy training at any age makes people more empathetic.

Once researchers showed that physicians who score better on empathy tests have better patient outcomes, some medical schools began requiring current medical school students to undergo empathy training as part of their curriculum.[8-12] Why? Because you can train empathy in people in a systematic way, and it works even in adulthood. Medical students with prior empathy training who are then exposed to emotionally stressful situations not only react in a more empathetic way, they also have lower stress levels than students without prior empathy training.[13] Thus, empathy training is not just good for patients, but it also benefits the health of these future physicians.

The Brain Basics of Empathy

To understand how you can deliberately cultivate empathy in your son or daughter, it helps to understand what's happening in the brain during an empathetic response.

- Brain areas responsible for empathy are spread throughout the brain. There's not an "empathy center." The neuronal connections and interplay between many diverse brain areas will either generate or prevent someone's empathetic action.

- The way your neurons are *connected* dictates your empathy experience. All empathetic thoughts and actions are completely rooted in neuronal pathways distributed throughout the brain. It's the interconnection between brain areas that is so important.

- These neuronal pathways grow stronger with use and weaker with neglect. Practicing empathy is no different from practicing any other skill, except you are strengthening connections between brain regions that regulate empathetic processes instead of enhancing the neuronal circuits in your motor cortex and cerebellum, such as when you practice a sport like soccer.

Increases in empathy, therefore, likely come from the strengthening of connections between neurons in empathetic brain circuits, such as those found in the medial prefrontal cortex. The function of the medial prefrontal cortex is to learn associations between context/place and to contribute to memory and decision-making. Practice also perhaps strengthens connections in areas that contain mirror neurons, which are specialized brain cells that get activated when we predict another person's actions or understand someone's intent. Empathetic networks have contributed to our success as a species and a society because when it comes to getting along with coworkers, colleagues, peers, and romantic partners, these connections are *very* important.

Types of Empathy

There are three versions of empathy:

> **Emotional (feeling) empathy:** When you feel an emotional pull

Cognitive (thinking) empathy: When you think about how someone feels

Applied empathy: When you act in a compassionate way toward someone else

Applied empathy is where empathy starts to mean something in the real world. You can't have it without first having one of the other two kinds of empathy—either emotional empathy or cognitive empathy.

As you might imagine, it's hard for scientists to conduct valid empathy research. It's nearly impossible to re-create relevant real-world social cues in a controlled laboratory environment. I certainly could not re-create the complexity of even third-grade girl playground dynamics in the lab. To answer questions about empathy, scientists try to break empathy into pieces, examine each piece, and then reconstruct the tower, but sometimes the sum is more than its parts. This is because so many other human processes (such as creativity, self-regulation, motivation, and attention) merge together to create a single feeling, thought, or action.

Using neuroimaging scans, we've figured out that emotional empathy and cognitive empathy are governed by two totally different neural networks: one network allows you to share others' internal states (experience sharing, or emotional empathy), and another network allows you to explicitly consider those states (mentalizing, or cognitive empathy).[14] These two basic types of empathy are *that* different. A situation that activates your emotional empathy brain regions may not change activity in the brain regions responsible for cognitive empathy.

We also know from people's behavior that emotional and cognitive empathy can fit together in different ways to spur compassionate acts. Researchers have recently started shifting the focus toward defining the more complicated neural pathways beneath prosocial behavior (compassion, or applied empathy). Perhaps more importantly, all acts of applied empathy require you to either think or feel first (see figure 6.1), but feeling and thinking do not always lead to compassionate acts.

Emotional Empathy

Babies can't regulate their emotions at all; even the sound of a nearby crying infant can cue a stress response in a baby. We call this effect emotional contagion. Your child is likely still in the emotional contagion stage if you agree with both these statements:

> When another child is upset, my child needs to be comforted too.

> When another child gets frightened, my child freezes or starts to cry.

It's not until the late toddler stage that kids can begin controlling their emotional responses. The first steps toward controlling emotional responses is simple attention to emotion. If the next two statements

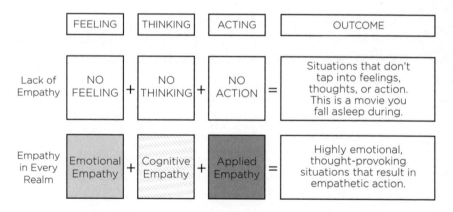

	FEELING		THINKING		ACTING		OUTCOME
Lack of Empathy	NO FEELING	+	NO THINKING	+	NO ACTION	=	Situations that don't tap into feelings, thoughts, or action. This is a movie you fall asleep during.
Empathy in Every Realm	Emotional Empathy	+	Cognitive Empathy	+	Applied Empathy	=	Highly emotional, thought-provoking situations that result in empathetic action.

Figure 6.1 Empathy is not all-or-none. We're used to thinking about empathy in black-and-white, but it comes in a lot of shades. When people don't initiate acts of compassion, or applied empathy, we think they have no empathy at all (top row). Other people seem to have high levels of both feeling and thinking empathy, which then results in empathetic acts (bottom row). But there are multiple ways of getting to compassion. Most of us have some elements of empathy that we can work with as a starting point, and all of us can be taught ways to be more compassionate.

(from the Empathy Questionnaire[15]) describe your child, then she already pays attention to emotion:

> My child looks up when another child laughs.

> When an adult gets angry with another child,
> my child watches attentively.

Emotions either happen or they don't. You can't force, or even teach, someone to feel sad or to feel happy. When someone feels an emotion, it springs up organically from the limbic system. In much the same way, emotional empathy in response to highly emotionally charged situations comes up from the limbic system unmanaged, and sometimes uninvited. Sue just heard an old college acquaintance's new baby is in the hospital, and she feels a small sadness. But when Caitlyn, the baby's godmother, hears the news, she has a gut response in which her stomach feels like it is dropping out. These are both examples of emotional empathy—raw and unfiltered, untinged with decision or action of any sort.

Karen's 5-year-old son is playing at the park. Karen sees a little kid at the playground aim and lob a handful of sand into her son's face. Karen's first impulse is to yell at the kindergartner who just gave her son a mouthful of sand, but the impulse is fleeting, and she'd be ashamed to admit it to anyone. Instead, Karen immediately rushes in to help her son clean up and work it out with the other boy.

Karen's first impulse to "mama bear" that sand-throwing boy at the park is from the unfiltered limbic system. She was barely conscious of even having the thought. Why? Those kernels of emotion flashed from the lower limbic system up through her thalamus in the midpart of her brain and ended up in multiple areas in her outer cortex—rough impulses, ready to be processed into full-fledged thoughts or actions (see figure 6.2).

Why didn't Karen's brief protective thought manifest into action? It was redirected due to the connections made in her prefrontal cortex. Self-control is a big part of developing a mature sense of empathy. In Karen's case, her prefrontal cortex also dampened her fight-or-flight response by allowing her to rationally think through a socially appropriate way to handle that playground incident, which allowed her to kindly bend down and help her son talk through the conflict. The connections within her prefrontal cortex allowed her to act in a way that we perceive as human.

The ability to emotionally empathize develops early and rapidly in children. Emotional contagion responses are the beginning seeds of emotional empathy. By 6 months, infants prefer dolls they have seen helping others over similar bully dolls. One-year-old toddlers will give a sad look to express concern or say, "I'm sorry," and they'll show interest in someone's distress by asking, "What happened?" These are pretty

Emotional Empathy

FEELING	THINKING	ACTING	OUTCOME
Emotional Empathy +	NO THINKING +	NO ACTION =	Situations that tap into innate emotions, coupled with nearly unconscious helpful actions.

Start/Finish

Emotional Empathy +	Cognitive Empathy +	NO ACTION =	Situations where you feel nothing but understand the circumstances are hard for the other person.
Emotional Empathy +	NO THINKING +	Applied Empathy =	Highly emotional, thought-provoking situations that result in empathetic action.

Figure 6.2 Emotions can sometimes leave us frozen or drowning in our own feelings (top row). Or perhaps they lead to thinking about someone we feel sympathy toward, but we don't make a move to help that person (middle row). These are both situations when emotions get in our way instead of working for us. But emotional situations can sometimes organically lead to compassionate acts even without thinking about it (bottom row).

sophisticated empathetic behaviors! By 2 years old, nearly all children will engage in some sort of helping behavior if someone is distressed, giving hugs and asking, "Are you okay?"[16-18]

Emotional empathy predates the development of cognitive empathy because the thought processes behind it are much simpler. Children don't have to put themselves in someone else's shoes in order to act in a helping way—they can simply *feel* the emotion themselves. Even lab mice respond with helping behaviors to fellow mice in distress, and I wouldn't say they're actively thinking through what it feels like to be the other mouse. Are they acting to relieve their own distress? Possibly. But that's why we care about emotional empathy: it's a route to compassionate acts. The motivation doesn't matter to the person who is being helped. And with practice, the helping behaviors will become second nature.

HOW TO CULTIVATE EMOTIONAL EMPATHY

The first step to helping your kids have more empathy is to choose it for your family. Emotional empathy can't be overtly taught, but you can help your child pay attention to emotional cues, and you can raise your child in an environment that fosters healthy development of emotional empathy, beginning in infancy. You, as a parent, can lay the foundation for your child's emotional empathy skill by being responsive, by being consistent, by not being reactive, and by being empathetic yourself.

Be Responsive

Empathy is particularly relevant to parents of a newborn, whose needs are enormous, even though the baby cannot yet speak. Being responsive to your newborn is your main job as a new parent. A newborn's earliest lesson in empathy is the way her mother responds to her, and the way we help our newborn deal with stressors is unbelievably important from a neuroscience perspective.

Research shows that the way you love your child—even in infancy—can forever change the way she responds to stress throughout her life. It's important to touch your baby, and touch her often. Be responsive to your child, and be aware that parenting methods like Babywise that advise you to let your child cry it out from a young age are not rooted in science, have led to multiple cases of child mistreatment and neglect, and establish an extremely poor empathy model during your child's early brain development.[19–21]

But what happens if you have a baby who cries even when you are responsive to her? Uncontrollable crying is the major risk factor for child abuse, and certainly there is little more stressful to new parents than a baby with colic or one who won't stop crying. Keep trying. Touching will help. One study showed that when mothers walked around carrying infants, it calmed the babies' crying and reduced the babies' heart rates more than when mothers simply held their baby while sitting. Infants who were in their crib cried the most. Interestingly, this same effect was found in animals, even when mouse pups were held and carried by the lab researcher instead of the mouse mother![22]

Being responsive is something we get to practice as parents for many years before our child begins his own social engagements with the world. You communicate a message that emotions are normal and understandable and can be expressed. Research shows that a warm and responsive environment allows your child to develop healthy ways to deal with his own emotions, like acceptance or positive thinking.

The way you respond to your child will turn on and off genes in his brain. Let's look at mothering behavior in rats, which is fair to do, since nearly all DNA regulation mechanisms are identical in mammalian species. The amount of maternal responsiveness and interaction with her infant is directly linked to adult psychological well-being. Rat pups that are raised by highly nurturing rat mothers (as measured by the amount of licking/grooming behavior) have expression differences in hundreds of genes when compared to low-nurtured rats. By the amount of licking, the mother is actually changing markers on her babies' DNA to alter their gene expression of glucocorticoid receptors, which respond to the stress hormone **cortisol**. (See appendix 2, "Epigenetics," for more details.) More licking adds **epigenetic tags** that open up the DNA, uncoiling the genes and allowing access to stress response genes, thereby changing the way the rat pups respond to stressors in ways that last a lifetime.[23]

In fact, high-nurtured female pups are much more likely to be high-nurturing moms themselves, so these epigenetic changes can even be passed down to the next generation, whereas the rats that received a less-nurturing upbringing remained more sensitive to stress throughout their life spans. We can see these results mirrored in humans as well: preterm infants who were exposed to 10 days of daily music and massage beginning 10 days after birth showed higher levels of growth factors that protect against neonatal diseases, including retinopathy of prematurity (a potentially blinding eye disorder) caused by low levels of the **growth factor IGF-1**, as well as decreased cortisol stress-hormone levels when compared to babies who didn't receive the extra stimulation.[24]

Abnormal stress responses often underlie some neuropsychiatric disorders (such as depression and anxiety), which suggests that the brain circuits that respond to stress are exceptionally vulnerable to external factors, starting very early in development. Child abuse victims have epigenetic tags on their stress response systems similar to the less-nurtured rats in the rat mothering experiment. In addition, suicide completers with a childhood history of abuse have decreased brain levels of these same glucocorticoid receptors compared to those with no history of abuse.[25]

The take-home message of all these studies is that we should parent with **epigenetics** in mind—not only mentally, but also physically. Hug the heck out of your child: there's no such thing as too many hugs. Hugs lower our blood pressure, reduce our heart rate, keep us from getting as sick, and make us more sociable.[26–28] Hug him when he does something great. Hug him when he has a tantrum. Hug him when he's sad. Reject the idea that not responding to your child is somehow in his best interests. And don't stop when he becomes a preteen.

Be Consistent

Studies show that parents who are consistently responsive and nonauthoritarian toward their young children will have more empathetic children.

Why? Your child can use her interactions with you to better predict others' behavior.

Imagine you are playing a basketball game in which every time you make a basket, you randomly receive between 0 and 3 points, depending on how the referee is feeling. It will likely take you a long time to figure out the rules. But if you consistently get 3 points when you shoot outside the 3-point line and 0 points when you shoot from out-of-bounds, you will learn the rules very quickly and will be able to predict how others will play basketball too.

It's the same with consistent parenting. Maybe you feel like you can't reason with a toddler, but you should practice empathy by telling your little ones the reasons every time you curb their behavior, which will provide firm empathy foundations for your child to understand and predict another person's behavior in the future (see chapter 11 for a discussion about discipline). Even at a very young age, reasoning with children about how their behavior affects others promotes empathy.

Clear expectations give your child an obvious path to victory or self-destruction, and the practice crystallizes the pathway between emotions and good decision-making. One of the simplest ways to respect your children is to offer them choices whenever possible. They don't always have to be equally desirable choices, but allowing children to decide for themselves is a freedom that humanity holds dear: it allows children to feel more powerful and allows them to own their choices.

Don't Be Reactive

Parenting often means not using your first response when reacting to a child's behavior. You don't want to be reactionary; you want to be deliberate, and that means controlling your own behavior as a parent. (See chapters 8 and 9 for self-control tips.) A misbehaving child interacting with a tired and cranky parent can easily lead to the child escalating her behavior so that it matches the parent's overreaction. The focus on the original behavior becomes completely lost.

Instead of learning the direct consequences for the original behavior, the child ends up reacting to the parent's reaction. Over time, the same spiral can occur no matter what the original behavior was. Keep the interaction as clear as possible. This is easier if you are (1) intentional about your parenting goals and (2) very clear about rules and consequences from the beginning. (This is covered in more detail in chapter 11.)

Be Empathetic Yourself

The burden is on parents to model empathetic behavior. The evidence clearly shows that parental empathy is crucial for raising healthy children and that it will foster empathetic behavior in your child. If you want your children to become empathetic adults, surround them with empathetic people, starting with yourself.

Empathy as a parenting method is a mind-set that takes some time to implement. Sometimes it's simpler to tuck your head down and plow through parenting, particularly when you feel overloaded or stressed (which, let's face it, can be often when you have kids). The long-term effects of *deciding* to be empathetic as a parent will spill into all aspects of your children's well-being, as well as into their interactions with others, for a lifetime. We need to work on some things in ourselves first, however.

It's hard to be empathetic to our kids sometimes. As parents, we're all grown up. We're staring at the screwed-up crying face of our toddler, down into his open mouth. In those moments, can you go back in time, to imagine you are small? Try to remember what you were doing at your child's exact developmental stage—for example, in kindergarten. How did it feel? What were your biggest joys? What did you struggle with?

Jen has to pause sometimes when dealing with her 2-year-old: "My daughter was way out of control. I was at the end of my rope because I was exhausted due to a kid all-nighter. I realized that she was probably reacting out of exhaustion too, and I realized she was feeling as crappy as I was. It helped me be more kind and understanding."

Conjuring up your own childhood memories allows you to keep perspective about what feels important to your child at each developmental stage. Surely you had no idea what dinner prep was when you were in elementary school, but you may clearly remember an amazing sticker trade or being reprimanded and shamed by a stern teacher.

Those were your big deals. Take the space to remember it, which may make you feel some emotional empathy toward your child. If not, you can still use that space to work toward cognitive empathy, a skill that will help you flip things around to see from your child's point of view.

Cognitive Empathy

Empathy is a spectrum, just like everything physiological. Some people start out with more than others. If your child doesn't naturally feel a lot of emotion for others and doesn't overflow with acts of compassion, it's okay; you just need to work with her from a different angle. You can teach your child the path from feelings to action, and you can teach her how to first identify an emotional situation and then how to think through it, bypassing emotional empathy entirely.

Cognitive empathy is a simple, rational thought process. And importantly, it's a deductive power that can be taught.[29] As parents, we have to start by teaching our children the basics: What does this person think? How does this person feel? What is this person likely to do? We can start by simply valuing not "being nasty."[30] Then we can make the leap to cultivating applied empathy in our kids.

To raise a compassionate person, we must teach kids not just how people feel, but also *what people are thinking.* If you have a child who is old enough to pay attention to the feelings swirling around the people in his personal space, there are two tests that will let you see if he can effectively read those signals.

Reading emotions test #1. Get some paper and draw three big-headed stick figures standing in a semicircle on a playground, but leave their faces blank. Draw one kid falling down in the middle, with a sad face. Maybe even add some stick-figure tears. Give your child the pen and ask him to fill in the faces of the other people on the playground. Do the results show that your child can somewhat predict the faces the kids would be wearing in that situation?

Reading emotions test #2. Find close-up faces with various expressions in magazine pictures. Cut out just the eyes, avoiding the nose but including the eyebrows. See if your child can identify how the person is feeling just by looking at the eyes. Are they sad eyes? Happy eyes?

How good is your child at reading the eyes? If your child is only saying "happy," "sad," and "mad," try to offer some other emotional suggestions, like "frustrated," "suspicious," or "nervous." (This can be used as an assessment to get an idea of your child's current abilities, but it's also a great way to boost people-reading skills.)

Cognitive empathy is how your child figures out what another person is feeling. It can be based on imagining how someone feels, reading another's facial expressions, or learning the social implications of a situation. Emotional empathy can be present even in babies, but cognitive empathy comes a bit later. Cognitive empathy requires you to process an emotion you've just felt or to project an emotion onto someone else based on cues that you pick up. This is conscious thought, plain and simple.

Cognitive empathy allows you to measure how you feel toward the person in distress, think about how you would feel being in that person's situation, and then project how that person may feel. In particular, it taps into the part of the brain that regulates both behavior and imaginative processes. This area of empathy is ripe for concrete teaching: you can show your children how to hunt for emotional cues, and you can teach them how to use those clues to predict an emotional state.

It's probably easier to act empathetically when a strong emotional empathy force guides your actions. But importantly, you can have cognitive empathy without feeling a thing for the other person: this is taught empathy (see figure 6.3). All you need to be able to do is imagine how it would feel if it were happening to you. Cognitive empathy can lead to the compassionate acts of applied empathy, without emotional empathy ever even showing up.

Children can be taught cognitive processes as a framework for positive social actions from an early age. They can be taught that when they see someone with a destroyed sandcastle, they should place a hand on the crying child's shoulder, ask if she is okay, and offer to help rebuild the castle with her. This human reaction should be practiced until it is automatic.

Cognitive empathy requires taking another person's perspective, so it is limited by the age and neurodevelopment of your child. Start small here. You first need to test if your child has a fully developed ability to see things from someone else's point of view, known as theory of mind.

This ability usually develops between ages 4 and 6. The following two tests can tell you whether your child has developed this ability.

Cognitive empathy test #1. Ask your child to predict what the next-door neighbor would think was inside a raisin box that actually contains a marble. If your child answers "raisins," he has the ability to see things from someone else's point of view. If your child gets the answer right to this first cognitive empathy test, you can give him the second one.

Cognitive empathy test #2. Use two dolls, Sally and Anne, to act out this scene: Sally places a toy in her basket and then leaves the room. While Sally is gone, Anne steals the toy and puts it into a box. When Sally comes back into the room, where will Sally look for her toy? To "pass" this seemingly simple Sally/Anne test, a child must have developed cognitive empathy (or understand what Sally believes) to know that Sally will look for her toy where she originally left it. A child has to be aware of the difference between what *he* knows and what *someone else* knows.

Children are usually unable to pass the Sally/Anne test until around age 4, so this seems to be a function of brain development. Most kids nail it by age 6.[31] If they pass, it simply indicates a readiness to have

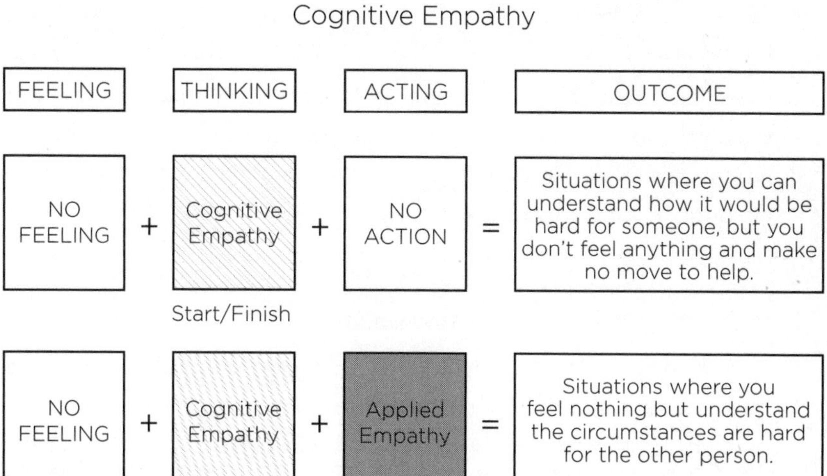

Cognitive Empathy

Figure 6.3 It is possible to have cognitive empathy with no emotional empathy. Empathy can be completely a thought process.

cognitive empathy. If not, they're not developmentally ready yet, but this doesn't mean you shouldn't actively work on empathy with them. It means you may have to use a slightly different approach to provide more structure or parental scaffolding for them.

Autism and Empathy Impairment

Individuals with autism have empathy impairments. In fact, the presence of empathy deficits is one of the criteria for diagnosing autism spectrum disorders. People with autism typically have deficits in cognitive empathy, or a central inability to read others' intentions, while emotional empathy may not be as affected, which leads to hope that empathy can be taught as a process that can be cultivated in at least certain ways.[32] Cognitive processes are trainable with practice, but more-basic human emotional urges are not as teachable.

HOW TO CULTIVATE COGNITIVE EMPATHY

Everywhere you look, there are opportunities for parents to keep a daily focus on empathy as an important life skill. It may involve reframing a normally occurring activity, encouraging certain behaviors, or simply setting a good example for your kids.

Minimize Differences Between People

One of the greatest challenges lies in teaching your children to empathize with another person even when they feel that person is different from themselves. In order to empathize with someone else, you have to be able to see that person as similar in some way.[33] This probably won't happen the first or even the second time your child encounters someone new. Having a child repeatedly practice looking at things from another person's point of view fosters more empathy than one-time or infrequent efforts.[34-38]

Cultivating openness to individual and cultural differences helps in developing both creativity and empathy, but it works better when you consistently minimize the gender, culture, and age differences in the people who interact with your child. You don't want to pass on your own preconceptions. Be aware that sometimes that means not mentioning differences at all. Stereotypes can be so deeply rooted that we're not even aware that they impact us, but consider the idea of "stereotype threat" (the risk of group members unconsciously conforming to negative stereotypes about their group). African Americans performed worse on a test if they were first asked to check a box declaring their ethnicity, and women did worse on a difficult math test when first reminded of their gender than those who were not asked for this information.[39, 40]

Emphasize that a child several grades younger can be a friend and invite him over, point out how your child and a TV character of a different ethnicity reacted in the same way to a problem, and make no comment when your 9-year-old son asks to do something with a female classmate. Fostering healthy cultural attitudes and openness is vitally important to a well-developed sense of empathy (as well as creativity, as discussed in chapter 5).

Having a buddy in a lower grade who kids see once a week is a great way to practice cross-age relationships in the school setting, as is providing older mentors (for example, an eighth grader mentoring a sixth grader new to middle school). Free Union Country School, an elementary school near Charlottesville, Virginia, does a great job with this. Every child in second through fifth grades has a younger buddy in pre-K through first grade. The buddy partnerships change each year, and as the children advance through school, they look forward to when they can finally be the big buddy.

This buddy system normalizes having friends of different ages, it allows kids to grow meaningful connections to individuals outside their normal social groups, it creates a broader sense of belonging, and it strengthens every kid's support network. Perhaps most importantly, it gives kids a chance to practice empathy through both teaching and looking at things from a different person's perspective.

Encourage Your Child to Read

A great book immerses you in someone else's life and helps you understand things from another point of view. (It's great for creativity too, as we saw in chapter 5). This includes not just the author's perspective, but also the perspective of the main character. Classic and literary fiction often contain in-depth portrayals of a character's inner thoughts and feelings and allow the reader to fill in the missing pieces about the character's motivation and perspective.

If you can lose yourself in a good book, you'll have higher empathy scores a week later, but if you read a book in which you are not engaged at all, you actually have lower levels of empathy.[41] In one study, people who read a short piece of literary fiction could better understand the mental states of others.[42] This result may or may not be transient, but it shows the remarkable plasticity of empathy.

This result is true for children as well as for adults. The number of stories preschoolers read predicts their ability to understand the emotions of others.[43] There are even types of video games that allow us to experience the world from someone else's perspective. Remember that empathy is not a wholly static trait but instead can be altered by our daily experiences.

Allow Your Child to Teach Others

Teaching something, however small, requires your child to anticipate what the learner does not know and to modify what he teaches to be on the learner's level. It's great for kids who need to practice empathy, as well as those who need a power boost. Try asking a child to share or demonstrate knowledge with another person, no matter how small the task.

Ask Jason to show the visiting student where the classroom puzzles are kept. Ask your younger son to teach your older daughter how to play the card game he got for his birthday. Allow your child to teach you the crazy way she is doing long division in class until you really understand it. Find something your child is competent at doing and then look for opportunities to let him share that knowledge. Doing so will not only empower your child, but it will offer practice at taking others' perspectives in order to effectively teach them what they don't know.

Increase Awareness about Emotional Cues

Ask your child to label his feelings in a healthy way. Articulate your own. Identify what a visibly angry person at the mall may be feeling, discuss the girl in the movie who is crying, and talk with the cousin who says nothing but has a worried look on his face when his mom is late to pick him up.

Teach your child how to read other people's emotional cues. Kids who bowl through social situations can be taught to pause and read the physical body cues of other people. They can practice looking into the eyes of the person who is talking, reading facial expressions and posture and evaluating tone of voice. You can also take selfies while expressing various emotions and have your child try to guess each emotion. Enhancing these skills will foster cognitive empathy. A child may or may not emotionally feel anything but can still be trained to be sensitive to the emotions of others. This type of non-verbal emotional cue training has been shown to increase empathetic behaviors in physicians after just three hour-long training sessions.[44]

One day at recess, McKenzie, a first-grade teacher, saw a group of her students chasing Amelia, another of her students. Amelia did not want to be chased. She was running, and tears were streaming down her face. But the other kids couldn't see her face from behind her, and amid their shouting they couldn't hear her crying. She ran and ran, panicked, until she was hyperventilating and standing before another teacher.

In response to what she'd seen, McKenzie erased her teaching plan for the afternoon and instead worked on emotional cues recognition with her students. First, she had her first graders take a mindful moment. Everyone lay flat on their backs to get centered. She asked them to see their lungs as balloons blowing up and letting air out. When everyone was sitting back up quietly, she asked them if they could remember a time when they were scared or when they didn't like something that was happening. Everyone nodded. Next McKenzie opened picture books and asked her class to look for body language in various illustrations. What does having fun look like? What does scared look like? She asked the kids if they could name what the characters were feeling.

McKenzie was not only teaching the class how to better recognize when a classmate does not want to be chased, but she was also (indirectly) teaching Amelia how to stop running and instead tell others very clearly how she feels and what she wants.

McKenzie also spent some time role-playing and discussing the options that each person has in this situation. Why? Because when children *practice* effectively dealing with an everyday playground occurrence like this, it sets the stage to avoid mistakes in the future, when the stakes will be higher if body cues aren't properly read and no isn't clearly articulated.

Practice Predicting Behavior Based on Clues

Unfortunately, the type of social content McKenzie taught in her class is rarely taught in schools, though this approach is the basis of a program called Responsive Classroom, which has been shown to improve student attitudes about school, decrease misbehavior, and increase test scores.[45–48] So it's up to you, Mom and Dad, to teach it to your kids!

You can ask your children to predict the behaviors of others in both real and hypothetical scenarios, navigating them through a process that sorts through the feelings on all sides: "If Morgan feels mad that you got a bigger ice cream than she did, what do you think she will do?" Asking kids to practice predicting behavior is especially helpful in conflict situations when they may not know the other person very well: "If you ask the kid on the swing next to you to stop sticking his leg out into your space, what do you think he will do?" This ability to reasonably predict the future is one way to empower your child in a situation where someone is being mean to him.

We can teach our kids how to function in society in a mindful way—to create children who are conscious of the effects their actions have on other people. For example, like many parents, Trish struggles to handle nightly conflict between her 3-year-old and 6-year-old, but regularly discussing and practicing behavior prediction helps. "When one of my children hurts the other, physically or emotionally, I always ask them to look at their sibling's face. I ask, 'What is it telling you right now? How does she feel about what just happened?'" By asking our kids to do something as simple as just labeling emotions, we can raise their awareness about the emotions they are feeling and the emotions that others are experiencing.

7

Applied Empathy
Is Compassion

APPLIED EMPATHY is actually *doing* something about the emotional problem that you recognize. It's initiating a compassionate act. Applied empathy springs directly from either emotional or cognitive empathy: whether you *feel* a problem or you *think* through a problem, you *do something* about it.

In a situation where a friend's baby is hospitalized, acts of applied empathy likely are filtered first through both emotional and cognitive empathy processes. It may take some time for you to funnel your emotional response into a thoughtful token of creative behavior, which could take the form of a donation to the parents in need, a letter of comfort, a quilted baby blanket gift, or an offer to pet-sit. Applied empathy will provide emotional or financial support to the distressed parents, but it will also make the empathetic person feel better.

The roots of what causes someone to *act* compassionately are more elusive than the neural networks that underlie emotional and cognitive empathy. But applied empathy is one of the most human things about us, and it's at the root of heroic acts and life-changing experiences.

Assessing Your Child's Applied Empathy Skills

Prosocial behavior is the way that psychologists measure applied empathy. These are active, observable compassionate acts. So where is your child on the prosocial behavior scale? You can conduct the next two tests to get an idea of how compassionate your child is.

Prosocial behavior test #1. Read your child the following story, previously published by researchers interested in altruism:[1]

> One morning, Chris was so late getting ready for school that he didn't have time to finish breakfast. By the time the lunch bell rang, Chris was really hungry. As he was unwrapping his sandwich, Chris noticed a kid sitting alone and looking sad and hungry. Chris thought that he must have lost his lunch or forgot to bring it. Chris didn't know what to do.

Then ask your child, "What would you do?" Ask your child to choose from the following choices:

A. I would tell the teacher.

B. I would not share because the other kid should learn to be more careful about remembering lunch and because I might be hungry in the afternoon.

C. I would share because I could imagine how I would feel if I were that kid.

Answer C shows the most prosocial behavior. But this situation is theoretical. The next test shows what your child might actually do in real life.

Prosocial behavior test #2. This one may take a little orchestrating on your part. Ask a friend whom your child doesn't know very well to accompany you and your child somewhere. Next, ask your friend to carry something heavy and bulky, like a big box, into a building or car. Make sure both his hands are full so that he isn't able to open the door for himself.

Follow behind with your child but pretend not to notice that your friend needs help. Pretend not to notice even when he bumps into the closed door several times. Will your child open the door for him?

Bonus points if your friend drops something like keys, and your child also picks them up.

It's not enough to work on "being nice." The world of empathy is a lot more complicated than that! To raise compassionate people, we need our kids to do more than sit and feel or sit and think. We want kids who *act*.

How to Cultivate Applied Empathy

If your child is already emotionally sensitive to others, applied empathy is easier to cultivate. However, the ability to exert control over emotional responses, or to regulate them, is essential for prosocial behavior.[2] You have to be able to hang those emotional responses on a framework. Likewise, if your child has a healthy amount of cognitive empathy, you can start there. But all acts of applied empathy must spring from either emotional or cognitive empathy (see figure 7.1).

The sections that follow provide six techniques for helping your kids develop and strengthen the neural pathways for applied empathy.

APPRECIATE ACTS OF APPLIED EMPATHY

The Making Caring Common initiative at Harvard University asked 10,000 middle and high school students to choose from the following what was most important to them: (1) achieving at a high level, (2) happiness (feeling good most of the time), or (3) caring for others. Only 20% of children selected "caring for others" as most important. Yet, in sharp contrast to this, most parents report that developing caring children is their top priority.[3] Either parents are not honestly reporting their priorities, or parents are not communicating the importance of caring very well to their children. I believe we, as parents, do place a high value on caring, but we don't know how to teach it, foster it, practice it, or reward it.

An easy way to start is by showing an appreciation for empathetic behavior you see around you. Recognize and reinforce the empathetic acts that you see in your child. Catching your child engaging in empathetic behaviors that naturally spring up will cause your child to act empathetically more often.[4–6] Many parents already do this. For example, I may say to my daughter, "You saw James had a heavy load, and you asked if you could help him carry the bucket. You're being kind to him, sweet girl." The goal here is for my daughter to view herself as a kind individual. You are teaching your child, "You are a person who acts kindly to others."

GIVE YOUR CHILD AUTONOMY IN SOCIAL SITUATIONS
When you start allowing your child to make social decisions, an adult needs to be available at first to manage conflict. You can't expect a

Three Ways to Reach Compassion Through Empathy

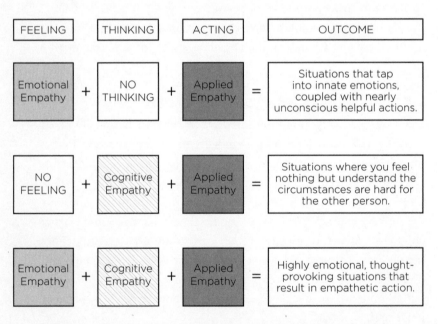

FEELING		THINKING		ACTING		OUTCOME
Emotional Empathy	+	NO THINKING	+	Applied Empathy	=	Situations that tap into innate emotions, coupled with nearly unconscious helpful actions.
NO FEELING	+	Cognitive Empathy	+	Applied Empathy	=	Situations where you feel nothing but understand the circumstances are hard for the other person.
Emotional Empathy	+	Cognitive Empathy	+	Applied Empathy	=	Highly emotional, thought-provoking situations that result in empathetic action.

Figure 7.1 There are three ways to reach applied empathy. To get to compassion, you can start with emotion and go directly to compassion (top row); or you can bypass feelings entirely, think through the situation, and then move to help someone (middle row); or you can go through all three types of empathy sequentially, starting with emotional empathy, then cognitive empathy, and ending up helping someone (bottom row).

child to be autonomous without guided practice first. The main job of the adult initially is to illustrate all the possible roads a person could take in various situations and to show everyone involved how things should have been done better and done differently. All play or interactions should stop until the conflict can be worked through. A discussion may be enough, or you may need to model an alternative way of behaving (especially with younger kids).

You won't have to do this forever, and the goal is to allow your children autonomy in social situations as soon as possible. Then let your children make decisions. Let them choose and choose again. Each decision strengthens your child's ability to choose well. It allows her to feel a social fail; it allows him to relish a social win. The ability to choose centers the power of learning right on the child. It does all this by strengthening synaptic connections. Practice makes it more likely that those used neural pathways will be reactivated when your children encounter a similar situation in the future.

Once you give your children the tools to handle social situations, you have to let them practice feeling emotional empathy and managing the sometimes unwieldy cognitive empathy. Older children are better able to empathize with others, predominately because they've made a bit more progress working on self-control and building imaginative processes. For example, the skill of empathy seems to be related to a child's ability to role-play.[7] Role-playing is fostered during free play, and imagination is required to successfully see things from another's point of view.

Free play empathy opportunities happen many times a day in your child's world. Recently, my older daughter was sitting still on the floor in her room, just listening to my younger daughter, who was inconsolably crying in the hallway over a toy that she couldn't find—one of those tiny, terrible Squinkies that are so cute and so easy to lose. I saw conflict on my older daughter's face for several minutes, and then, with a sudden burst of movement, she bolted out of the room and offered one of her Squinkies to her crying sister—one that she knew her sister had her eye on. I felt a little twist in my chest. We can make these moments happen more often when we teach our children how to think socially. Then socially acting is a natural consequence.

BRING IN MINDFULNESS AND REFLECTION

Quiet moments can be incredibly powerful tools for the development of empathy, but they'll be more effective if you've already taught your children how to observe social cues. These reflection spaces provide room for intention. A mindful moment lets kids check in with themselves. It allows them to pivot, if needed, to make a different decision.

Here's a pivot example that came out of intentionally leaving space for someone to feel another person's point of view in a conflict situation: It was a typically harried school morning, with the kids packed three across the backseat by 7:30 a.m. But it was no normal school morning. Katherine woke up to find her beloved pet rabbit dead in its cage outside. I suppose it seemed like her whole 9-year-old world should have stopped then, but instead we had to pack all our lunches and pile our book bags into the car in 10 minutes flat.

As I helped Katherine buckle into her seat, I found an old yellow stress ball on the floor and handed it to her. "If you feel sad, squeeze this ball, and it might make you feel a little better," I told her.

Sure enough, a few minutes into our journey, she pulled out the yellow ball and squeezed it with both hands as hard as she could, eyes shut tight.

Next to Katherine sat her younger sister, Jessica. Jessica's bunny was still very much alive and healthy.

Jessica spied the crushed yellow ball and screamed, "That's *my* ball! Stop squeezing it!"

It was then that I noticed the ball had a smiley face on it.

I tried to explain, "Honey, she's really sad right now, and I gave her that ball to help. It won't hurt it to be squeezed. That's what it's meant for."

"No!" Jessica shrieked. "It's alive! She's hurting it!"

I wanted to force Jessica to share the ball, but I stopped myself. Their conflict filled the car, and we just drove on, stuck, until Jessica reached over and snatched her ball back.

I tried again, "Jessica, you know Katherine's going through a really hard thing right now, and anything you can do to make a difference to her is a good thing." And then I left it there, with Jessica clutching the ball and Katherine weeping, face turned to the window.

If you allow for it, there can be a space for weighing or balancing right after conflict. It's a space where kids can sort out feelings and thoughts in the aftermath of screaming. In our fast-paced lives, we normally just zoom straight through it. And yet, it's in this small space—the space that feels really bad—where kindness and compassion can happen. Jessica's response to her sister after what I'd said had to be Jessica's decision; if it were forced, there would be no genuine kindness in it.

It's situations like these that make us who we are. And if we fail to let our children have these moments, they will grow up without us giving them the opportunity to decide who to be. They'll miss out on the chance to truly define themselves by those decisions.

We want to foster deliberate kindness in our children. And deliberate action is nearly always preceded by mindfulness. It takes space to feel and think through things. Cultivating this type of awareness—sometimes called mindfulness training—can promote empathy in people of all ages. The space doesn't have to be a weekend filled with silent meditation. It can happen in the minutes you wait in the checkout line, while you hunt for a raincoat, or while you're driving to school.

Your kids are not always going to make the decisions you want them to make, but sometimes they will. I could barely see Jessica from the driver's seat as she slid the ball over and pressed it back into her sister's palm. This time, giving Jessica space for reflection worked. I gave Jessica a thumbs-up in the rearview mirror. She was smiling.

Sometimes the first obstacle to having empathy is simply making the space for it. Particularly in new social situations, there is often a need for children to have a quiet space either before, during, or after conflict. Without this pause, your child may miss recognizing the emotions he feels, or he may not take the time to see the situation from another's perspective.

ENGAGE IN SCAFFOLDED PRACTICE

Some kids need more practice with social situations than other kids. Scaffolded practice is similar to immersing kids in the framework for working through conflicts, but in the absence of other children. It can be reflective, to sort through something that happened at school that day, or it can be prospective, to better prepare a child for handling social conflict in the future.

Parents with more than one child have an advantage in that they can somewhat control both sides of conflicts, since most of these involve siblings. But a lot of times, particularly for parents of single children, social situations will be processed after they happen.

Having more practice making hypothetical social decisions may make it easier to make social decisions in real life, just like a boy who grows up playing race car video games and is a better driver once he's finally gotten his license. Choose a situation that your child may encounter and ask him to make choices all the way to the conclusion of the imagined scenario. Find an example in a film or book, especially if it's controversial in some way or if you think the character chose poorly, and ask your child to choose differently for the character. It doesn't have to be a special situation. You'll find opportunities everywhere once you start looking.

SPREAD ACTS OF KINDNESS WITH YOUR CHILDREN

Paying the toll for the car behind you can result in similar monetary acts of goodwill for other people down the road.[8] In the same way, other acts of kindness and generosity can start a chain reaction that results in more acts of compassion. Compassion is contagious, but someone needs to start it. Find a place in your community where you and your child can give your time and energy, whether it's at the local animal shelter, a school reading-buddy program, or a food bank.

If you have trouble finding an organization that will allow you to volunteer in a meaningful way with your child, you can create your own ways to make a difference. The simplest way is devise a plan to raise money to donate to an organization, such as selling art to help send a disadvantaged kid to camp. Another way is to use your time to ask others for needed supplies, such as collecting coats during a cold winter to give to a local shelter.

Not long ago, I found a new way to work with my kids to help others. About a year ago, individuals began holding signs—ripped cardboard with words drawn onto them with black marker at stoplights—in my small city. One man held up one that said, "I hate to be a bother, but down on my luck."

My children noticed. "What does his sign say, Mama?"

"Not lazy. Need food or work. Anything helps." I read.

"Oooooh, what can we give him?"

I thought to myself: "We're not giving him anything." And then I felt bad.

The signs make me feel terrible—they do. Why? Because I'm not in the car alone: it's my children who watch me drive past, who listen to my reasoning about how "those people" will choose to spend the money they get, who watch me say no. And I am acutely aware that they are watching. These signs force my parenting hand: my action or inaction teaches my children in that moment no matter what choice I make—whether I ignore the man standing there with the sign, give him money, or talk to him. And at first, feeling pushed made me also feel mad.

Still, I kept thinking about that one sign: "Sorry to be a bother." This one man wasn't the bother. It's the homelessness, disabilities, poor life choices, addictions, and our own suspicions that are the distasteful, guilt-ridden, and awkward things that we shove to the periphery. It's hard to talk to your kids about ugly things and even harder to solve the problems.

Finally, my daughter and I came up with an idea. So many things make the person standing on the curb different from my daughter, so we focused on what is the same. She drew a card and thought for a long time about what to write inside it. She wrote: "Sometimes people don't treat you well, but there can also be a hidden friend." We packaged up the card with some nuts, a granola bar, applesauce, and water to give to the man.

Now we have similar bags that live packaged up in our backseat, ready to go. If my daughter's in the car and sees someone standing at the stoplight, she'll scramble to get one ready, slide the window down, and hand it out. And when I look back in the rearview mirror after the light turns green, she's always beaming as we drive away. The "happy bags" make *her* happy.

Simply thinking about a close personal bond with someone else makes people feel more altruistic. It makes them say they're more likely to help a stranger in need. Social connection makes people more likely to help monetarily. For example, asking people to read words that have to do with social connections has been shown to boost generosity toward organizations like the Red Cross.[9]

Giving things away has been shown to make people happier. Toddlers are happier when they give Goldfish crackers away from their own stash to toy puppets than when they don't share, and giving away their own snacks made them even happier than when they gave the puppets Goldfish from an adult's stash.[10] Researchers have shown that giving has the most benefit for the giver when the act meets three interconnected criteria: (1) when you connect to it in some way that is relevant to you, (2) when it actually fills a need or makes a difference, and (3) when you're not forced to do it.[11]

When people were given $20 and asked to spend it, those who spent the money on others were, at the end of the day, happier. If they kept it, they felt shame and had increased levels of the stress hormone cortisol. And yet, when asked, the study participants said spending money on yourself will make you happier. Our outlook is misplaced; we don't value giving enough, and as a result we will likely keep money for ourselves, thinking it will lead to our own happiness![12]

Studies like this help nonprofit leaders create great marketing strategies. They're also a reminder that kids who feel loved and well connected are more likely to give away their time and money to help others, and more giving leads to happier kids.

PRACTICE RESTORATIVE JUSTICE

Restorative justice is a framework to handle conflict. It's a way of seeing crime as not just breaking the law, but also as something that causes harm to relationships and communities. Restorative justice focuses on repairing the harm caused, ideally by letting the involved parties decide how to make it better together.

Restorative justice principles are used in a variety of settings, including schools. Effective enough to be explored as an alternative to incarceration, it has been implemented in a large-scale way by the Youth Justice Board for victims and young offenders in England

and Wales to target the underlying causes of crime. Research suggests that the victims also benefit from face-to-face restorative justice encounters.[13]

Joy, a middle school psychologist, recalls a time when a student, Jackson, used a permanent marker to write terrible things about another student on the bathroom wall. Part of his restorative justice resolution was a group circle process, where Jackson was present along with everyone who had been affected by his actions. The student he wrote the terrible thing about was there, the janitor who had to clean it up was there, the principal who had to discipline him was there, and the teacher who dismissed the student from class during the disciplining was there.

Each person in the circle took a turn explaining how Jackson's action had affected him or her. The janitor, for instance, stated that it had taken him over an hour to scrub off the words. Since it's impossible to give time back to someone, the facilitator asked Jackson if there was something else he could do. Jackson offered to come twice after school to help the custodian with his work. And from that, a friendship between Jackson and the custodian emerged. Restorative justice freed Jackson from the shame of his actions in all directions, allowed him to forgive himself, whether others did or not, and gave him a clean slate.

Parents need a system in which to actively and consistently weave empathy skills into their family's lives—a system that unites emotional and cognitive empathy and leaves space for applied empathy to emerge. There's a deep need here—a gap in social education that desperately needs to be filled. But you can't just teach this once, like you'd recount a story. You need to weave it into daily life, like retelling a favorite fairy tale every night before bed.

Parenting with Restorative Justice

In our house, we're drowning in creative but terrible ways to say, "I'm sorry." These apologies are thrown at the other person as if they're insults, tweeted in a singsong voice to show how little they mean, muttered under someone's breath barely audible but full of anger, or said with chin thrust up and eyes narrowed into slits.

As a parent, I'm frankly tired of it. I don't want "I'm sorry" any-more; I want you to not throw sand. I don't want "I'm sorry;" I want you to not hit your brother. I want your behavior to change.

"Sorry" doesn't undo events, and "sorry" doesn't really take care of the rift between two people. At its best, it's an overture, a bridge over troubled waters. An apology is nearly always a prerequisite for reconciliation, but it is not necessary for forgiveness, and—importantly for parenting—it does not indicate that the same behavior won't happen again.[14]

Ownership of the actions is the first step toward different behav-ior. Studies show that admission of guilt and contrition do help the situation, but taking responsibility for the action followed by repara-tion has the most positive benefits for the confessor.[15] In other words, saying "I'm sorry" doesn't really help the troublemaker, but making amends does.

In adults, it's the conversation that happens after the "I'm sorry" that usually makes the situation better. But for kids, this conversa-tion is nearly impossible to have without guidance. Without follow-up, the olive branch of an apology is a wasted opportunity to change the future. Children need someone to wade into the waters with them.

Apologies are particularly problematic when one person has hurt the other on purpose. If it wasn't an accident, then there's not a knee-jerk "Oh, I bumped you. I'm sorry." There's intent to hurt. A lot of times, I can tell that my child is not sorry at all. But everyone else around is hoping that the behavior doesn't happen again, and we all know the other person deserves better. So, what to do?

Instead of asking my kids to say they're sorry, I ask them to make things right with the other person using the OUT framework (see "The OUT Framework" sidebar). We keep it specific to the incident, even if it sounds a bit ridiculous. (Some of the things kids do *are* ridiculous.)

Don't let your kids off the hook if they can't think of what to say. Give them the words and make them repeat after you. Importantly, the OUT framework doesn't require a response from the other person, so you can use it on the playground if your child has hurt a stranger, whether inten-tionally or not. It gives you a way to model empathy for both your child and the stranger. If both kids have been unkind at school or in a sibling interaction, you can have each child take a turn speaking.

The OUT Framework

I use the acronym OUT as a three-step framework to help my kids decide how to make things right:

> **O**wn the action.
> **U**nderstand how it affects people.
> **T**ell how you'll do it differently next time.

Here is an example of what kids might say within the OUT framework:

> **Own the action:** "I licked your peach when you weren't looking."

> **Understand how it affects people:** "You were probably mad and had to go wash off your peach."

> **Tell how you'll do it differently next time:** "I won't lick your peach again."

It's powerful enough to work with bigger stuff too:

> **Own the action:** "I walked away from the swing set when Connor tried to take the swing from you."

> **Understand how it affects people:** "You probably felt really sad and lonely."

> **Tell how you'll do it differently next time:** "I won't walk away when someone's being mean to you again. I'll tell him that's not okay."

In my family, we can get stuck on the first step. Sometimes it's hard to see or admit to culpability in a situation. Take, for example, when my son chased his sister through the master bedroom and up over our bed. He leapt at her, and she jumped off the bed to escape, landing directly on my clothes hamper and shattering it. He disappeared. And when I tracked him down, he maintained that his sister broke the hamper. And she did. But getting him to see his role in it turned into a legal argument about whether he is an accessory, an accomplice, or (as he'd have it) a bystander. So, we implemented the "It's a Wonderful Life" principle, after the famous Christmas movie. If he were never born, if he were never there, would it still have happened? If the answer is yes, then he's not responsible for it. If the answer is no, then he's accountable and has to own it.

Use Time-Outs Differently

When you place your child in time-out, instead of making him stay there for a specified time (for example, 1 minute for each year of his age), ask him not to come out until he is ready to make things right. Asking your child to make amends for behavior gives him a bit of direction during that quiet time—he has to think about what he will say and what he will do—and it will be more effective than simply requiring an "I'm sorry" ticket to get out.

Your child could make things right with words, using the OUT framework. He could do something to fix the toy he broke. He could offer to share his new art supplies instead. His ticket to freedom is either (1) an act of applied empathy or (2) talking through the cognitive empathy of the situation using the OUT framework and explaining how he'd choose differently next time.

Typically, if the action is deliberate, he should always walk through the OUT framework. If he can't make these statements without being rude, he's not ready to leave time-out. Once this conversation has happened, the person affected by his behavior can choose to forgive or not, but you're giving your child the gift of having it be over, of letting him move on, of blank space to make the next decision in. Time-out is a mindful moment, if used properly.

Bullying and Conflict Resolution

Nearly 30% of middle and high school children surveyed reported being bullied during the 2010–2011 school year.[16] At a middle school in my area, teachers pass out a questionnaire several times a year that asks students to write the names of fellow students they think are either bullies or are being bullied. If a name pops up under the "bullied" category more than four or five times, the guidance counselor calls the bullied student in to see if there's some way to offer support.

This school uses a system of bullying identification called RIP. The acronym stands for:

> **R**epeated incidents
> **I**mbalance of power
> **P**urposeful or deliberate

Bullies get virtually no support through this system, though they can be punished with school suspension for repeated offenses. Surprised that I'm worried about support for the bullies? Research supports the idea that mandating restitution from people who have wronged others, or requiring the offenders to "make it better," is more effective than incarceration.[17]

Sometimes judges can use creative punishment to try to curb future behavior, but it's important to provide choice to the offender—that is, the offender has to be willing to participate. For example, Ohio judge Mike Cicconetti offers a choice to people convicted of speeding in a school zone: a 90-day driver's license suspension or a shorter suspension combined with 1 day working as a school crossing guard. He says that shuttling kids safely across the street keeps down the number of speeding reoffenders. He also asked a group of high-schoolers convicted of vandalizing school buses to throw a picnic for the younger students whose outing was canceled due to the incident.[18]

Reforming behavior is about awareness and practice. With parenting, the scale may be different, but the idea is the same. How we treat offenders—or bullies—tells us a lot about how we function as a society. Helping the bully today will help your child tomorrow. An unreformed bully will target your child, or someone else's child, again.

And that unreformed bully may grow up to be your child's boss or someone else's child's boss one day. Or, heaven forbid, your child may be the bully, since everyone has the capacity to make those choices, especially in situations where social power is involved.

There are a lot of ways to have social power: you can have knowledge, wealth, physical skills, or personal skills that give you an advantage over others. (See page 51 for more information about power.) And, as one way to look at bullying, social power can have profound effects on empathy measures. Typically, the more powerful people are, the less empathetic they are. In one study, people who reflected on a time when they felt powerless activated their mirror neurons more than people who recalled being in a power position.[19] Remember that mirror neurons allow you to better anticipate the reactions of others. It appears that power does indeed "go to your head" and can transiently change the way the brain works, making it hard to relate to others.

BULLYING IN ELEMENTARY SCHOOL AND SUBTLE BULLYING

Unfortunately, bullying isn't limited to middle and high school, and it isn't always overt. Let's say a young girl, Wynn, starts at a new elementary school for gifted kids. She's blonde and freckled, artsy and accommodating, a lithe ballerina type. But she's having a hard time with kids in her class. There's one girl in particular, Delaney, who is domineering on the playground. Wynn is afraid of her. Delaney plays a game called "bus," where the other girls line up to take rides on her back. Delaney's the bus, and she carries passengers around. It probably looks sweet to the teachers who stand and monitor play at recess. In this game, Delaney charges for rides. Not real money, of course, but the girl who goes before Wynn today gets charged an imaginary 5 cents. It's Wynn's turn now. Wynn gets charged $100 to take her ride. Why? Because Delaney says she's really heavy.

It's not just Wynn, though. Parent complaints flow in to Delaney's classroom teacher, a very caring, lovely individual who admits that she, too, is overwhelmed with the classroom dynamics. The solution?

Another parent, fed up with her own daughter being picked on, makes up T-shirts that say "Delaney Is a Bully" and tries to pass them out at school. So, in the midst of the rather toxic social dynamic that has spread from the children to the parents and throughout the elementary school, how can we help Wynn? We can teach her—and her classmates—the essential life skill of handling and resolving conflict. Kids will sometimes find themselves in situations that are bigger than themselves. It's important to show our children not just how to try to fix things, but also how to change their reaction to the situation if they find they are unable to alter someone else's behavior.

GIVE YOUR CHILD TOOLS TO HANDLE CONFLICT

When bullying behavior occurs, we can start with the teacher or guidance counselor. But what if you get an inadequate response from the school or other parents? Or what if you have a child who does *not* want you to talk to anyone about it? The following conflict resolution tools can help your child get through bullying (not just in one piece, but to actually grow through the experience).

Conflict Resolution Tool #1:
Teach Your Child to Communicate Very Clearly
Effective conflict resolution is problematic because, as adults, many of us still struggle with this very same thing. We never learned how to properly resolve conflict when we were young. We hid from it. We yelled. We were bossy. But even if you're not great at handling conflict, in order to successfully arm your child, you need to teach her to be her own mediator and her own advocate. This will come naturally to some kids, and others will struggle with it. And no matter what school your child attends, these skills are not taught enough in schools.

What do you do if your son starts to have a problem with another boy at a park when you're there? You could talk solely to your son and ignore the rude behavior coming from the other kid, or you could leave. But pushing through and doing the harder thing—talking directly to the other child—is better. Why? First, remember that the way you interact with that tiny perpetrator shows your child how to handle conflict—even if you're bad at confronting conflict. What better way to start than with a young child? It's probably easier for you: the child will be more forgiving of your clumsy efforts. Conflict is like a foreign language for some of us, and to get better at it, we have to practice. Model it for your kids.

But what if your child needs help navigating troublesome situations herself? For my daughter who felt lost in conflict, we came up with an acronym so that she could remember the exact steps to take if there is mean play directed at her or if she is being excluded by others. The acronym is STAFF, and it is support for the bullied:

Say how you feel.
Tell them what they're doing is not okay.
Ask for what you want to have happen. Give space for the
    other person to respond to you. If that doesn't work . . .
Find someone else to play with. It's your choice if you
    decide you don't want to play with that group. If that
    doesn't fit the situation . . .
Find a grown-up. Some situations shouldn't be handled
    completely by kids.

Conflict Resolution Tool #2:
Make Sure Your Child Knows Where to Go for Help
"Find a grown-up" is a last resort, but it's still important. We don't want to raise a generation of kids whose first impulse is to get a teacher. But your child should know where a safe space is in every situation, whether it is in class, at lunch, or outside a school setting.

Conflict Resolution Tool #3: Practice Creative Problem-Solving
In conflict situations, parents can come up with some creative redirection for a younger child. But this makes the early parts of parenting so exhausting: you're not only physically tired, but the creative burden is still on you. As early as possible, we can provide our kids the scaffolding to talk through what is happening and predict

an outcome: If Ben is repeatedly being poked with a pencil by a girl in his class, he can do several different things. But first, he can think through the outcomes in his head. Ben can poke back. Ben can cry. Ben can tell the girl to stop, or he can change seats. Make it Ben's job to come up with creative alternatives to the situation (see the examples of creativity in chapter 5) and then reinforce the solutions you want to see stick around.

This won't always work because sometimes, no matter what your kid tries, a bully still acts like a bully. In that situation, ask your child to think of ways he can change his own behavior to be happier. Ask your child to come up with a way to get the bully to understand her actions enough to change them, whether he is able to implement this or not. Ask your child to plan a way to help other children who are bullied at school. Write these things down and then help your child to act proactively to change his world.

Conflict Resolution Tool #4: Foster Compassion for the Bully

Having empathy for the bully is an important part of developing a mature sense of empathy in your child. Remember that research shows it's harder to understand someone's perspective if you view that person as very different from yourself. Try asking your son to explain the bully's actions as if the bully were his best friend. Talk about feelings—both your son's feelings and the bully's feelings. Make your child a detective: have your child try to read the bully's body language, find patterns in the bully's behavior, find a motivation. Have your child draw the bully's face and write word bubbles that say what the bully might be thinking.

There is a program called Cognitively-Based Compassion Training (CBCT) that uses mindfulness training to enhance compassion in children—yes, compassion even toward bullies. The CBCT is run by researchers at Emory University and involves spending a few minutes daily simply reflecting on how we are all interconnected, with the objective of becoming more altruistic and compassionate.[20] When our children deal with people they perceive as threatening, the body stress response is not so different from what the response to a bear might be.

Inserting these mindful moments into classrooms helps decrease this stress response in children, and it follows that there is great benefit in having these mindful moments at home as well.

Here's an example: Siblings Carson, age 4, and Liam, age 9, were complaining about the "big bully" car in their monster truck video game. "He's so mean, and he butts in front of us all the time and doesn't care about the rules. I don't like him," said Carson. Their father, Bradley, who played the video game with them enough to have unlocked a level for them just yesterday, said, "Oh, it's okay guys. He's just trying to win. I think his mom is in the hospital, and he's trying to win money to pay for her doctor bills." Carson paused and looked at his dad. You could see him processing that. "Nuh uh," said Carson. "He is not." "Yep," continued Bradley. "She's old and sick, and he's going to do everything he can to win because he loves her so much. She'll be so proud of him when he wins. Maybe after the race is over, we can all go visit her in the hospital together."

Teaching your child to take an empathetic position gives her a big individual power boost. First, she will better understand the situation, so she is able to predict other people's behavior based on their emotions. Second, she is more likely to act if she appreciates the emotional distress of others and has tried it on herself. Third, her ability to choose whether to act or not can shift the entire balance of power between the bully and the bullied. The key to useful empathy rests in the power of control over situations—the power of applied empathy.

FRENEMIES

Most of the negative social interactions your child will go through will not be with unknown bullies. Instead, your child may have mean friends, or frenemies—so common are these relationships that there's a special word for them.

Frenemies are the bullies you know well. These relationships are unbelievably tricky because intermittent reinforcement is the strongest type of reinforcement: I like you. I hate you. Studies have shown that viewing a bully as similar to you helps generate empathy. So in many ways, it's easier to teach your child about empathy with mean friends because your child identifies with this person, or they wouldn't be friends to begin with. However, especially when young children are first learning where personal friend boundaries should be, kids need help with mean friends.

It feels nearly impossible to tell our children how to react to mean play when it happens, especially in situations where no one is breaking any rules but someone still feels bad when she walks away. It's impossible for teachers and staff members to physically be present for all school interactions, so we need our children to start sorting through these types of things on their own. You have to give tools to your children if you expect them to be socially independent and to be good at it.

Let's take Laura as an example. Laura's 8-year-old daughter, Ava, cries every day when she gets home from school because of Charlotte. Charlotte is a mean best friend, a bit of a queen bee. Laura's talked to Charlotte's mom on the phone about it; Charlotte's mom was nice enough but clueless about the situation. In the meantime, Ava is plotting how she can change schools or whether she can study hard enough to skip a grade to escape her nemesis.

Laura buys the classroom some books on relationships and bullies. She talks to the teachers. She talks to the school administrators, who are caring and listen. But things stay the same. Ava asks her mom to come to recess, and Laura does come one day but doesn't see anything amiss. She gets what the teachers are saying: these frenemy relationships can be nearly invisible.

But one day, Laura is dropping off a lunch at the school and sees Ava in a tight circle of girls at recess. When Laura gets closer, she hears the teacher's aide encouraging Charlotte to tell Ava and Jillian about her feelings—how they were being mean by excluding her at recess. Laura had seen the 34 text messages that came in from Charlotte the night before, threatening to defriend Ava if she was too slow to text her back; knew how Charlotte had ridiculed Ava's star-print boots last week so that Ava had hidden them under her bed; and saw Charlotte barrel down a slide right through Jillian's playground game yesterday yelling, "Dramatic ennnnntrance!"

It somehow always ended up being all about Charlotte's feelings anyway. And yet, when Charlotte started crying, Laura started to feel nearly as lost as the girls, as lost as the ineffective teacher's aide trying to talk it out. She felt bad for Charlotte.

Social power, or personal charisma, is something that these mean girls, or frenemies, often have. The RIP method of bully categorization typically defines power as numbers (a group of kids picking on someone) or power in age (an older kid picking on a younger one) or size (a muscular football player type picking on the scrawny nerd). But social power is also power. And it's formidable. And if you count Charlotte's fine-tuned people skills as power, then Charlotte's behavior is bullying too.

Yes, even if she is crying. No one said bullies are happy people.

And if you are a powerful person, like Charlotte, it's easy to get others lost in *your* feelings—even if you are only 8 years old. In fact, social power is a highly desirable attribute, even in elementary school—this is our queen bee. Without a framework, it becomes a cesspool of emotions. It's easier to see this clearly when our kids are younger. These kids don't want this conflict. The bully's not happy, and the picked-on, controlled kids feel terrible.

As kids get older, emotions and situations become more complex, and we may need to clearly define the elements we want our kids to pay attention to in social situations. We can't stay in a world that just discusses feelings. We start there, but then we have to show kids how to think and how to act. Conflicts are an opportunity to practice empathy, as well as creativity and self-control.

So how should Laura respond? She (or the teacher) must not only give the girls a solution but also give them opportunities to practice, so they don't slip back into the way things were. She needs to let them help her establish some ground rules, some structure—a template for how to act and react. Here's an example of rules they might agree to:

> **Help the girls set the ground rules for inclusion.** "Ava and Jillian, you can't exclude Charlotte. Don't run away when she comes over."

> **Help the girls set the ground rules for fair play.** "Charlotte, you can't come in and change the rules of the game they're

playing. If you come into their game, you can change only one thing."

The girls should know that they don't have to play if it's not fair. "If Charlotte comes in and changes more than one thing in the game you were already playing, you don't have to play with her."

Then the teacher should follow up and check in with the girls. But Laura doesn't have to wait for the teachers to do it. It's okay for parents to check in on the scaffold they created, and it's great to model conflict resolutions for your kids. Do a hot cocoa date with them. Start by listening. Let each kid talk for 2 minutes. See how it's going. Ask if they are adhering to the ground rules that were set up. Hold people accountable. Change the rules if you need to.

part 4

CULTIVATING
SELF-CONTROL

8

The Neuroscience
of Self-Control

WHY IS SELF-CONTROL so hard for kids? It's because management of the self is not easy, and developing the skills necessary for
self-control is a long process. Self-control is a state of inaction. It's the
ability to stop behavior that seems to be a near certainty; it's the ability
to pause the default settings.

Self-control requires a person to be both a farsighted planner and
a doer in each moment.[1] Imagine your child as both the owner of an
NFL team and the head coach. Every time a conflict comes up, the
owner and the coach need to have a conversation. They're both in
charge of the same team, but when making decisions, they must come
together and do what's best for the team by balancing the present and
the future. That team is your kid, and she is in charge of it all.

Neuroimaging studies show us that the development of more
mature, controlled behavior continues throughout adolescence and
into adulthood. These self-control skills fall under the term *executive
function*, and they encompass the majority of the tasks parents are constantly reminding their children to do: pay attention, listen, remember,
keep track of things.[2]

Younger kids don't regulate their impulses at all. Instead, they'll
just act on whatever pops into their minds. Eventually, children will
begin to inhibit their unacceptable behaviors when there is something
in their immediate surroundings that prevents them from acting in an

objectional way: they may not throw the ball into the water if there is little chance of getting it back or if their mother is standing right there and they know they'll get in trouble for doing it. An older child can anticipate negative outcomes—for example, his mother will be upset with him or he will be upset with himself for letting his temper get out of control or for disappointing his mother. Some of this is due to developmentally regulated differences in the neurons that get myelinated; remember that, as we saw in chapter 2, the last neurons to mature are the ones responsible for mature judgment, impulse control, and decision-making.

Yet individual differences in the ability to delay gratification and engage in goal-directed behavior for long periods of time exist as early as preschool age, and these abilities appear to remain quite stable over a lifetime. The children who could delay gratification in a lab situation were able to cope better with frustration and stress during adolescence.[3] There's a classic study from 1970 that asked 1,000 4-to-6-year-old children to either choose a small reward (one marshmallow or cookie or pretzel) now or wait longer for a larger reward (two marshmallows).[4] A few children ate the treat almost immediately, but most were able to wait varying amounts of time in an attempt to gain two treats. The older the children, the longer they were able to delay gratification.

As these 1,000 children were followed into adulthood, researchers found that the amount of self-control a child had at preschool age is predictive of adult health, wealth, and crime rates—and can predict those things better than intelligence or social class can. The "high delayers" had higher SAT scores as adolescents, and when a follow-up self-control test was administered 40 years later, the individual differences appeared stable throughout life.[5]

In this follow-up study the researchers tested whether the subjects were able to inhibit impulses when they receive conflicting social cues instead, since marshmallows as a reward presumably hold less attraction for adults in their 40s. The natural impulse is to respond when you see a happy face, but the subjects in the follow-up study were told not to respond. Neuroimaging in the follow-up study found activation in both the **striatum** and the frontal cortex during this task, but the "low delayers" had greater striatal activation (a lower brain region), and the "high delayers" had greater frontal cortex activation (a brain area associated with reasoning and processing of the input coming up from the striatal areas). These results looked about the same between 4-year-old Kendrick and 44-year-old Kendrick. Self-control doesn't appear to change much over time.

Wait. Self-control is the same in your 40s as it is at age 4? Uh-oh. Julia's son, Pietro, is extremely intelligent, but he also has trouble with impulse control. He has a tough time regulating his own behavior to meet the requirements of others around him (think teacher who is lecturing or coach who is trying to run through a play), and only very selectively is he able to delay gratification. For him, goal-directed behavior must be structured in a way that engages him or it won't work. In other words, he has to care about the goal. Pietro would eat the first marshmallow in a heartbeat, smile, and kick his legs while he ate it. The marshmallow study is making Julia very concerned.

The Terms Self-Control and Willpower

Self-control and willpower are essentially the same thing, but typically we think of self-control as the ability to reign in our desires and impulses so that they don't negatively affect other people, and we think of willpower as the ability to control our desires and impulses so that they don't negatively affect ourselves. Self-control means "Hey, get yourself under control" in a room with twenty other people so that you stop bothering them, whereas willpower refers to the battle you have with yourself about whether to have one or three pieces of lemon pound cake. When you call it willpower, the only casualty of failure is yourself.

Kid Self-Control Is Low and Going Down

It's not only Julia who's worried about her kid's impulse control, though. Lots of studies have established how important self-control is for life success. Now, disturbingly, consider that children's capacity for self-control has diminished over the past few decades.[6–9] A recent study replicated a study first done in the late 1940s. Researchers asked kids ages 3, 5, and 7 to do a number of exercises, including asking the children to stand perfectly still without moving. In the 1940s, the 3-year-olds couldn't stand still at all, the 5-year-olds could do it for about 3 minutes, and the 7-year-olds could stand still pretty much as long as the researchers asked. When researchers repeated this experiment in 2001, they found very different results: according to psychologist Elena Bodrova, today's 5-year-olds act at the level of the 3-year-olds 60 years ago, and 7-year-olds now act the way 5-year-olds did 60 years ago.[10]

When that famous marshmallow test was given to non-American kids in 2017, the results looked somewhat different: Nearly half of the American kids can "pass" this test (that is, wait 10 minutes without eating the first marshmallow in order to receive a second one), whereas only about 30% of German kids can. The real rock stars here are the 4-year-olds from Cameroon. Nearly 70% of Cameroonian kids were able to wait the full 10 minutes for the second marshmallow. No one knows exactly why that difference exists, but Germans tend to engage in more sensitive, child-centered parenting, whereas Cameroonian parents expect high self-control from infancy and discipline in a more consistent way. Cameroonian kids grow up helping with subsistence farming and looking after younger siblings from a young age. This study shows that the way kids are raised has a huge impact on their performance on the marshmallow test.[11]

Tests for Self-Control

As a group, our kids don't have enough self-control. What about your child? There are a lot of ways that you can test self-control at home, but sometimes it can be difficult to interpret the results. There are two common ways to test self-control: subjects can fill out a questionnaire that looks at relevant behaviors (self-report), or they can take some tests with a psychologist (lab observation). Contrary to a large Australian study that correlates self-control behavior with good life outcomes, scientists have shown that neither of these self-control assessment measures closely correlates with reoffending in nearly a thousand adolescent male first-time offenders, but self-report measures are a better indicator of reoffending than performance on lab tests.[12, 13]

Wondering about impulsivity? As a past neuropsychological technician, I see a great deal of utility in parents using commonplace assessments to see whether their child's behavior is something that needs to be worked on.

Self-control test #1. Here's an easy self-control test for when your child is old enough to answer questions on a sliding scale. Ask your child to respond to the following statements using a scale of 1 (*false*) to 5 (*true*):

> "I do things without giving them enough thought."

> "I become 'wild and crazy' and do things other people might not like."

> "When I'm doing something for fun (for example, partying, acting silly), I tend to get carried away and go too far."

> "I say the first thing that comes into my mind without thinking enough about it."

> "I stop and think things through before I act." (This one is reverse coded, so here *true* is 1, and *false* is 5.)[14]

This assessment is the impulse-control part of the Weinberger Adjustment Inventory. The average item score for more than 15,000 young people aged 12 to 28 from eleven countries was 2.48 (range 1–5, where higher scores mean less self-control).[15] Add your child's scores and divide by 5 to see how close she is to the 2.48 average.

Taking one of these assessments can provide a quiet moment for reflection on behavior. Is your child acting the way he wants to act?

For younger children, guardian/teacher reports are the most common way of assessing self-control issues. But as mentioned, self-reports turn out to be a better way of predicting outcomes. Your child knows himself, including his own thoughts and feelings, better than anyone else.

In addition to having your child answer the questions, I'd recommend also completing this test independently for him as the parent and then comparing your score with his score. It's worth a conversation to see if your scores match up. Does he accurately represent his behaviors when self-reporting?

While self-reports are susceptible to false reporting, you can't fake results with psychologist-administered tests. Such lab observations might test, for example, a person's ability to delay gratification (like in the famous marshmallow test), the ability to sustain concentration, or the ability to inhibit a response, such as with the Go/No-Go task, which we'll look at next.[16] But testing self-control in a laboratory setting only lets you assess one aspect of what we've already established as a multifaceted behavior.

Self-control test #2. You can do a version of the Go/No-Go task at home by teaching your child a game with simple rules. The game goes something like this: When I point at you, you give me a peace sign back. If I give you a peace sign, you point back at me. That's it. Once your child has the hang of it, you change up the rules. So now, when I give you the peace sign, you point back at me, and when I point at you, you do nothing. It's this second round that is actually the Go/No-Go task. How does she perform when you change the rules on her? You have taught your child to play the game in a certain way, and it's hard to override those first impulses when the rules get changed.[17] Once it's clear she understands the change, is it difficult for her to play by the new rule?

Psychologists think that of the available options, tests like the Go/No-Go response inhibition tasks are probably the most useful for getting at the true nature of self-control because they tap into relevant areas of the frontal cortex that are involved with moderating first impulses or gut reactions.[18] But again, measures of self-control are only accurate if the subject is properly motivated—that is, he is willing to do the tests and he is trying his hardest. Otherwise, there's a motivation issue, not a self-control issue.

However, like many tests of self-control, the idea of motivation is hard to capture. No child is at his best when seated before a neuropsychological technician. And it's not performance in the psychologist's office that counts. It's the self-control performance in life that counts. Thankfully, this skill continues to develop long after preschool is over.[19]

Beyond That Marshmallow Study

So if a child's ability to wait for a marshmallow predicts adult success in so many realms, perhaps we should cultivate our kids' ability to wait for a marshmallow. But is timing how long a child can wait for a marshmallow actually testing self-control? This study does test the ability to wait, to delay gratification. Researchers properly define that as self-control, but this is a narrow definition to apply to the results of this study. If you look closely, the study also tests the obedience of the child and compliance with authority. It tests whether a child thinks the person in charge is telling the truth and has trust in society. It tests how much a kid likes sweets as a reward. It tests what a kid values.

The question "Will Pietro wait for the marshmallow?" depends on two things. First, *can* Pietro wait? If Pietro really wants to not eat the marshmallow, yet can't keep himself from doing so, that's a giant problem. There are absolutely situations that require kids to be able to delay gratification. Sometimes waiting is required, and sometimes it's simply worth it. Take heart because although it's somewhat of a developmental process, self-control can also be improved. We can help kids wait when it matters: we can teach them to pretend, we can teach them to meditate, and we can teach them to play games, to be creative, to think about empathy.

Second, does Pietro *want* to wait? It's important to raise a kid who can be obedient, but it's important only when that obedience lines up with what he values. As a parent, I really don't care if Pietro complies with the authority figure who tells him not to eat the marshmallow in an experimental condition. In fact, I want him to trust his gut instincts about whether he feels a person can be trusted and whom he chooses to obey and respect.

Marshmallow Waiting Is Not a Simple Self-Control Test

It may not surprise you to learn that the ability to wait for that second marshmallow is shaped in large part by economic and social background. A new analysis of the marshmallow study shows that even great self-control might not be enough to counteract the long-term effects of growing up poor and with less household education.[20] The ability to wait for something as simple as a marshmallow ties into past experiences associated with poverty (for example, if you're unsure of whether there will be food in the kitchen tomorrow, you're probably more likely to go ahead and eat what's in front of you right now) and translates pretty well into bigger ideas about delayed gratification and rewards (if you don't expect to ever go to college, you may be less likely to set money aside for that large expense). Being poor or being uneducated may force you to live in the *now*.

Compliance is helpful in a classroom, but it doesn't mean the child is learning or growing, and it would be a tough argument to say that compliance with expectations is the best measure of a child's success. In fact, it seems many success stories are of children who buck the trends and do not comply at all (think Bill Gates not completing college).

But, for example, what if Pietro didn't want to wait in a situation where eating the marshmallow meant Jacob and Rowan didn't get one? If Pietro can't clearly see and respect the socially appropriate thing to do in a situation like that, it's problematic, and we need to work on it. At the root of our kids' self-control problem is the bigger challenge of how to instill valuation and motivation in another person. We don't want to teach our kids to wait for marshmallows. We want to teach our kids to choose their rewards in a life-smart way, to decide what's worth the wait for them.

Crossing the street, for example, is delayed gratification where it makes sense. Don't wait until your kid tries to chase a ball across the road to teach this lesson. Instead, weave it into your daily life the next time you walk somewhere together. As you approach a street, talk through the reasons that you will have to stop and wait before you cross. Let her listen to you and then allow her to decide when it's safe to cross and then follow her lead (assuming she chooses correctly!). This is a well-placed, well-timed decision on her part. It takes 2 minutes, and it sets her up for success for more than just street crossing. It teaches that there's room in her life to pause and make a good decision even without the drama of an emergency. She makes the decision, so she retains the learning better. She practices being in control of her actions with real consequences. She is empowered. And *you* are on the way to stepping back as the parent.

Brain Areas Involved in Self-Control

You can't have good self-regulation unless you first have great executive functioning skills: you have to get a handle on not only self-control, but also attention, decision-making, willpower, goal-directed behavior, and impulse control before you have a shot at using those tools to work toward a goal. That is a very big list.

Importantly, these processes are developmentally regulated as the brain shifts from a more youthful bottom-up to more top-down processing.[21] This means that as we age, the brain areas controlling higher thought actually start to send feedback down to control the gut impulses coming from the lower brain regions, like crushing the impulse to snatch the biggest cookie for yourself or stifling the urge to run away from the haircutting scissors. Proper executive function depends on maturation of the frontal lobes in the **cerebral cortex** and the synaptic remodeling and myelination that continue to occur during this process.

From an evolutionary point of view, the development of newer brain areas doesn't change the function of the older areas. It simply allows the newer brain areas to change the way the entire organism behaves by limiting or promoting the activity of the older system beneath it.[22] We use our top-down approach, our newer brain areas, to control the impulses coming from the older brain. We have a way to modify our own behavior for our own benefit.

Neuroimaging shows an interaction between the **ventromedial prefrontal cortex** (newer brain) and the ventral striatum (older brain) when subjects have to wait for a reward. Research of this brain activity suggests that impulsive individuals have greater activation of the older brain and are more sensitive to immediate reward value, or perhaps they experience pleasure associated with reward more strongly.[23]

But even within the newer brain, self-control taps into two different brain pathways as the brain plays the role of both NFL owner and head coach: (1) signals are created from the valuation circuitry found in the rather "shortsighted" ventromedial prefrontal cortex, and (2) these value signals are interpreted by the decision-making circuitry—the "farsighted" **dorsolateral prefrontal cortex**—which is involved in cognitive control, working memory, and emotional regulation. Neuroimaging studies about self-control show that systems within the prefrontal cortex are activated when subjects exert self-control while making food consumption decisions.[24]

For example, if you are choosing food to eat, you might value taste or healthfulness or how quickly the meal can be prepared, and these values will likely line up with your eating goals. Self-control is used when the farsighted part of your prefrontal cortex is required to integrate several different values within the more shortsighted part (for example, you are very hungry, and healthful food takes longer to prepare). Self-control differences may depend on the extent to which the farsighted dorsolateral prefrontal cortex can mediate the shortsighted ventromedial prefrontal cortex. Interestingly, these farsighted areas are also involved in emotional regulation and cognitive control, so that may begin to explain why these skills and, in fact, overall intelligence are correlated with self-control.[25]

9

How to Help Kids
Develop Self-Control

LIKE EMPATHY, SELF-CONTROL can be influenced by the immediate situation, but it is relatively stable at the same time. Self-control can be thought of like a muscle—exertion in the short-term can leave you feeling depleted and tired. But over time, exercising self-control will strengthen it and deepen your resources.[1]

Why do people think self-control might be a limited resource? Self-control comes at a cost: First, it requires emotional sacrifice. You must delay gratification now to get something later (you pay to attend college now because you know that college grads will make over a million dollars more during their careers). But second, self-control also requires physiological sacrifice. When the brain must work to make something happen, there is actually an additional expenditure of energy required.

Self-control *can* be depleted: we've all been there. For example, in one study, people who first forced themselves to eat radishes instead of chocolates ended up quitting unsolvable puzzles faster.[2] But the depths that we can reach into for just a little bit more self-control differs from person to person and from hour to hour. The brain doesn't have limited capabilities, like a computer. Because there are infinite ways that neurons can deal with situations, we often can reach deeper than we thought. It turns out that self-control is an attention- and motivation-driven process, highly dependent on our own thoughts about the way self-control works. In short, we can teach our kids to trick themselves into having more self-control.

Strategies to Boost Kids' Self-Control

There are a bunch of different ways to boost self-control in the short-term after it's been depleted or to keep it from being depleted in the first place.

Regular exercise of self-control will increase self-control, just like a muscle that gets stronger with repeated use, and improvements in one area can bleed over into other areas.[3] One study showed that college students who spent 2 weeks practicing self-control (working on their posture or monitoring their eating habits daily) had deeper self-control reserves than students who didn't practice. After this training, all students were asked to *not* think about a white bear for 5 minutes, which requires self-control to avoid doing, and then, in a presumably depleted state, they were asked to take a grip-strength test that again required self-control to keep gripping even when they wanted to relax their hands. Students who had practiced self-control did better on that grip-strength task.[4]

Repeatedly practicing these techniques in the short-term will allow self-control pathways to strengthen in the long-term. We can increase our children's self-control by showing them how to either distract themselves or trick themselves into it. Self-control comes off seeming like a party trick—like when you teach a dog to hold a treat on its nose until you say "okay."

But since improvements in one form of self-control can also leak into other areas, which means that, as a parent, you can pick an easy thing to work on and start there first, confident that the results will translate. For example, a study showed that if people regulated their money usage for several weeks, they saw an improvement in their savings. But those same people also reported that they began to study more regularly and effectively, became more scrupulous about completing household chores, smoked fewer cigarettes, and seemed to exert self-control more effectively in other spheres as well.[5]

MODEL SELF-CONTROL IN YOUR PARENTING

We start self-control practice with *ourselves* because the way we respond to our children can change their developmental self-control trajectory. Modeling good self-control in a way that means something to your kids is maybe harder than dabbling in creativity or even empathy. It means not yelling at your kids, not spanking, not being reactive, and so on. And some days, that can be hard to do.

Not surprisingly, fostering parental creativity and empathy also helps us parent with more self-control because we have more tools at our disposal. If you can figure out how to solve a problem creatively, you may avoid a head-on confrontation with a tired, hungry toddler after daycare pickup. One-year-old children who had responsive mothers who talked about emotions and were supportive while also encouraging independence did better on self-control tasks 6 to 12 months later.[6]

Jessie is a new parent. She feels she hasn't started working on these skills with her baby yet, but she's working on them in herself: she sees self-control as "being able to put the baby down during a crying session instead of yelling or getting frustrated." It's much better to take a moment's break from your baby if a crying session is overwhelming than to take your frustration out on the baby. Jessie is giving herself a mindful moment to recoup before digging back into the hard parts of parenting. Without thinking too much about it, she's also modeling empathy in her parenting, and these values will be passed on to her child.

Fiona sees self-control as "knowing that a certain reaction is going too far and having the wherewithal to stop yourself." Even with her baby, she knows self-control is an important part of parenting: "I have to regularly work on self-control with my 7-month-old, who often doesn't want to eat dinner. It's the end of a long day, we're both tired, I'm trying to feed her a lovely puree I've made, and it's very frustrating when she refuses to eat. But I remind myself that it's okay if she doesn't want to eat it. She's tired and teething and may not be hungry. I usually give up and give her a yogurt and try again at lunch the next day." This, again, is modeling a bit of creativity in the solution, as well as showing empathy for how her preverbal daughter might be feeling.

FUEL YOUR CHILD'S BRAIN

If your child is having a meltdown, first make sure she's not hungry. Researchers have shown that willpower-depleted individuals might be low on fuel. The brain is a high-energy organ, powered by a steady supply of glucose (blood sugar). Some researchers have proposed that brain cells working hard to maintain self-control consume glucose faster than it can be replenished. In other words, hungry children have lower self-control.[7] And indeed, people who had to use self-control in lab tasks had lower glucose levels afterward than control subjects who weren't asked to use self-control.[8]

So, a day of repeatedly using self-control at school only to have a tantrum right before dinner makes total sense. Luckily, restoring glucose appears to help reboot run-down willpower. One study, for example, found that drinking sugar-sweetened lemonade (that contains glucose) restored willpower strength in depleted individuals, while drinking sugar-free lemonade did not.[9] So feed your tantrum-thrower ASAP.

CHANGE YOUR KID'S SELF-CONTROL ATTITUDE

Your child's thoughts and beliefs about his own self-control and motivation to control his own behavior are important. The perception of being depleted is even more important than the actual depletion.[10] This means that if you think your willpower is endless, then it is. Thinking this way will make it a reality: it will let you step up your goal-directed efforts, even when it gets tough, and end up making you happier.

Educating kids about the ways they can change their own self-control resources is the first step toward making meaningful gains in self-control in this generation. Kids get the message loud and clear that their DNA makes them who they are. They think: "Who am I to fight my own genetics in a daily battle?" It's easy for them to shrug off personal responsibility and accept genetic makeup as the most powerful force that guides their life. With a cultural emphasis on genetics, parents, too, can focus too much on what kids inherit: "Oh, depression runs in the family, so no wonder you're having trouble adjusting." Kids can remain wholly unaware of the ways that they can alter their own neurology, and that's a shame, because people who believe their willpower is limitless strive for higher goals and are happier.[11]

Teach your children that self-control is not necessarily a limited resource. Teach them how pathways are formed in the brain and how they are in charge of who they become by what they practice being. Show them how to talk themselves into action and out of action.

The brain is dynamic in a way that no computer can ever be. It can pivot and is ever changing, and importantly for self-control, it can manipulate itself and change its mind. The brain can surprise us.

ENGAGE IN SELF-TALK AS A SELF-MANAGEMENT STRATEGY

Self-talk has been actively promoted in another area where practice is a big deal: athletic performance. Coaches promote self-talk as a psychological skill that can increase athletic performance. Self-talk can boost decision-making skills, increase focus/attention, and decrease interfering thoughts, and positive self-talk even has a positive effect on performance.[12]

Encourage your kids to use self-talk to remind themselves out loud to stay focused when they're following directions in a sequence. Provide verbal cues—like a cleanup song—to help kids stay on task. Verbal self-reminders help kids in complex rule following, too. Self-talk can help children resist responding in the old way when the rules to a game change in a way that requires impulse control, like when they're playing a game where they have to switch to clapping when they see a square instead of stomping their feet.[13]

PUT YOUR CHILD IN A GOOD MOOD TO HELP WITH WILLPOWER

People in one study who got to watch a comedy show or who got a surprise gift, such as a thank-you bag of candy, showed less self-control depletion.[14] Being in a happy mood helps to replenish self-control after a particularly taxing task. Be nice to your kids, try to make them laugh, be silly, stop for an ice cream recharge. Happy kids have better self-control than sad kids.

LET YOUR KIDS HAVE AN EMOTIONAL OUTLET

One study showed an upsetting movie to people and asked some participants to suppress their feelings about it. The ones that held their emotions in did worse on a subsequent physical stamina test than people who were asked to freely respond to the emotional impact of the film.[15] Talking about emotions is good for us, as is having a framework to process those emotions. Discussing emotional content with kids may boost self-control, while it also helps them learn to recognize those emotions in others and predict how others might be feeling.

GIVE KIDS CONCRETE REMINDERS
ABOUT WHAT THEY NEED TO DO

Sometimes, young children need to be reminded of things they are supposed to do to stay on task. For example, if kids are supposed to be taking turns reading with a buddy at school, have the reader hold a picture of lips and the listener hold a picture of an ear as external reminders about what they are supposed to be doing. When this technique was used in an immersion curricula called Tools of the Mind, the pictures weren't needed anymore after a few months.[16]

Normal activities can be easily modified to enhance self-control skills and incorporate creativity. For example, if you are trying to work through a conflict about who gets to jump on the trampoline next, you can have your kids take turns holding the lips and ears pictures while you talk it through with them. Ask them to come up with concrete ideas about how to keep track of the trampoline jumping sessions. They may come up with the idea of switching off wearing a jumping bracelet and a waiting bracelet; they may ask you to give them a 10-minute session timer; they may say that the nonjumpers get to eat a snack while they wait; or they may say that the person waiting can spray the jumper with the hose if they go over the session time. The bracelets and the timer function as concrete reminders, the snack would change the power balance and provide a distraction, while the hose could turn the conflict into a fun game (but could also potentially create more conflict). Make sure they come up with the solutions, or at least agree to them wholeheartedly, and make sure you agree with them too, since you'll have to clean up the conflict. You are still the parent and need to approve their solutions.

Have your older children make their own checklists of things they need to get done or help them set their own reminders on their phones. Let's use the tools we have to stay on track.

ALLOW CHILDREN TO SELF-MONITOR

Set up situations that encourage your child to both self-monitor and co-monitor behavior. Have one child perform a task, such as counting suits of cards in a deck before a game is palyed or sorting laundry for multiple family members, and ask a second child to then check his partner's progress. Both the sorter and the listener have to stay on task, and they have a buddy to help them do it.[17] Co-monitoring is good practice for self-monitoring, since (1) it requires children to practice waiting, and (2) it gives children practice monitoring other people's behavior (which can be hard to do, as parents know). It gives kids a better benchmark for appropriate and inappropriate behavior when they see it mirrored in someone else. Trust the kids to do it. They like accountability, they accept the responsibility, and they may surprise you.

When my son was 13, a neighbor asked if he wanted to babysit for her two children. My son really wanted to do it, but when he babysits his siblings in our household, it never goes so well. I asked him to do a practice session by watching his brother and sisters during a parent-teacher conference for an hour. I told his siblings that they could write a reference for their brother that we'd give to his potential employer. They could check "Recommend," "Recommend with Reservations," or "Not Recommend." The babysitting hour went well, all the siblings checked "Recommend," and they filled up the pages with helpful examples about how he helped when someone lost a shoe and other important things to pass along to the neighbor. By the time he had his first babysitting job with the neighbor, he felt prepared to be there. His siblings were essentially co-monitoring his job, feeling powerful as they provided feedback they knew someone would actually listen to, and learning how to co- and self-monitor.

TRY PRAYER

Many religions have self-control as a pillar of behavioral expectations, so they've been figuring out how to be good at self-control for centuries. The simple placement of subconscious religious concepts like "God" or "divine" was able to offset self-control depletion effects in study participants.[18] But prayer can actually prevent self-control from being depleted in the first place. One study showed that 5 minutes of directed prayer before being asked to exercise self-control was stronger than 5 minutes of free thought. The researchers asked subjects to not laugh at something funny in order to deplete self-control, and then they used Stroop test performance as the measure of subjects' self-control. The Stroop test asks you to read color names that are written in a different color font, so you have to repress your response to the font in order to correctly read the color names. Irrespective of how religious people were coming into the study, the people who prayed first did better on the Stroop test after depletion.[19]

Self-Control Versus Self-Regulation

Despite the 1,000-kid marshmallow study, our focus shouldn't be solely on self-control for life success. Self-control is about *not acting*—not speaking out in class, not telling your aunt she looks fat, not hitting back. But we need kids who can *act* as well as not act—kids with great self-regulation skills, not just with good self-control.

Self-regulation allows you to both work within someone else's rules and to make up new rules that enable you to get what you want. Sometimes that means self-control, or refraining from action, but many other avenues are also open to you.

Self-regulation is about more than just sitting on your hands. Self-regulation is defined as the "processes that enable an individual to guide his/her goal-directed activities over time and across changing circumstances."[20] Someone with great self-regulation is flexible and self-aware. She has not only the self-control to stifle her gut first response if necessary, but she can also then weigh complex cognitive and social aspects in the situation and think creatively about how to act differently. She is self-aware enough to decide to act in a different way. Self-regulation taps into not only decision-making, but also creativity and empathy. We can start with self-control, but the main goal as a parent is to move toward great self-regulation, which we'll explore next in part 5.

part 5

SELF-REGULATION
FOR THE WIN

10

What Is
Self-Regulation?

SELF-CONTROL IS A RESOURCE that can hypothetically be used up; self-control depletion is that moment you give in and grab the last piece of pizza while on a diet. But self-regulation continues whether you still have self-control reserves. Even when you can't tap into self-control anymore, you can still work purposefully toward your goals using self-regulation, defined as "any efforts undertaken to alter one's behavior."[1] Let's apply this definition to a conflict situation in the classroom, where Ben is repeatedly being poked with a pencil by his classmate. Ben may run out of self-control pretty quickly. Once he can't sit there for a moment longer without poking back, we'll say his self-control has run out. He can poke back. Or he can use other ways to *regulate* his own behavior.

We don't want kids who simply have amazing self-control. We don't want our son to just sit there being poked with a pencil for an entire class period by virtue of his impressive willpower. No, we want our son to be a problem solver instead. We want him to decide to resolve the situation creatively, with empathy, with respect for all parties involved, even when he has depleted self-control. Self-regulation is a much bigger deal than simple self-control. It's not just the ability to pause behavior, but it's having the flexibility to pivot behavior. Self-regulation is the ability to blaze a trail toward a goal, while still preserving trust and reciprocity in those around you.

Ongoing self-regulation has these three main components:[2]

Forethought or planning

The action itself

Self-reflection afterward

As a society, we often focus only on the second component—how an individual behaves. Action means that he ate his brother's Halloween candy when he came home from school hungry or that she bit her classmate after harsh words. We can do a much better job on the forethought component to prep our kids, setting them up for success the first time they independently tackle these scenarios in real life. And we can introduce more self-reflection, to help our kids process how things went and how they can do better next time. This helps our kids master these basic social interactions early on, leaving them more mental space available to pivot behavior, to create, to empathize, to be thoughtful about their trajectory and life choices (see figure 10.1).

Self-control, then, is just another tool on the way to competent self-regulation. Self-control taps into many of the same brain processes that govern empathy and creativity. And just like creativity and empathy, self-control is a skill that gets better as we practice it. You can see how interconnected these systems are, culminating in self-regulation. It's a precise juggling act to be completely in charge of yourself. And both you and your kids have to feel like the work is worth it.

How to Help Kids Develop Self-Regulation

The ability to self-regulate is not an innate or permanently fixed trait. Self-regulation is a skill that can be practiced, but our kids need our help because they're not getting this practice in our schools.

Kindergarten in the United States has changed so much in the last two decades that it is nearly unrecognizable. A large study comparing American public-school kindergarten classrooms in 1998 and 2010 showed that current teachers have higher academic expectations: they spend more class time on literacy, math, and assessment and less time on art, music, and science. Current kindergarten teachers devote more time to teacher-directed instruction and less time to child-selected activities.[3] The increased focus on academics means there is very little play embedded in our kindergarten programs and less school time dedicated to teaching other kinds of skills, such as social awareness, personal decision-making, and the ability to self-regulate and to resolve conflict. These changes effectively mean that kindergarten is the new first grade—or even second grade.

So much of our formal schooling structure and our assessment methods are dependent on our children being able to pay attention and focus on what we are teaching. A recent study shows that when children enter kindergarten at age 6 instead of at age 5, they have lower levels of inattention and hyperactivity at age 7, and these differences are still there at age 11.[4] This study is a blazing red flag that shows us we have to do kindergarten differently.

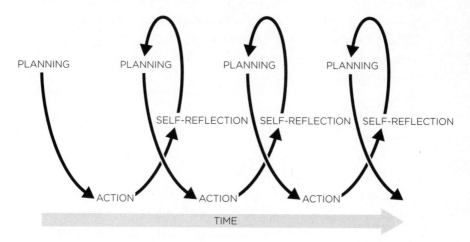

Figure 10.1 Self-regulation is a continuous spiraling process that goes through three separate but connected stages: planning, action, and self-reflection. Planning is when you set goals, come up with a strategy, or simply have an intrinsic interest in a situation. The action requires you to focus your attention and monitor yourself in the context of making a decision. Self-reflection is when you think about your performance, your reactions, and—importantly—what you can do next time to be better. Each step is an important element of self-regulation.

This readiness study was done in Denmark, where there is universal access to pre-K programs, so Danish parents can choose to wait a year, keeping their children in an environment with more playtime and a more developmentally appropriate curriculum. But what about in the United States, where pre-K programs are harder to access and expensive? School attendance at age 5 is required by eight US states and the District of Columbia.[5] American parents with a 5-year-old can be faced with four choices, none of which are ideal: (1) placing their child in an academic environment too early, (2) paying for a year of extra preschool and having an "older" kindergartener the next year, (3) paying for private kindergarten with a different educational philosophy, or (4) homeschooling/petitioning for an exemption. Our kids shouldn't be in a situation where play is sacrificed for structured academics and parents shouldn't have to consider holding kids out of school for their own good.

There is another option here: if we redesign our academic content delivery in a way that also fosters child choice, experience, play, ownership, and self-regulation, we could teach kids how to learn and live at the same time. This option starts with evidence that these skills can be taught in a school setting and it ends with pointed curriculum reform keeping neuroscience in mind.

SELF-REGULATION TRAINING PROGRAMS FOR KIDS

Evidence shows that at least two immersion school curricula can improve self-regulation in young children. These curricula both use play-based learning, but in different ways.

The first program, called Tools of the Mind, focuses on ways to build self-regulation skills in preschool children and is centered on Russian psychologist Lev Vygotsky's theories that sociodramatic play in early childhood could contribute to the development of self-regulation.[6-8] Tools of the Mind facilitates children's executive functioning skills (working memory, attention, and behavior control) in both preschool and school-age children, including children diagnosed with ADHD.[9] And it works: at-risk preschool kids who were in a Tools of the Mind program for 1 to 2 years had better executive functioning skills than those who were not in the program.[10]

The second program, Montessori education, is based on Italian physician and educator Maria Montessori's ideas about the normalization of behavior, moving from "disorder, impulsivity, and inattention to self-discipline, independence, orderliness, and peacefulness."[11] Though play is encouraged, the focus is less on sociodramatic play; instead, children engage in activities (for example, instead of playing restaurant, children may actually cook). Follow-up evaluation has shown that at 5 years old, Montessori children have better executive functioning skills than peers attending other schools, as well as superior social and academic skills. By age 12, these differences had disappeared, but Montessori children still showed more creativity in essay writing than children enrolled in other types of schools.[12] The results clearly show that really young children can be taught self-regulation skills, and the classrooms were less stressful places for both teachers and students. As parents, we can find one of these educational programs for our kids, or we can decide to make some changes at home in light of this evidence-based research.

SELF-REGULATION TOOLS

What works to enhance self-regulation in our kids if they aren't in one of those immersion programs? Here is where most of the tools we've already talked about all come together.

Mindfulness and Reflection

We need to slow our kids down. When one teacher integrated between 10 and 30 minutes of mindfulness/yoga exercises into the classroom daily for 6 months, researchers found improvements in attention, delay of gratification, and inhibitory control. The best thing about this study is that kids who were the worst at self-regulating their own behavior at the beginning of the year made the most gains. In other words, the "difficult" kids benefited more from the training.[13]

On the first day of school in my son's first-grade class, the teacher lit a tiny candle and placed it in the middle of the carpet where the kids sat in a circle. It was settling-in time. No one talks, no one makes faces at the kid across the circle. Kids are supposed to stare at the candle and be still, listen, observe, reflect, and check in with themselves. It's part of the Responsive Classroom curriculum that a mindful moment should start every child's morning off right. But could this actually work with 6-year-olds? Two minutes went by. There were some squirmers, a few gentle whispered corrections from the teacher. And then they were done and on to the morning greeting.

I liked it. I thought about using it with my college students. I appreciated the grounding in that very moment. But it wasn't until I went back to attend morning meeting again in May that I saw the amazing thing that had happened. The teacher lit the candle, the kids got quiet, and the candle stayed flickering and flickering, and the kids stayed quiet. I stared at the candle for longer than I felt I needed to and then looked around, amazed at what this teacher had done in those few months.

Jasper, who talks and thinks a mile a minute, was a bit squirmy but quiet on the teacher's lap. Nevaeh, who had a tearful morning separation from her mother just moments earlier, was staring intently at the candle, rooted to the floor. Tyler, who never wants to be told what to do, was looking down at the carpet instead of the flame: I kept waiting for him to thrust his shoes obtrusively into the center of circle or bustle against Theo next to him, but he never did.

As I sat there, those original 2 minutes stretched into 5 and then 10. The power of those extra minutes was overwhelming. And every single child did it. I guarantee not one child could have done it on the first day of school. But they had practiced every morning. What a gift for that second-grade teacher next year! And what a skill to give those children—the ability to just *be* for 10 minutes. Without a game. Without picking up their phone. They can just be alone with themselves.

There's no particular magic about developing this skill in a school setting. In fact, teachers only have to work on it because kids are walking into their classrooms without the self-regulation skills they need to be a functional part of the learning experience. Every parent knows it only takes one or two kids to disrupt learning for everyone in the room, and constantly taking instructional time to manage one child is annoying. But we can easily teach this to our children at home.

Mature Play

Play is a great way to let your kids practice executive functions in everyday life by regulating their own behavior and having opportunities to hone their self-control skills. The best time to do this is when it doesn't actually count: during play. Early childhood play experiences allow a child to explore life in a manner not regulated by adults. Once they enter school and instruction begins to focus on reading and math skills, their activities become adult-led, and even their afterschool activities and sports are often adult-directed. There are few opportunities for self-regulation and practice of executive functions. Free play is a childhood space that should be held sacred. You will never pretend with such abandon again. And it will never be as important as a learning tool.

It's not enough just to free play, though. We want *mature play* in order to foster self-regulation skills.[14] During this type of play, kids practice making choices, and they have to plan ahead. The Tools of the Mind program encourages mature play by asking kids to think before acting and to plan out their play by drawing the scenes and the role they will play. Once they start playing, teachers will check in with the group to see how it's going.

This isn't a game of tag or a 10-minute session of playing house at recess. Mature play has rich recurring characters with backstories—nurses who perform triage on pretend patients who present with life-threatening symptoms, shopkeepers who experience power outages and offer free ice cream to the neighborhood kids before it all melts. In mature play, the games can span weeks and involve complex social communication between children. Children are able to role-play, which requires self-control to stay in character and inhibit impulses to behave in ways that don't fit their role in the game.[15]

The amount of playtime our kids have is less than it used to be, and researchers are observing less mature play when kids do get to play.[16-18] But it takes *time* to develop mature play—time that our kids aren't getting these days. They have to get good at playing—first they pretend to chop vegetables, then they become the chef, and then they might finally open a restaurant. When we only offer our kids enough playtime to start this process, we arrest them in the stages where they are still veggie choppers.

If we don't give them enough time, they'll never win the imaginary *Battle of the Chefs* reality TV competition and then donate the million dollars to the local food bank. You don't jump right to the end; it's a process. The fact that our kids get so little play is disturbing when we also look at the fact that self-regulation levels are declining in young children, since we know that this sort of play enhances self-regulation skills.

Creativity and Self-Control

Creativity is all about bending the rules, but you must be able to play by the rules when the situation calls for it. Adaptable kids can do both. How do we teach our kids to wait effectively when they must wait? We can teach them how to read situations, how to create, how to predict, how to escape in their minds, how to trick themselves. This type of self-manipulation is a form of self-control. Knowing how and when to use it is key.

Research shows that children exhibit greater self-regulation while role-playing and acting out a situation. Take the incredibly hard task of standing still. Parents know this is nearly impossible for kids to do for long periods of time (or for some kids, impossible to do for 10 seconds). Preschoolers can stand at attention far longer when they are pretending to be guards supervising other children in a pretend factory than when simply asked to stand still for a period of time. If you ask young children to pretend to be "lookouts," they can stand still for longer than if you just ask them to be still. In one study, "lookouts" had a mean of 12 minutes versus 4 minutes for other kids, which is an amazing difference.[19]

Adding creative play elements to tasks that are rather mundane allows kids to practice self-regulation in a guided way. For example, children in one study could move individual matches from one pile to another for a much longer period of time (a monotonous and pointless task) when the researcher added an imaginary friend who was watching to see if they followed the directions.[20] Doing things like this with your kids will help make self-control a habit. You can practice games where you have to inhibit impulses to win, such as red light/green light, where you must stop running when someone says "red light" or go back to the start. Things done during play are still practice, and they still build skills.

Making things a game isn't coddling your kids. Instead, it's a tool to turn waiting into internal thought and a way of teaching your kids to find meaning in situations devoid of it. A study with children aged 6 to 9 showed that those with a more active internal fantasy world were able to remain still longer than children who didn't have much of an internal fantasy world.[21] Imaginative processes are powerful tools that can control attention in younger children and can provide strong inspiration for proper planning skills in older children because in order to make a sequential plan for behavior, you must be able to envision the outcome. This is another compelling reason to foster creativity in kids and to make room for play in spaces that aren't earmarked for playtime.

The boring things in life don't get less boring. Grown-ups just learn to cope with them better. We may not even be better at waiting, actually. With the advent of the smartphone, no moment is ever "wasted." At this point, we may be asking children to do something that we as grown-ups can't even do—wait without fillers.

Using fantasy or role-playing while parenting obviously takes some creativity on the part of the parent, but it can make situations where your young child is required to wait more tolerable. We trick them into short-term self-control by tapping into creative processes, and eventually self-control will stick around long-term as it becomes a habit. Kids will begin to regulate themselves sooner if you provide that sort of guided practice.

It may seem like creativity and self-control are opposing concepts, but they build on each other. Exercising self-control leads to enhanced creativity because it allows for flexibility when the normal options may be taken from you. For example, if you are asked to write a story but also asked not to use the letters *a* and *n* while you write, you will come up with novel ways to express your thoughts.[22, 23]

Empathy and Self-Control

Self-control is largely about the impact that our actions have on other people, and it's easier to make actions meaningful if we place them in this context. To appreciate someone else's perspective in a situation, it helps to overtly think about it and to think about the different ways you could handle a situation. You're already working on this awareness when you say to your toddler, "We don't hit. Hitting hurts Mama."

It helps to observe, it helps to synthesize what you see with what you already know, it helps to try to anticipate the future, and these skills get better every time we use them. Creative role-playing helps with this. This is as simple as asking, "How would you feel if someone hit you?"

These social-emotional skills are important to work on early because the ease of the transition to elementary school largely depends on them.[24] Social-emotional skills will define aspects of executive functioning, in combination with other skills, including theory of mind (being able to see things from another's point of view), long-term memory retrieval, and, of course, self-regulation.[25–27]

We're used to talking to kids about the impact of their behavior on other kids when they're little, but we don't keep talking to them about it. Sometimes it's a part of early elementary school education, but then we assume that kids get it, teachers move on to academic content, and adults become annoyed with a disruptive kid pretty quickly.

Consideration of others' feelings is a part of life adjustment. You can see how teaching empathy is important to resolve self-control issues. There has to be a *reason* to not act that way, so motivation becomes important here. You can control your behavior to reach your own long-term goals, or you can control it out of consideration for other people's feelings. As a parent trying to teach your kid life skills, *where* the motivation comes from isn't as important here as actual neuromechanisms beneath the *practice* controlling the behavior. We want our kids to have the proper behavior spring up from well-oiled brain machinery. The goal of practicing is to have them do the right thing as effortlessly as possible, so they can save their energy for higher-level thinking, for creativity, for applied empathy, for problem-solving, for changing the world.

Enhancing Self-Regulation Through Mindfulness
Troubling social interactions are inevitable in this world, and many people wish they had acted differently the moment they get out of a conflict situation. Parents can use mindfulness and scaffolding to help

relieve the stressful impact that conflict can have on our kids. But we also want to use these experiences as a learning tool to enhance future self-regulation—no matter what side of the conflict our child is on. The following five elements of body, mind, emotions, facts, and reflection will help you use creativity, empathy, and self-control to enhance self-regulation in trouble spots. This complete process can take some time, so it doesn't all have to be done in one sitting.

A calm body. To get to a calm mind, first focus on helping your child calm her body. This might mean asking her to sit and focus on the physical sensations of breathing in and out for a minute or so.[28]

A calm mind. Next, your child can work toward stillness in her mind. The bridge between stillness in the body and the mind is sensation. Help your child practice awareness by asking her to focus on the stimuli around her and to silently try to think of three things she hears, three things she feels through touch, and anything she smells.[29]

An accurate sense of personal emotions. From there, foster an awareness of how she *feels* by having her identify three emotions she's feeling. You want her to understand her own feelings, and labeling them can be helpful for this process.

An acknowledgment of the facts. Next, you can talk your child through a narrative of what has happened in the sticky situation. This awareness must first be factual before she can move to predicting other people's emotions or potential implications. She can consider all the options she has for action in this particular situation, but she needs to own or accept what happened first.

Critical reflection and prediction. Finally, she can move on to critical reflection about the situation: How can she act differently to change the outcome next time or how can she potentially solve this problem? This is when she may need to use cognitive empathy and perhaps some creativity to determine future actions, which may also require some future self-control. By preparing your child ahead of time, you are priming her actions and making her more of an expert on this specific situation: she'll have a course of action to follow. You have helped her preplan her own self-regulation.

How Do We Make Self-Regulation Second Nature?

Neuroscience for everyone:

- All teachers and parents should have training about normal brain development and learn how practice changes synaptic connections.

- Children should be taught how neurons work. This will help our kids understand that the qualities of creativity, empathy, and self-control are not traits but instead skills that they can work at and get good at, no matter who they are.

Changing the way we teach:

- Teaching approaches from preschool through college should incorporate creativity as a common method of learning.

- Creativity should be a normal part of teaching self-regulation and empathy so that kids can generate better choice options and therefore have more control over their personal situations.

- The focus in early education should be on self-regulation skills rather than self-control.

Changing how kids spend their time:

- Every kid should spend at least 30 minutes per day engaged in play that is self-directed and not toy-directed.

- Every classroom should have a social education component to it, including conflict resolution.

- Mindfulness, or just quiet space, should be required at some point in every child's school day.

Enhanced parenting resources:

- Parents should have easy access to expert advice when they're stuck on parenting issues—where someone could walk them through what to do at that very moment and also help strategize for a future game plan.

- Parents should have resources to develop creativity, empathy, and self-control skills of their own. Our adult status doesn't mean it's too late for us to get better at these things, and if we demonstrate them in our own life interactions, our kids will be much more likely to practice these behaviors too.

- Parents should have the information in this book before they put kids on medication for behavioral issues, especially for attention-deficit disorders, because use of any kind of methamphetamine in the developing brain can be problematic.

11

How to Win at Parenting

Motivation, Discipline, and Game Theory

SOMETIMES OUR KIDS have ample motivation to do what we consider the right thing, but more often, the business of parenting becomes a struggle to get our kids to act (in the words of psychologists) in a way that will not harm themselves or others. To make self-regulation worthwhile for kids, you have to get them to believe and support the idea of self-regulation in the first place. And to do that, you have to make self-regulation appealing, predictable, and rewarding—not just in the short-term, but in the long-term.

As parents, we can help with motivation in a lot of different ways, including placing our kids in situations where self-regulation is rewarding, using discipline/consequences, and even using game theory to generate rules that will work best with our child. Self-regulation tools come in lots of different flavors, and they all work to give our children strategies and practice controlling behavior and funneling wants and desires into actions that can serve them in socially conscious ways, fostering personal happiness in different realms.

Motivation: How to Motivate Your Child

Motivation is an influence that impacts why you choose to do something, how long you choose to do it, and how hard you will pursue it.[1] In order to figure out what motivates kids, you have to understand why they might be willing to put forth all the effort that self-regulation requires. Motivation falls into one of two categories: internal or external.

INTERNAL MOTIVATION

Internal morals are your natural way of doing something, guided by unseen forces that we now know are neural networks driving a person's character. Kids internalize standards of behavior and know how to conform to them, holding their behavior up to a sort of moral compass inside them. Children are able to internalize their "mommy" rules and conform to a standard of behavior. Parenting can be easy when motivations line up and you have a compliant kid.

But what about when your child's moral compass points elsewhere? To be sure, internalization of ideals that parents think are important is a valuable thing, but there's got to be a way to instill our morals in kids who have different objectives and still value their point of view.

Take Pietro: he has his own very strong moral ideals, and they don't always line up with other people's. He has a very developed sense of fairness, and he often roots for the underdog in a loyal and caring way, but it can blind him to the feelings of people he thinks are already on top. Pietro's mother, Julia, will have to continually work on aspects of empathy with him, because in some situations he has empathy in great quantities, while it appears to be absent in others. She'll model it, scaffold it, practice it. She'll need to work on it with him more than with her other kids.

For example, one morning Pietro threw a temper tantrum when he ended up with "unload dishwasher" as his morning job. It was obvious to Julia that his temper tantrum was at least partly fake, but two of his three siblings felt bad enough to offer to switch jobs with him. Was he throwing a tantrum to manipulate them? Sure. But he was also wielding a superpower: empathy.

The word *manipulation* brings to mind everything that is the opposite of what we usually associate with empathy. But manipulation and empathy are very closely related. It's a carefully orchestrated brain performance to be not just aware of others' feelings, but to also have the added awareness of how your actions can change those feelings.

When Pietro was a 2-year-old, he was a bit young to have a rational conversation with about the pros and cons of each behavior, though Julia certainly tried to have such conversations. But now that he's 11, she is tired of having to constantly repeat the same things to him. Julia's starting to feel like she's doing something wrong. Pietro has become the little boy sitting in a corner and thinking to himself, "Yes, it was totally worth it." Meanwhile, there's crying all around him.

Julia's always telling Pietro he should use his powers for good and not for evil. He might not fully understand what she means by that, but with repetition and examples, he will. She can shift her highly cognitively empathetic child from being a "manipulator" to being a "leader" by teaching him thoughtfulness about every action.

Julia knows Pietro *can* make the shift. But how can she make him *want* to do it? Starting from the ground up, she can work on building his valuation system by practicing empathy. She can capitalize on the fact that creativity is one of his strong points in order to help him solve conflicts. She can be clear about both the rules and the standards that are acceptable in society, model what he should do, and have clear rules about consequences. Presenting children with alternatives to wrong ways of behaving and asking them to choose differently will take up a large part of early childhood. But in the meantime, Pietro needs more work. Julia needs to figure out something else. And so do all the other parents of low-motivation kids. When internal motivation isn't overflowing, parents have other options for helping it along, and here's where external motivation comes in handy.

EXTERNAL MOTIVATION

External motivation is exactly what it sounds like: kids do things for a reason outside themselves. External motivation is where children know how they are expected to behave and then choose the "reward" that is offered for good behavior.[2] One of the biggest things we can do as parents is to encourage our kids (with practice) to gradually move things from the external motivation bucket to the internal motivation bucket. Things become internal when they are second nature to us.

And they become habit when we practice them. We can help our kids practice by using tools to encourage self-regulation behaviors.

Require Practice of Ownership

The internal and external motivation perspectives differ on the idea of ownership, or "responsibility," where external motivation usually results in less ownership of behavior. Let's think about parenting like a company where you are the CEO, and your children are the employees. Psychological ownership is an effective tool used in the business world: it's a theory that says the greater amount of control an individual has over the goal, the more ownership she feels about the goal and working toward it.[3] Psychological ownership encompasses five things: a sense of responsibility, identity, accountability, self-efficacy, and belongingness—all things we want for our kids. Using this tool in a business environment retains talent and results in better attitudes (including commitment levels and responsibility), self-esteem, self-efficacy, self-identity, motivation, accountability, performance, and sense of belonging.[4, 5] There's no reason it won't do the same thing for your family life.

You want your kids to own their behavior from start to finish. Require that of them. When you have a situation that you're talking through with your child, and you know for a fact she was in the wrong, don't allow it to be over until your child has basically confessed. Requiring that your kids take ownership of their actions is essential for changing kids' behavior. The deliberate way that you specify the behavior as something that we *don't* want leaves room for identifying what we *do* want. And that is the next step: you need to ask your kids how their behavior will be different next time, and they need to come up with solutions. Leave time to pause family life until this conversation is complete. If they stall or can't think of anything, ask that they come up with three ways that their behavior impacts other people; that's often a great starting point for identifying concrete ways to change behavior.

Ownership is a powerful psychological tool. Consider this simple psychological study: Subjects were asked to move picture cards into either their own basket or into another person's basket. Afterward, subjects remembered more of the cards in their own basket than in the other person's.[6] We remember things more if we own them. Your child will feel more in control of her choices if she perceives that she has been the one making them all along by helping craft the rules and consequences.

But no one always follows the rules, and when they don't, make your kids walk through the right way to do things (as described in "The OUT Framework" in chapter 7). This is *practice* for the real world. Remember, the world you create for your children is the only place they're ever going to get to practice these life skills in the absence of real-life consequences.

Encourage Goal-Directed Behavior

A great way to encourage ownership is to ask your child to set goals for himself. Goal setting is the process of setting an intentional outcome (a goal) to serve as the aim of one's actions, and it's one of the oldest tricks in the book for increasing achievement.[7] This has been known for decades. Setting goals is old news and has been shown again and again to be effective in educational settings.[8, 9] But parents still don't do it enough. Setting goals increases motivation, and setting really specific goals works better to increase motivation than simply telling people to "do their best."[10–12] It's important to help your kids set goals early when they have something they need to work on.

We recognize that our goals for our kids are more long-ranging than perhaps their own goals for themselves will be. Not many kids will have the goal of growing up to be a kind and respectful person. That's our job. We can teach them to establish goals and work toward those goals by telling them our goals as parents and explaining how we're going to get there. These kids are more a part of the process than we are. The changes are happening in them: there's every reason to keep them involved in the parenting process and not keep your motivations a mystery. Your parenting is the first model they have for how to change long-term behavior and how to consistently work toward a goal.

Go Ahead and Bribe

Bribery *is* external motivation. At the core of external motivation lies the question, "What do I get?" When second-grade teachers break out the reward systems of stickers and pizza parties for good behavior,

Take Advantage of Childhood Neuroplasticity

An addiction researcher offered his daughter $1,000 to not try any drugs until she was 21 years old. Notice he didn't say to *never* try drugs. He knows that during brain development, circuits are very susceptible to being rewired based on activation, especially dopamine-reward pathways.

Your children could wait until they go to college to work on self-regulation, but it will be much harder for them to learn it then. They will always default to the pathways that were activated while their brains were actively forming. These are strong connections, reinforced by years of use, making these neurons more likely to fire.

Though it's not impossible, changing these defaults will take repeatedly choosing to activate different pathways, and this change will be harder in brains that are in later stages of development, or once brain development is predominately over. It's harder to make an alcoholic out of a person who doesn't start drinking until adulthood.[13]

What if you could pay an organization $1,000 to craft self-regulation pathways in your child? That would be a booming business! The best business plan would start when your child is young and would work for a few minutes with him every day. Save your $1,000: you are that organization, and you've got this.

all the "good" parents cringe and think: *I* would never bribe my child to be good, but I guess it might work for those *troublemakers* in the classroom. But bribing, as a form of external motivation, makes neuroscientific sense. Bribing is absolutely worth using to craft brain development at sensitive times.

We know practice strengthens pathways. Regardless of what motivates you to act, in the end, your decision to do so uses the same neuronal connections, and practice activates those same neural pathways. You could literally just activate the neural pathway with an electrode placed in the brain, and it would have the same effect. Those pathways will grow functionally stronger. And once used, they're more likely to be used again the next time.

For bribes to work you'll need to keep two things in mind:

> **Trust matters.** Individuals are less likely to wait for a reward if they don't wholly trust the source of the reward.[14] As parents, we can work toward establishing a trustworthy relationship with our children. You need to deliver. If you promise a reward, give it. If you promise a punishment, be clear about it and then follow through.

> **The reward matters.** It has to be something that matters to your child. And in the beginning, reward consistently. If your children consistently know the rules of the game, then they play a better game.

Discipline

Okay, I'm going to talk about the *D* word now: *discipline* (verb) means to "Train (someone) to obey rules or a code of behavior, using punishment to correct disobedience."[15] Discipline is an essential part of crafting neuronal synapses. But think about discipline as a noun instead. We all want to raise a child who *has* discipline. Let's parent with that sort of discipline in mind—raising kids who work toward a goal, who have great self-regulation. Let's bring the verb *discipline* in line with what the noun means. They are the same word, after all, and discipline is about much more than simply punishment.

Discipline is the combination of (1) telling our kids no, while also (2) forcing them to say yes to things they don't necessarily want to do. All of this is done, of course, for their own benefit. We construct an artificial version of the world full of "rewards" and "consequences" to mimic the way life actually works. Discipline is full of potential pitfalls and escalation, however, and it's very easy to get it wrong when we become reactive. But it's an essential part of parenting to craft the proper neuronal connections.

TEACHING NO

We need our kids to hear no, and we need them to practice responding to no. You should say no every time his behavior will impact other people negatively. Or the flip side of that, you should force a yes from him when he has to do something he doesn't want to do but should do for personal development, to practice an important life skill.

Most nos in life aren't hard stops, but rather they are puzzles that you have to sort through to get to your end goal. It's important to hear and accept a no—not necessarily as an end point, but as a setback. Parents have a couple of easy options to incorporate the acceptance of the occasional no into daily life, including helping your kids to wait, to practice autonomous behavior, and to listen to what other people want.

Make Them Wait

Waiting isn't a part of our culture anymore. We can binge-watch TV shows now, we eat oranges out of season, and we see the dots on text messages that mean someone is texting us back right now. But waiting for something means you value it more, and it's tied in to goal-oriented behavior.

Waiting can be hard for everyone, so sometimes while you're asking your kids to wait, teach them how to use creativity to make waiting easier. Activities like guessing the occupation of strangers who pass in cars on a long road trip are things we do to "pass the time." But passing the time *is* the art of waiting, and it's a very important skill to have.

It's also important to teach your children to read social cues when they have something to say. Don't let your kids talk whenever they want to. If you're in the middle of a conversation, they'll need to wait for a stopping point. Their opinions are worthwhile, but everyone else's opinion is important too. This will diminish their perceptions of self-importance, while still allowing for a healthy sense of self-worth when they get their turn.

Don't Let Them Always Win

Nobody likes to lose. But winning all the time is a completely unrealistic way to have children experience the world, so make sure they experience both winning *and* losing when you play together. When you tag them, you tag them. If everyone knows you're great at golf, you should win most of the time at Putt-Putt. But when you get home, you should play something that your kids may actually be better at than you, like who can find their favorite bedtime book first. Setting them up to win is very different than letting them win.

This is the way life is: sometimes you win and sometimes you lose. And once the game is over, use empathy to frame the situation so that your children can see it from both the winning and the losing side. Don't wait until there's crying to start this conversation.

Don't Fix It for Them

Sometimes competent kids act helpless. If you don't step in to help, they are forced to try it themselves, whether it's zipping up their coats, cleaning their rooms, or talking to a classmate who is upset. Require creative solutions. Make a rule that you'll only rescue them after they make an effort.

When the parent must repeatedly come up with creative solutions for problems, parenting becomes exhausting, and your child isn't practicing creativity. Instead, provide the scaffolding to talk through what is happening with your kids: Why might your classmate be poking you?

What on earth can be done about it? Flip it back on them. Make it their job to come up with creative alternatives to a situation.

Teach Affirmative Consent

We have an issue in our society with the idea of consent: How can we give it, and how can we hear it? This is a problem exacerbated by two things: (1) entitled kids who aren't used to hearing no and (2) kids who have poor conflict-resolution skills. If our society relegates affirmative consent only to the world of sexual interactions, we ignore what a powerful social tool affirmative consent actually is.

Affirmative consent is not just about sex. It's about respect, and as such affirmative consent is a tool that parents should be practicing with their kids from the very beginning. Children need to know what consent looks like way before they're teenagers—not just how to ask for consent, but also how to give consent.

Parents have many opportunities to teach affirmative consent. For example, Kelly recently took her two boys to the lake. Her 11-year-old, Kyle, laid out two giant water shooters and asked his 5-year-old brother, Brady, to choose one. When Brady just stood there, Kyle grabbed a shooter and sent a gushing stream of water into his brother's face. He threw Brady the other one and waited for him to pick it up. He then proceeded to wade into the water and shoot Brady multiple times directly in the eyes. But Brady seemed to take it in stride, picking up the other water shooter and aiming back at Kyle.

"Brady, do you want to play this game?" Kelly asked.

"Um, not really," he said through the streaming water.

"Kyle, this game is over until Brady asks you to shoot him," Kelly said.

There was a look of relief on Brady's face, and multiple protests from Kyle, but the rule was firm because a kindergartener had not given affirmative consent.

Using affirmative consent as a parenting tool means we must get our children talking to each other about uncomfortable things. It's not enough to watch body language or infer from social cues. Perhaps Kyle couldn't tell that Brady was feeling pressure to participate in the water fight. Brady seemed fine, after all. Our children must not only learn how to say, "Do you want to play king of the mountain?" to other kids before they shove them off the sand heap, they must also be okay with a no.

If they get in the habit of asking for consent when they're young, it will help alleviate confusion later, when they need to navigate the muddled mess of adolescence and young adulthood.

Let's get the idea of affirmative consent in preschools and in high schools, and let's practice it in our homes. When it comes to personal contact, kids need to understand that consent is part of the equation. They need to know that whether they're twirling the ponytail of the girl sitting in front of them, slapping the hand of the boy they're playing tag with, or receiving a giant hug from Uncle Harry, consent must be obtained.

From a moral perspective, consent not only protects people from unwanted trespassing on body and property, but it allows us to define the things that we will cooperate with. At the lake, Brady eventually asked his brother to shoot him with the water gun, but he got to make that deliberate decision to start playing. "Yes means yes" is a way of maintaining social balance, teaching the more assertive kids to be considerate of others, and giving control and confidence to the kids who are more passive and diffident.

We shouldn't wait to let our children learn about consent at college. They need to understand the idea when they're much younger. We need to infuse our cultural parenting attitudes with the idea that affirmative consent is not just an edict that governs sexual relations. It's a way of being a good person.

TEACHING YES

Sometimes you just have to buckle down and get it done. Julia had a conference at Pietro's very loose progressive school. That conference was delightful in so many ways: the teacher really knew Pietro's bright spots and had great things to say about his helpfulness and creativity. But Pietro wasn't turning in homework, and he wasn't completing classroom assignments. Julia wanted him to stay in at recess to complete them. But when the teacher said, "It's my wish that he will eventually really want to complete these assignments," Julia knew that a wish from afar would never work to get Pietro where he needed to be. He needed to practice doing things he didn't want to do and practice every day. How do you make kids do things they don't want to do?

The Dreaded Homework Nightmare

Homework is the worst part of the day with a kid who struggles with self-regulation. Studies show that for kids in grades 7 through 12, there is a correlation between homework and better test scores, but this correlation is weaker for younger kids.[16] Because this correlation is weaker for younger children, there is room in effective schools for early elementary school kids to spend their time after school doing things other than homework.

To make a balanced child, there is an overwhelming need for children to practice things that are not academic after school, to play and to regulate their own behavior. Ideally, there'd be no homework until fourth or fifth grade. This is a hard sell in the land of standardized testing in elementary school, but waiting until kids can developmentally get the most from homework will allow kids to practice overlooked but important life skills (like self-regulation) and still prevent kids from losing any potential academic advantage.

Too much homework, too early, can lead to negative attitudes toward education and constrain the amount of time that kids can just be kids after school, which limits the time they can spend outside or directing their own activities. Completing homework does translate to better test performance, but this has nothing to do with the *amount* of homework that is assigned. If your child is assigned so much homework that she hates homework and hides in a closet when it's time to start, then homework turns into a battleground, and your child is learning how to avoid things or how to do barely enough to get by.

By the end of elementary school, she'll need to begin practicing doing homework and doing it well to develop good study skills. But practicing self-regulation skills through play can enhance self-regulation, and, in turn, kids will be better at homework when they eventually start tackling it after school. When the right amount is assigned at the right time, practicing self-regulation skills in the context of homework can pay off.[17]

Teach Them to Share the Load

Children shouldn't be the center of family life, but they shouldn't be treated as second-class citizens either. Kids should participate in the care of the household. They don't necessarily need specific chores or schedules, but sometimes this is a good way of getting started. Finding ways to help that aren't mandated is a more real-life way of teaching household responsibility, and perhaps more rewarding, but it's trickier to enforce and regulate. Always point out helping opportunities to your kids. They're never too young to learn that shared responsibility applies to them, too.

Show Them What Service Feels Like

Kids who give to others learn that giving is rewarding, especially if children get to see their gift making a difference. Service learning is popular in education not only to support learning course content, but also because it provides giant opportunities for personal growth. Pick up trash on the beach, even if it's not your trash. Help the homeless you see in your own community. Donate old toys and clothes. You don't need to find a formal volunteer organization to provide a service to our world: part of the lesson is that anyone can make a difference at any time. (See "Spread Acts of Kindness with Your Children" in chapter 7 for more ideas.)

Using Game Theory to Parent

To get kids doing things they don't want to do, we can view parenting as a game that we play to win. To do this, we need to use game theory when we parent. Game theory is a kind of math that focuses on competitive interaction, but it's also neuroscience. People have been using game theory for all of human history, even before it was first called game theory in the mid-twentieth century. And your parenting can be strengthened using principles of game theory, since—let's admit it—some days parenting feels like a competitive interaction.

Let's understand the rules of gaming using the rock-paper-scissors game with two people. Game theory says that if you play a game using a "mixed strategy," where you randomly throw either rock, paper, or scissors each time, and you never know what the other person will do, then no one will ever truly win the game because it will even out in the end, resulting in a tie. This idea assumes that humans are able to be random (which we are not), and also that we would never try to predict what the other person might do.

If parenting were as easy as playing a random game of rock-paper-scissors, we wouldn't need this book. But real life isn't played that way, and neither is parenting. We can't parent effectively when we "tie" with our children; we need to *win*, and to do so we need to be aware of the social constructs that change the game. Economic models assume that all people are both rational and selfish, but when we add another social layer onto our game theory, the outcomes are different. All of our choices are driven by past experience and by future direction, so when we play—or when we parent—we have to take into account the decisions that we think our kids will make in return.

Parenting is, by nature, a cooperative game, in which the players can make bargains or agreements with each other. Those agreements are sometimes unspoken, but they are always linked to a real consequence that can be enforced. Cooperative games have an element of moral obligation to them, and perhaps potential guilt for, say, stealing your mom's phone charger when you lost your own, or overt consequences, like losing your phone privileges for a week for valuing your phone battery life over hers.

What is clear from game theory research is that social aspects change the game in rather surprising ways, so we don't always do what is best for us. For example, in the game called Ultimatum, two people are given $10 to share, and one person gets to make the decision about how to split the money between them. The other person can then accept the offer, or neither gets any money. In practice, the median offer amount is about $4.00, and it is likely to be accepted.

From a rational point of view, if a person is offered any amount of money, even a penny, then they should accept it, because they are clearly better off than they were before. However, when you place the constraints of social expectations on this situation, researchers have found that anything under about $2.50 is likely to be rejected by the second person. In other words, the receiver is saying, "It means more to me to have you lose all your money than for me to get $2.50." This is a type of cooperative social contract. And the person making the money-splitting decision has to weigh what they think the other person will do.[18]

What makes this so interesting is that there's another version of this game in which a "dictator" is given $10 and can give whatever he'd like to the other person and keep the rest, ending the game. On average, the dictators give $2.50, even though they don't have to give anything. So in the Ultimatum game, when we get nothing if our offer is rejected, we'll offer about 40% of the pot. If we're a dictator, we'll offer 25%, even when nothing is at stake for us. That 25% represents the goodness of our hearts, or our altruism. But the 15% difference between what people offer when they play the Ultimatum game (40%) versus the Dictator game (25%) is our own motivation not to be rejected. With game theory, every decision that you make has a value and a payoff attached to it, even the idea of being "nice."[19, 20]

A lot of game theory depends on the perceived fairness of the situation. Some studies have only focused on recordings from single neurons or brain areas such as the **amygdala** and striatum, which are activated when you expect a reward and find the social aspects of a game to be rewarding. Game theory research shows that activity in an area of the striatum can be modulated when a player is considering the moral character of another player and deciding whether to trust her in the game. In particular, reciprocated cooperation during a game increases brain activity in the striatum, but activity decreases when that cooperation isn't paid back.[21]

In each parenting situation, we use game theory with our kids, whether we know it or not. We're trying to predict what they will do, trying to get them to follow the rules. But the most effective way to do this involves setting up a situation where they accept what we're offering. As parents, in every sense of game theory, we have entered into a cooperative agreement with our children. We are teaching them how to play the long game, how to make social bargains, and how to uphold them. And yet we must be careful here because in this setup, we can function as the opponent, the coconspirator, the police, the jailer, and the liberator. Our role is enormous, and the level of fairness that we play with—that we parent with—will impact the way our kids learn to play themselves.

A disciplinarian makes sure a kid obeys. It's easy to be a disciplinarian in the beginning, but it's exhausting to implement over the long-term. It's a much tougher job to guide our kids' valuation and motivation system from the ground up in a way that has kid buy-in, but once done, it's much easier to parent this way in daily life. Game theory is on our side, but it means we need to both craft and understand what motivates our children. To be successful parents, we can't play rock-paper-scissors using the mixed strategy. We have to adapt and react to each parenting situation and to be deliberate. In truth, we must get buy-in for both the rules and the consequences ahead of time, or the parenting road is hard.

RULES

It's a fact that kids will pick which rules to follow and which to ignore. Kids will only resist moral rules about 10% of the time, but about 70% of the time kids will not want to follow rules that are made in areas of their life where they feel they should have autonomy, like how they dress and who they're friends with.[22] Choose the aspects of your child's life that require rules carefully. Give as much autonomy as possible (in the form of choice). The perception of control here gives you that buy-in. And as your children grow and they become more practiced, you will release more and more of the decisions of consequence to them, until control over their own lives isn't practice anymore, but is real.

Kids who have self-regulation issues need to be given as many choices as possible. If our kids were cool with people telling them what to do all the time, then we wouldn't have this plummeting self-control problem. These children are the "I'm going to eat your marshmallow now anyway, and it's delicious, and what's next?" kind of kids. So, let them make the rules, as long as you agree with those rules. We asked our preteen son to come up with rules for his phone. We tweaked his rules only a bit and then happily posted them: use only in common areas, no more than 30 minutes at a time, only after homework and chores are done.

Parents can post simple rules and ask their children to read them out loud. Research shows that posting written rules makes kids more likely to follow them. A study showed that when kids are given conflicting print and verbal directions, they'll choose to follow the rules that are written down, especially early readers aged 3 to 6 years.[23] (If kids haven't started learning to read yet, the act of writing rules down makes no real difference to them.)

CONSEQUENCES

Kids with self-regulation issues need enough structure so that they can predict the consequences of their own behavior in as many circumstances as possible. So, hand in hand with the phone rules, we asked our son to come up with the consequences for breaking the rules. He decided that the consequence for breaking the rules is that he loses his phone for a week. He's owned the rules. He *has to* because he made the rules. Now, when we stumble upon him breaking the rules, we tell him it's not okay, ask him what happens now, and he'll answer that he'll see his phone again in 7 days. Then we take it away. His rules. Your agreement. His choices. He's made our job easier, and we're not necessarily the bad guy. Remember that just because the rules and consequences are clear doesn't mean there won't ever be drama. But the structure is there and will remain unless we sit down and work on the rules together again.

Let your kids make rules and consequences for not just themselves, but also for other people. If my son hurts or insults a sibling, we often let the wronged party choose his consequence, and his sibling's are usually so much nicer than I ever am. You want peace in the house. You want kindness to others. If there's conflict during hide-and-seek, and you make your son sit out for 5 minutes from hide-and-seek to solve it, then the problem will still be there at the end of those 5 minutes.

Your kids are reentering the same battlefield. If you tell your daughter that her brother can only come back into the game when she is comfortable with that, then suddenly he is quite nice to her. He doesn't apologize exactly, but he shifts things in a way where she is central instead of ostracized. The balance of power has moved, and it rests in her hands. And when she permits him back in the game, the game is different.

GAME THEORY TEACHES SELF-REGULATION

Teach your kids game theory concepts. They are a great way to teach your kids how to make good decisions within a social context: even kids who aren't especially interested yet in the feelings of others or in developing empathy can get hooked on game theory—the idea that we are all in an intricate game all the time is engaging to kids. Remember, with game theory, it's all about value and payoff. Thinking about behavior in this way will help kids make deliberate decisions.

Though we are beginning to understand the brain areas involved, elucidation of the actual pathways is more difficult. The neuroscience behind social decision-making when other people are involved is even more complicated than the neuroscience behind personal decisions. Game theory takes into account that people want to maximize their self-interests (that is, we want to *win*), but it also acknowledges that humans have consideration for the well-being of others, and that consideration can be modulated by different things. When you put the added social layer on it, these interactions become more than just self-control issues. They become complicated self-regulation puzzles. These puzzles involve empathy: you can see that theory of mind, or the ability to understand what the other player might do, is absolutely key to successful game theory strategy.

These self-regulation puzzles also involve creativity. Ask your kids to imagine the rules of a particular social situation as if it were a movie. What do you think is going to happen when the main character breaks the rules? When you talk to kids about social situations, tell them they can often increase their chances of getting what they want by negotiating the rules or goals. That's game theory. And then use it in your parenting. If a rule keeps getting broken, something isn't working.

Screen Time Is No Substitute for Real-World Experience

Too much screen time is bad for our kids' self-regulation skills—not so much because staring at the screen is bad for their brain, but because TV and video games take up so much room in their lives when they should be having valuable hands-on experiences instead. When kids are being led through the story, there's no internalized cause and effect. There's no opportunity for a "choose your own adventure." Even if they are learning about the world, they are not experiencing it, and there is no substitute for experiencing the world and making their own decisions about how to interact with it. Television should be used judiciously, with the recognition that it is not a substitute for hands-on learning or activities. In older children, it can be a useful tool for introducing new concepts and facts, but the best way for children to learn is to actually explore the world around them, not a virtual representation of that world.

Conclusion

Parents Shape Future Free Will

THE NEWLY EMERGED field of neuroscience has given us amazing answers about how the brain works, has shown how learning happens on a cellular level, and has provided techniques that allow us to see inside someone's head. These studies are incredibly important to the parenting community. All parents should know how children learn. Lots of data says that metacognition, or thinking about your own thinking, improves both teaching and learning, and children have a huge jump in the ability for metacognition between the ages of 12 and 15.[1, 2]

Importantly, children should also be taught about how neurons work and how practice can strengthen pathways and neuronal connections, since this knowledge has an enormous impact on the perception of free will and how much control we have over the people we become.

The mantra of kindergarten classrooms everywhere is "Make Good Choices," but in a 2009 *Nature* article, Harvard scientist Robert Doyle declared that "free will is a biological property, not a gift or a mystery."[3] If all thoughts and intentions arise from a person's neuroanatomical background, then our kids' actual behavioral choices are limited by the premade neuronal pathways they have when they walk into that kindergarten classroom. And this is why the way experience crafts our neurons is so important.

René Descartes's idea that humans have a freely given mind—totally separate from the body—has vanished like a mirage in the wake of modern neuroscience techniques. Neuronal recording experiments show that simple actions, such as pressing a button, can be detected before the subject is even conscious that they've decided to press the button. If a person's actions are governed by neural pathways that aren't accessible by consciousness, then that person's choices and actions may not be governed by true free will. And the most compelling part of this for parents is that as neuroscience research pushes toward mapping the way neurons are connected, we're learning that if we can trace brain circuits, we can also predict behavior with nearly 100% accuracy.

According to the basic principles of neuroplasticity, kids are born with a vast network of synaptic connections—a wealth of possible connections that are then eliminated one by one as they lie unused. And in exchange, the pathways that *have* been activated—one to learn the letter *g*, another to recognize the smell of an oatmeal cookie, and yet another to understand it's not okay to hit a playmate—are strengthened and remain, since neuronal pathways get stronger when used. As a result, with each year of maturity, a child begins to shed free will in its most pure and honest form.

Freedom of decision is possible, though it's governed by neuro-anatomy that can't change instantaneously. We are defined by our neural circuits, and those circuits are defined by use, but these pathways are constantly undergoing synapse modifications to make them more efficient.

However, if what we call free will is a natural biological process, then not only can neuroscientists track it, but parents are placed in a unique position to craft it. As parents, we have this miraculous opportunity to lay down those critical brain pathways for our children by simply deciding what they practice. When repeated practice makes something a habit, neurophysiology changes, and future behavior choices narrow.

While we may think of free will as a grocery store full of life choices, in reality, free will is more like a vending machine, where the most probable choices are ones that have been preselected for us. True change is still possible, just as multiple calls to your food supplier may result in a new type of Pop-Tarts appearing in your vending machine a few days later. But you step up to bat with a certain set of skills, and meaningful change requires multiple activations to set you on a different path.

Experts argue that the illusion of free will is not one society is ready to relinquish: when faced with the idea of free will slipping through our fingers, people are more likely to act immorally. People who don't believe in free will are less likely to help others, less likely to perform well academically, less likely to think life has meaning—all the things we desperately hope our children will do one day.[4, 5]

Luckily, parents can do more than just help young kids build great habits. We can use these same neuronal principles to help kids of all ages deal with their own preprogramming. We can cultivate self-control to empower our children to stop bad habits, and we can foster creativity to help our kids come up with better solutions. Both self-control and creativity are life skills that can be improved with practice, and both work together to make high-functioning individuals.

So, are our kids free to choose? The answer is that their ability to choose shrinks with age, unless kids can stop their first instinct and unless they are exposed to something different. We pin all our hopes for our children on the fact that they will make good decisions, but, in the end, our kids will be governed by the neuroanatomy of their brains and must function within the landscape that we've helped them create with our daily parenting throughout the incredibly plastic period of childhood. All we want as parents is for our children to make good decisions. But by the time our kids are old enough to articulate questions about their own true neurological independence—such as, "Do I control my brain or does my brain control me?"—their pathways will be mostly set.

No brain is made in isolation but rather is a product of the genes and environment that it is raised in, which forces a collective community view regarding the idea of free will. The way you parent your children obviously influences the way their brains develops, but realize that as experience crafts their habits, it also manipulates their future free will.

Freedom is having the ability, means, and desire to do that which makes you happy in the most farsighted future you can dream up.[6] All parents want their children to experience true personal freedom in adulthood. But this concept rests on the assumption that our children's decisions will not limit their future choices in a negative way. So in the process of teaching our kids to make decisions, parents need to set their children up for success by also teaching the three skills essential for life success: (1) self-control, so that doors to desirable life places don't slam shut on them, (2) empathy, so the desire to enter into places bigger than themselves is there, and (3) creativity, so they have the ability to clear roadblocks that impede progress toward their goals. These three things are inexorably linked through self-regulation. They feed on each other, support each other, and form a stable footing on which to build a life of meaning.

APPENDIX 1

Commonsense Neuroanatomy

Ten Building Blocks to a Human Brain

IT'S EASIEST TO think about neuroanatomy as various problems that nature has presented and the ways the human body has solved these problems. Humans need a way of interacting with the world, and to do this we use our brains. To build a human brain, we need ten basic things.

1. **Starting material.** Humans have a natural process of carving out a piece of the developing embryo to become the brain and spinal cord, regulated by both genetic cues and signals from surrounding cells. This process, called neurulation, is the defining feature of early development: The embryo starts as a ball. Then as the cells differentiate into neural material, the ball lengthens out, and the future spinal cord appears down the embryo's back.

2. **Basic functions: breathing and heartbeat.** These unconscious activities are taken care of by the brain stem, the natural progression of your spinal cord as it fans out into your brain. Breathing allows you to pull oxygen into your lungs and then into your bloodstream, and the heartbeat allows you to pump the oxygen and nutrients around your body to your cells. In particular,

brain cells pull large amounts of the sugar glucose from the blood to fuel their metabolic needs. Your brain is just 2% of your body weight, but it uses over 20% of the glucose you ingest.[1]

3. **The ability to move.** Motor control (control over movement) is taken care of mostly by the cerebellum, the small circular structure on the lower part of your brain that almost looks like a miniature brain in itself (see figure A1.1). It specializes in balance and gait, but studies of people who have something wrong with their cerebellum

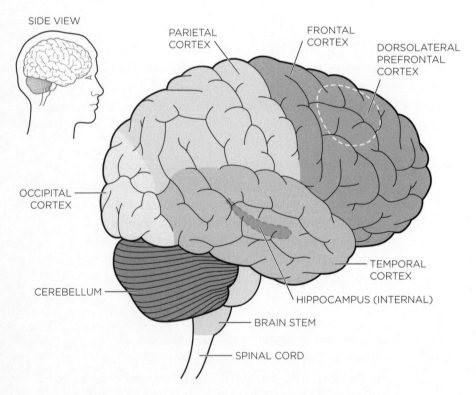

SIDE VIEW

PARIETAL CORTEX

FRONTAL CORTEX

DORSOLATERAL PREFRONTAL CORTEX

OCCIPITAL CORTEX

CEREBELLUM

TEMPORAL CORTEX

HIPPOCAMPUS (INTERNAL)

BRAIN STEM

SPINAL CORD

Figure A1.1 The brain and spinal cord make up the central nervous system. The brain stem handles basic functions like heartbeat and breathing, while the cerebellum specializes in balance and movement. The cortex can process and coordinate the activities of the brain stem and the cerebellum.

show us that the cerebellum is also involved in whole-brain activities, like cognition and emotion, through intricate feedback loops that link the cerebellum to the rest of the brain and facilitate communication. The simplest explanation of a feedback loop is that it's like a circular relay race that never ends, and when you pass the baton, you also offer a bit of running advice to the next runner about how to hone their running skill to be more precise or effective. "I tell you something, and in return, you send me back a message that can change the way I tell you things."

4. **The ability to receive environmental input.** Humans, and all animals, do this through sensory input. You have your five basic senses (taste, touch, smell, hearing, and sight), along with a sixth sense—proprioception, or the ability to know where your body is in space. The input comes in through a variety of entry points, depending on the sense, is processed in a central location called the thalamus, and is sent to different areas in the cortex to be pondered. For example, touch information can come in from any part of your body, gets passed through the thalamus, and then is processed in the somatosensory (body-sensing) area of the parietal lobe in the cortex (located on the top of your head right below where you would wear a royal crown).

5. **A way of actively sorting through information and deciding what to keep.** We can't remember everything we experience each day. So we sort through it all in a very individual way by filtering our environment for things that are important to us: we pay attention to what we're interested in, and we remember only what we pay attention to. All memories have meaning for us; otherwise, they wouldn't have been incorporated into our brains. Sometimes meaning is as simple as the items in a scenario that we paid attention to—the items we picked out as being somehow important in a sensory landscape filled with details. We go through

a lifelong, daily process of picking out what is important to us in our environment. Other times, a memory has an emotional component to it that cements it in our minds. Sometimes the basic instincts that we have for survival dictate what we remember.

6. **A way to store information.** The most well-known memory structure is the hippocampus, which allows short-term memories to be consolidated into long-term memories based on what we pay attention to and rehearse. The hippocampus, along with areas in the cortex, is responsible for memory storage. But there are also many other ways the brain can remember things, such as procedural memory (how you remember to ride a bike) or learning though conditioning (knowing that if you touch a hot stove you will get burned), factual knowledge (remembering the name of your elementary school), and visuospatial memory (knowing the way to get from your house to work). All of this information is stored in different places in the brain.

7. **A way to get the information back out.** Memory retrieval is the ability to access information over time. We can't retrieve the information unless we remember it, and we remember it only if we've paid attention to it in the first place. The task of remembering something uses different brain circuits than memory formation does.[2]

8. **The ability to change and adapt.** With neuronal communication, the old way of doing things must be discarded at times for a new system, and this is called learning. Learning requires concerted collaboration between multiple brain areas.[3] This is the heart of human neuroscience—the interactive nature of the connections. The types of connections that are formed in your brain underlie learning, and your identity wholly rests in these connections (see figure A1.2).

For humans, it doesn't seem that the act of remembering is what makes us distinct from other animals. In fact, the cellular basis of learning and memory, called long-term potentiation (LTP), was originally described in the sea slug and appears to occur in a similar manner despite the species. The description of how a memory physically changes the brain earned Austrian-American neuroscientist Eric Kandel a Nobel Prize in 2000.[4]

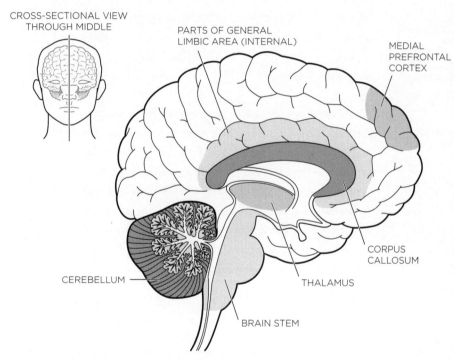

CROSS-SECTIONAL VIEW THROUGH MIDDLE

PARTS OF GENERAL LIMBIC AREA (INTERNAL)

MEDIAL PREFRONTAL CORTEX

CORPUS CALLOSUM

CEREBELLUM

THALAMUS

BRAIN STEM

Figure A1.2 We have looked at the "higher" brain processing centers in the cortex, but we aren't able to see many internal brain structures unless we cut the brain in half right down between the eyes and look at it from the side. Viewed this way, you can see that some of the brain areas responsible for gut instincts and emotions, such as the limbic system, are indeed "lower" in the brain. You can easily see the central thalamus that routes incoming signals to the right cortical areas for processing. But some brain structures remain hidden, such as the hippocampus (responsible for memory formation) and deeper parts of the limbic system. In self-regulation, there is constant interplay between limbic areas and cortical areas.

9. **The ability to process emotional responses.** Emotional responses stem largely from a connected community of brain areas collectively called the limbic system. Structures from multiple areas of the brain are part of this limbic system, and though they each have separate roles, they work together to coordinate feelings of emotion. As an example, we know the amygdala handles fear and aggression, because when the amygdala is removed or damaged the fear response is blocked. During neuroimaging studies, amygdala activation is seen when subjects report feeling afraid.[5] That is not to say that the amygdala's only role is to modulate fear. It is, like all brain structures, intricately linked to other functions, including regulating memory and social interaction.

10. **The ability to sometimes stop emotional responses.** Our first emotional response isn't always our best option, but it makes us undeniably human. Controlling the emotional input coming up from the limbic system is the key to sound judgment, self-control, and what we call "mature" behavior. This ability is housed in the cortex, particularly the prefrontal cortex, and allows us to modify our actions to fit with what is socially acceptable and in line with our own goal-directed behaviors.

APPENDIX 2

Epigenetics

The Intersection of Nature and Nurture

THE SCIENCE OF INTERACTIONISM, named epigenetics, is an unfolding explanation of how nature and nurture cooperate. Environmental events can turn genes on or off during development and adulthood. Epigenetics is one of the coolest discoveries of the last few decades. It's the idea that nature and nurture can interact with each other within your body. Your experiences can actually change which genes are "turned on" in your cells. And while your genetic makeup is always the bottom line, if genes aren't turned on, then they won't have much effect on you.

Everyone has a set number of genes. Genes make proteins, and proteins determine everything. And yet, did you know that your body can turn the genes on and off? It's a phenomenon that scientists are only just beginning to untangle. Although your child is born with a relatively unchangeable DNA code, the environment your child is raised in can dictate whether her genes are expressed and become physical and character traits, or whether those genes remain silent.

David Hume, an eighteenth-century Scottish philosopher, proposed the idea that children are born into the world as a *tabula rasa* or a blank slate. This type of environmentalism was the predominate view until scientists in the nineteenth century focused on the inheritance of human ability, ignited by the writings of Charles Darwin. The flag bearer for the "nature" side of the nature/nurture debate was Sir Francis Galton, who pioneered the field of eugenics and firmly believed, along with many of his colleagues, that nature alone determines who a child will become, as evidenced in his 1869 book *Hereditary Genius*:

> I have no patience with the hypothesis occasionally expressed, and often implied, especially in tales written to teach children to be good, that babies are born pretty much alike and that the sole agencies in creating differences between boy and boy, and man and man, are steady application and moral effort.[1]

Consider the views of John Watson, a prominent twentieth-century behavioral psychologist who comes down abruptly on the "nurture" side. In his 1930 book *Behaviorism*, he makes the following statement:

> Give me a dozen healthy infants, well-formed, and my own specified world to bring them up in and I'll guarantee to take any one at random and train him to become any type of specialist I might select—doctor, lawyer, artist, merchant-chief and, yes, even beggar-man and thief, regardless of his talents, penchants, tendencies, abilities, vocations, and race of his ancestors. I am going beyond my facts and I admit it, but so have the advocates of the contrary and they have been doing it for many thousands of years.[2]

Viewed now through the lenses of modern genetics and neuroscience, we can see that no one can rightly choose between nature and nurture. Our environmental experiences can place epigenetic tags on our DNA to change which genes are turned on or off in a cell. These tags are the sum of all the signals that the cell has received and responded to over the course of its lifetime. These tags are important because cellular signals are transient, and the cell needs a way to "remember" what kind of cell it is and what its genes should be doing. In this way, our experiences are recorded on top of our existing DNA.

This **epigenome** provides another layer of structure to the genome: it tightly wraps inactive genes, causing them to become unreadable, and relaxes active genes, allowing their DNA sequence to be transcribed, translated into protein, and used by the cell. Cells turn genes on and off using regulators, and the regulators are held in check by other proteins. The next frontier is figuring out how to turn on the genes that are desirable within the DNA, and as you can imagine, this is an area of great excitement in neuroscience research.

The role of the pregnant mother is largely to be vigilant about epigenetic processes to support correct reading of the genetic code. The minute you take prenatal vitamins, you have actively participated in regulating the way your child's genes are expressed. A great example of epigenetic regulation is how folate can influence the process of neurulation (the formation of the very early brain/neural tube). Studies have shown that folate is required for the genes that control neurulation to work properly.[3] In fact, about 60% to 70% of neural tube defects appear to be sensitive to folate.[4]

Since low folate levels are a risk factor for neural tube defects, this has led to an effective campaign educating pregnant women to supplement their diet with folic acid (the more bioavailable form of folate).[5] Folate is part of the B-vitamin group, which our bodies can't make; instead, it must be ingested through food or supplements.

The most common epigenetic tag is a methyl group, and folate is so important because it allows the body to effectively make those methyl tags. A methyl group will block the attachment of the proteins that normally turn on genes. Methyl is like a stop sign: it binds up DNA—turns it off—in a desirable way that lets neurulation occur.

If food can change epigenetics, then early nutrition has the capability to program long-term health in our kids. In fact, based on what we know about epigenetics, a mother's diet during pregnancy becomes unbelievably important to the eventual adult health of her child. Our bodies can't make methyl groups; they have to come from our food, or, in the case of a fetus, from the mother's nutrition. When you can't hold your baby yet, what you eat makes a difference.[6] For example, researchers showed that the methylation status of key genes at birth is linked to the child being overweight nearly a decade later.[7] And the introduction of toxins during pregnancy (whether intentional, like smoking, or via accidental exposure) will induce a number of epigenetic changes in your baby as well.[8]

Our DNA is fixed for life, but epigenetic mechanisms can respond rapidly to cues in the environment, including seemingly mundane things like social interactions, physical activity, diet, and hormones. Early in development, epigenetic signals come from other cells, the mother's diet, and the mother's stress levels. After birth, your baby's social interactions, physical activity, diet, and (in adolescence) hormones influence your child's epigenome.

Gene Regulation

Brain plasticity is the dynamic neuronal ability to rapidly adapt to the input coming from the outside world by (1) making specific changes in synaptic connections and/or (2) making changes in myelination. To do this, a neuron must constantly be monitoring what's happening and turning genes on or off to meet the needs of the cell. Epigenetic tags aren't the only way to do this. There are also gene regulator proteins in every cell—molecules that can turn DNA on and off in a very quick and responsive way to support neuronal connections.

This is largely how synaptic and myelin plasticity are governed. For example, when a neuron receives a signal that a synapse is actively being used and should be strengthened, we turn genes on to make the necessary components to build up that synapse. Neurons turn genes on and off using regulator proteins, and the regulators are held in check by other proteins. This process is constantly happening in the cell, since every neuron has genes, and every gene is regulated.

This is the fundamental way that neurons learn: long-term memory requires that genes are turned on to support the strengthening of a new synapse. So, every time your child learns something, every time you learn something, gene expression must change.

The Environment Can Turn Genes On and Off

We don't know everything about epigenetics, but we do know that epigenetics sometimes works by turning off harmful genes. For example, your child may have genes that predispose her to schizophrenia, but if those genes are never turned on, she likely won't get schizophrenia.

In fact, gene silencing is being explored as a treatment option for some tough-to-treat conditions, particularly in the brain where the blood-brain barrier makes drug delivery difficult. It's simple: when you turn off a disease-causing gene, then it can't cause disease.

There's a constant battle going on in the cell for genetic control, for the right to express certain genes and silence others. As we've just discussed, what a pregnant mother eats and what a child eats changes epigenetic tags of the child's genome in a way that persists into adulthood. Researchers found that high-fructose diets can negatively change nearly a thousand genes in our brains (including in the hippocampus learning/memory center and the hypothalamus metabolic center).[9]

For parents, this information is disturbing, since fructose is found in countless processed foods as high-fructose corn syrup. It takes careful effort to come home from the grocery store these days without foods containing high-fructose corn syrup. But in the same dynamic way, many of those negative gene changes caused by high-fructose consumption can be undone by DHA (an omega-3 fatty acid). DHA works to supplement proper vision-system development, but it can also reverse some of the epigenetic modifications made by fructose.

As scientists started researching how and when gene regulation can happen, we figured out that environmental substances can also act like switches to turn gene expression on and off. These epigenetic changers are everywhere and can be inadvertently absorbed through exposure, such as exposure to bisphenol A (BPA).[10] That's why BPA, a chemical used in making polycarbonate plastic (typically plastic numbers 1 and 2), is such a big deal. BPA is an estrogen mimic that turns good genes off, negatively affecting the developing brain and behavior. Widespread use of BPA means that people in developed countries are nearly continuously exposed to it: it coats the receipt you're handed at the grocery store, it's in much of our food packaging, and it's detectable in the urine of 95% of people.[11]

Epigenetics Is the Most Powerful Tool Parents Have

Epigenetics has fundamentally changed the way we think about genes. A gene is a tool to be used, not a dictator of fate. But being a good parent in today's world can be exhausting. The food our kids eat, the chemicals they are exposed to, and the way we act as parents have the power to change the way our children use their DNA. But the amazing flexibility of this system is both our burden and our saving grace as parents.

Epigenetics probably explains disease phenomena like autism, obesity, and asthma, whose rates have risen faster than changes in DNA sequence can occur in the general population.[12] It's not that new bad genes are popping up, but it's that the genes our kids already have onboard are being used differently. While the sudden rise of these types of disorders is problematic, it's actually encouraging to know that there may be an environmental cause. It's nearly impossible to change a person's genetic sequence, but we *can* pretty easily alter a person's environment, and this in turn changes which genes turn on or off.

Genetic flexibility within the brain is based on two facts: First, neurons maintain a living, breathing interface with the environment. The world will activate or inhibit a neuron in a certain way, and that neuron can respond and change. The second part of this epigenetic flexibility is that these genetic changes can be reversible if we intentionally expose our kids to things that we know turn beneficial genes on and/or turn harmful genes off, and limit exposure to things that do the reverse. Together, these two facts mean that what we do as parents makes a difference. We make a huge difference. We aren't given these kids preprogrammed. Instead, it's our task to help our children use the resources they have been granted to the very best of their ability.

We're in early explorations into how epigenetics changes people's behavior and how to use it to our best advantage. Epigenetics allows people to use genes differently today than they did yesterday, or even use them differently from a moment before. These epigenetic processes can be understood and used with intention by parents. Purposefully tapping into epigenetic processes can foster major changes in attitude, proficiency, weight, or reflexes and produce visible changes within an individual. As parents, we can capitalize on the idea that at every second, nature and nurture are interacting in our children's brains. Experience dictates the structure of neurons, the structure dictates function, how the neurons function dictates behavior, and behavior makes your children who they are.

APPENDIX 3

Neuromyths Versus Neurofacts

WHILE READING THIS BOOK, you will come across some deconstructed brain myths, some of which are deeply ingrained in parental society. Why are myths about the brain so plentiful in pop culture? Overwhelmingly, these neuromyths arise from an oversimplification of a difficult neuropuzzle. Sometimes there is a single study that spawns a popular idea; sometimes a trend can be oversimplified to the point that it is distorted; or perhaps the results of one study resonate with people in a culturally poignant way, such as in the search for a cause of autism.

A good illustration of a myth gone viral is the "Mozart Effect." In 1993, researchers found that college students experienced a brief, transient boost in abstract spatial reasoning scores on the nonverbal portion of an IQ test after listening to a Mozart sonata.[1] These results morphed into the idea that "listening to Mozart makes you smarter," and a subsequent wave of passive music-centered "learning" crashed down on America.

Who wouldn't want an easy way to make kids smarter? In 1998, Georgia governor Zell Miller began an initiative to ensure each Georgia newborn received a classical music CD titled *Build Your Baby's Brain: Through the Power of Music*. Unfortunately, listening to classical music *doesn't* make you smarter. The wildfire spread of the Mozart Effect idea is an example of runaway media. The Mozart Effect is, in fact, no effect at all, unless you teach your children to play Mozart themselves on a musical instrument. Learning to play the instrument is where the long-term brain benefits come in, not in passive listening.

Once propagated in the general media, the most recent single study can seem larger and more relevant than the literature that came before it. Ideas about the brain can become so pervasive in popular culture that it is even difficult for scientists to sort through the evidence. When the original author of the study protested at the way the Mozart Effect results were being presented in the media, it made little difference; the train had already picked up momentum.[2]

A pressing human need to understand how our brain works is beneath it all. As a society, we are eager for brain information. We want to embrace the knowledge, and we're ready to apply the findings to everyday life. Research shows that when something is explained using a bit of neuroscience information—whether the scientific information is accurate or not—it skews the way people evaluate and accept these explanations. One study showed that when you present nonexperts with psychological phenomena and explain it away with any bit of neuroscience evidence, even if it's not logically connected, people become way more satisfied with the explanation.[3]

This means that it's hard to sort out brain fact from fiction. There are a lot of "brain-based" programs out there, and there are a lot of parents willing to consume them because they want to do the best for their children. Assumptions about the brain are pervasive in our culture, and as a parent you need to be able to evaluate these claims. For example, how do you choose the best tutoring help for your struggling child? How can you get information about a program? You can start with the company's website, but since that's likely to be laced with marketing, you need to find your own evidence of effectiveness. If there's science behind a claim, then it will show up in a search of a peer-review journal database. Those databases are where you can see what the scientists think.

Before buying in to any brain-based program for your kids, try the following:

- Type your subject into the search engine Google Scholar, which will automatically find peer-reviewed journal articles, meaning that experts in that particular field have read the study and found it to be accurate and trustworthy.

This is important because it means you don't have to take a company's word for it. Sometimes Google Scholar can find full versions of articles that other databases don't have freely available.[4]

- The What Works Clearinghouse, run by the Institute of Education Sciences, looks at the peer-reviewed evidence for educational programs and practices. This site provides great evidence snapshots.[5]

- Try searching for biology- and medicine-based articles about your subject in PubMed (which accesses the archives of the US National Institutes of Health's National Library of Medicine).[6]

- Search the American Psychological Association's PsycNET for psychology- and behavioral-based articles. You can search as a new user without logging in.[7]

You may get the information you need from the abstract (article summary) in these last two databases. If you want more, and the full article isn't available for free on those sites, copy the title of the article and do a Google Scholar search to try to get the whole article.

You can also use the following resource to get information about neuroscience-related conditions:

- The Online Mendelian Inheritance in Man (OMIM) is updated daily by the National Center for Biotechnology Information with peer-reviewed findings about genetics. This site is searchable for genetic conditions based on appearance or behavior. It is intended to be used primarily by physicians and genetic researchers but is also available to the general public.[8]

Glossary

action potential   A change in voltage caused by the movement of charged ions across the membrane of the neuron, an action potential causes the neuron to "fire" a nerve impulse, which is an electrical signal that travels down the length of a neuron.

alleles   Alleles are versions of genes. Everyone has two alleles for each gene: one is inherited from the mother and one comes from the father. The alleles you end up with are your DNA genotype, and how they are expressed determines what you look like or how you behave (your phenotype).

amygdala   This inner-brain structure is part of the limbic system and is associated with fear and aggression.

association cortexes   The association areas of the cortex are where we process sensory information that comes in and make meaning of it before we decide to act on it. Association areas often have many connections with other parts of the brain.

axon   The axon is a long projection from the neuron that allows action potentials to travel through the body to other neurons, sometimes across great distances.

cerebellum   This brain area is found in the lower back of the brain and primarily coordinates precise movement, though it's also responsible for some aspects of learning and pain processing.

cerebral cortex   The cerebral cortex is made of tightly packed neurons. It is responsible for most aspects of higher thought, reasoning, judgment, consciousness, and attention, as well as for the processing of sensory information and motor output. You may see it referred to as simply "cortex." The outermost layer is known as the cerebrum.

corpus callosum   The left and right hemispheres of the brain are connected through axon tracts. The main communication pathway between the hemispheres is called the corpus callosum.

cortisol   Cortisol is a steroid hormone that we naturally produce in response to stress.

dopamine   Dopamine is a neurotransmitter released by neurons to carry messages to other neurons. Dopamine modulates the way we regulate emotions and movement, how we determine the value of a reward, and how we are motivated. It is a key chemical involved in the brain's reward pathways, so dopamine is often implicated in drugs of abuse.

dorsolateral prefrontal cortex   The dorsolateral prefrontal area of the cortex is responsible for many aspects of executive functioning (planning, attention, working memory, cognitive flexibility), decision-making, and self-regulation. Located right above your eyes, the dorsolateral prefrontal cortex is one of the last brain regions to mature.

epigenetics   Epigenetics is the study of how gene expression can change (to turn genes on and off) without changing the underlying DNA sequence. Epigenetic changes can occur throughout development and can be passed to the next generation. Epigenetics is the study of how "nurture" can affect "nature."

epigenetic tags   Epigenetic tags are the most common epigenetic changes. These tags allow tight control over our genes and retain a cellular memory of all the things we've responded to over the years. When a neuron adds a methyl tag to a section of DNA, it physically closes it up to turn off gene expression. Adding an acetyl tag can do the opposite—it will open up that specific section of DNA so that protein can be made from the gene. More methylation means fewer active genes; more acetylation means more active genes. These tags are responsive to environmental stimuli in an ongoing way and can be reversible and inherited.

epigenome   The epigenome is the collection of chemical tags and proteins attached to the DNA that tell the genome what to do. This cellular memory is the sum of all of the signals that the cell has received and responded to over the course of its lifetime.

excitatory neurotransmitter   Excitatory neurotransmitters are chemical messengers that cross the synapse and bind to receptors on the next neuron, making it more likely that the next neuron will fire.

frontal lobes   The frontal lobes are responsible for many aspects of personality, speech, planning, reasoning, and voluntary movement. The frontal lobes are the largest of the four lobes of the cerebral cortex.

growth factor IGF-1   The production of insulin-like growth factor 1, a hormone important for childhood growth, is epigenetically decreased in premature babies who develop the eye disorder retinopathy of prematurity.

hippocampus   The hippocampus, along with areas in the cortex, is responsible for memory storage. Specifically, the hippocampus allows short-term memories to be consolidated into long-term memories, and hippocampal damage can prevent the formation of new long-term memories.

limbic system   The limbic system, often referred to as the "old brain," is a collection of structures at the core of the brain, including the striatum, hippocampus, amygdala, hypothalamus, and thalamus. These structures provide a framework for the brain to link our emotions, memories, and body regulation systems together and send this content up to the cortex for further processing.

myelin   In the central nervous system, myelin can coat the axons of mature neurons to make the signals transmit faster. The white myelin is actually an extension of neighboring oligodendrocyte cells that wrap the neuron's axons in an insulated, coiled sleeve. This myelination speeds up the conduction of electrical nerve impulses.

neuron   The neuron, or nerve cell, is the basic conduction unit in the brain. It is an electrical cell that links structures over a lifetime to retain pathways and communication avenues between the environment and the brain. It typically does not divide and is composed of several parts: the dendrites (which receive information), the cell body, and the axon (which sends information).

neuroplasticity   Neuroplasticity is the ability of the brain to continuously change over its lifetime through reorganization, differences in brain activity, alterations in the amount of myelination, compensation for injury, or synapses weakening or strengthening (synaptic plasticity).

norepinephrine   Norepinephrine is an excitatory neurotransmitter similar to adrenaline that is released during our stress response. Norepinephrine is also involved in the creative process and cognitive flexibility.

oligodendrocytes   Oligodendrocytes are glial support cells found in the central nervous system that primarily function to insulate axons of nearby neurons with myelin.

striatum   As part of the "old brain," the striatum is involved with regulating both voluntary movement and reward systems, including the ability to wait for reward, pleasure-seeking behavior, and the valuation of rewards.

synapse   A synapse is the tiny space between two neurons, typically about 20 nanometers (billionths of a meter). To pass a signal, chemical transmitters traverse this minute gap and bind to receptors on the next neuron.

synaptic plasticity   Synaptic plasticity is a version of neuroplasticity that focuses on the neuron's ability to strengthen synapses that are being frequently used and weaken synapses that are infrequently used. This streamlining of resources causes changes in neuronal architecture that can translate into functional changes in the way that neurons work and how they are linked together.

temporal lobes   The temporal lobes make up one of the four lobes of the brain. Located on either side of the head above the ears, the temporal lobes house the hippocampus (responsible for memory formation) and process hearing and understanding of speech.

theory of mind   Theory of mind is the ability to attribute mental states to others, including the idea that others' ideas, opinions, values, and expectations are different from your own. It is developmentally regulated and an important element underlying cognitive empathy.

ventromedial prefrontal cortex   The ventromedial prefrontal cortex is the part of the frontal lobes involved in judgment and decision-making, including regulating the information coming up from the lower brain areas, such as the striatum.

Notes

CHAPTER 1: CREATIVITY, EMPATHY,
AND SELF-CONTROL

1. Elizabeth Dias, "Creativity Conference," *Time*, April 26, 2013, business.time.com/2013/04/26/the-time-creativity-poll.
2. Lev Semenovich Vygotsky, "Imagination and Creativity in Childhood," *Journal of Russian & East European Psychology* 42, no. 1 (2004): 7–97, DOI: 10.1080/10610405.2004.11059210.
3. Dias, "Creativity Conference."
4. Robert J. Sternberg, ed., *Handbook of Creativity* (Cambridge: Cambridge University Press, 1998).
5. Robert Franken, *Human Motivation* (Pacific Grove, CA: Brooks/Cole, 1993), 396.
6. Alfred F. Carlozzi, Kay S. Bull, Gregory T. Eells, and John D. Hurlburt, "Empathy as Related to Creativity, Dogmatism, and Expressiveness," *Journal of Psychology* 129, no. 4 (1994): 365–373, DOI: 10.1080/00223980.1995.9914974.
7. Jean Decety and Philip L. Jackson, "The Functional Architecture of Human Empathy," *Behavioral and Cognitive Neuroscience Reviews* 3, no. 2 (2004): 71–100, DOI: 10.1177/1534582304267187.
8. Henry C. Evrard, Thomas Forro, and Nikos K. Logothetis, "Von Economo Neurons in the Anterior Insula of the Macaque Monkey," *Neuron* 74, no. 3 (2012): 482–489, DOI: 10.1016/j.neuron.2012.03.003.
9. Micaela Santos et al., "Von Economo Neurons in Autism: A Stereologic Study of the Frontoinsular Cortex in Children," *Brain Research* 1380 (2011): 206–217, DOI: 10.1016/j.brainres.2010.08.067.
10. Jaime Craig and Simon Baron-Cohen, "Creativity and Imagination in Autism and Asperger Syndrome," *Journal of Autism and Developmental Disorders* 29, no. 4 (1999): 319–326, DOI: 10.1023/a:1022163403479.

11. Jason Low, Elizabeth Goddard, and Joseph Melser, "Generativity and Imagination in Autism Spectrum Disorder: Evidence from Individual Differences in Children's Impossible Entity Drawings," *British Journal of Developmental Psychology* 27, no. 2 (2009): 425–444, DOI: 10.1348/026151008x334728.

12. Luigi F. Agnati et al., "The Neurobiology of Imagination: Possible Role of Interaction-Dominant Dynamics and Default Mode Network," *Frontiers in Psychology* 4 (2013): 296, DOI: 10.3389/fpsyg.2013.00296.

13. Jean Decety and Julie Grèzes, "The Power of Simulation: Imagining One's Own and Other's Behavior," *Brain Research* 1079, no. 1 (2006): 4–14, DOI: 10.1016/j.brainres.2005.12.115.

14. David B. Hay et al., "Using Drawings of the Brain Cell to Exhibit Expertise in Neuroscience: Exploring the Boundaries of Experimental Culture," *Science Education* 97, no. 3 (2013): 468–491, DOI: 10.1002/sce.21055.

15. Mark H. Davis and H. Alan Oathout, "Maintenance of Satisfaction in Romantic Relationships: Empathy and Relational Competence," *Journal of Personality and Social Psychology* 53, no. 2 (1987): 397, DOI: 10.1037/0022-3514.53.2.397.

16. F. Giorgia Paleari, Camillo Regalia, and Frank Fincham, "Marital Quality, Forgiveness, Empathy, and Rumination: A Longitudinal Analysis," *Personality and Social Psychology Bulletin* 31, no. 3 (2005): 368–378, DOI: 10.1177/0146167204271597.

17. Janet B. Kellett, Ronald H. Humphrey, and Randall G. Sleeth, "Empathy and the Emergence of Task and Relations Leaders," *Leadership Quarterly* 17, no. 2 (2006): 146–162, DOI: 10.1016/j.leaqua.2005.12.003.

18. Thomas J. Long and Edward W. Schultz, "Empathy: A Quality of an Effective Group Leader," *Psychological Reports* 32, no. 3 (1973): 699–705.

19. Rebecca P. Ang and Dion H. Goh, "Cyberbullying among Adolescents: The Role of Affective and Cognitive Empathy, and Gender," *Child Psychiatry & Human Development* 41, no. 4 (2010): 387–397, DOI: 10.1007/s10578-010-0176-3.

20. Gianluca Gini et al., "Determinants of Adolescents' Active Defending and Passive Bystanding Behavior in Bullying," *Journal of Adolescence* 31, no. 1 (2008): 93–105, DOI: 10.1016/j.adolescence.2007.05.002.

21. Minet de Wied, Susan J. T. Branje, and Wim H. J. Meeus, "Empathy and Conflict Resolution in Friendship Relations among Adolescents," *Aggressive Behavior* 33, no. 1 (2007): 48–55, DOI: 10.1002/ab.20166.

22. L. Melita Prati et al., "Emotional Intelligence, Leadership Effectiveness, and Team Outcomes," *International Journal of Organizational Analysis* 11, no. 1 (2003): 21–40, DOI: 10.1108/eb028961.

23. Elizabeth W. Dunn, Lara B. Aknin, and Michael I. Norton, "Prosocial Spending and Happiness: Using Money to Benefit Others Pays Off," *Current Directions in Psychological Science* 23, no. 1 (2014): 41–47, DOI: 10.1177/0963721413512503.

24. Cassie Mogilner, Zoë Chance, and Michael I. Norton, "Giving Time Gives You Time," *Psychological Science* 23, no. 10 (2012): 1233–1238, DOI: 10.1177/0956797612442551.

25. Loren Toussaint and Jon R. Webb, "Theoretical and Empirical Connections Between Forgiveness, Mental Health, and Well-Being," in *Handbook of Forgiveness*, ed. Everett L. Worthington Jr. (New York: Routledge, 2005), 349–362.

26. Dean M. Busby and Brandt C. Gardner, "How Do I Analyze Thee? Let Me Count the Ways: Considering Empathy in Couple Relationships Using Self and Partner Ratings," *Family Process* 47, no. 2 (2008): 229–242, DOI: 10.1111/j.1545-5300.2008.00250.x.

27. Duncan Cramer and Sophia Jowett, "Perceived Empathy, Accurate Empathy and Relationship Satisfaction in Heterosexual Couples," *Journal of Social and Personal Relationships* 27, no. 3 (2010): 327–349, DOI: 10.1177/0265407509348384.

28. Davis and Oathout, "Maintenance of Satisfaction," 397–410.

29. Tess Byrd O'Brien et al., "Couples Coping with Stress: The Role of Empathic Responding," *European Psychologist* 14, no. 1 (2009): 18–28, DOI: 10.1027/1016-9040.14.1.18.

30. Hui Liu and Debra J. Umberson, "The Times They Are a Changin': Marital Status and Health Differentials from 1972 to 2003," *Journal of Health and Social Behavior* 49, no. 3 (2008): 239–253, DOI: 10.1177/002214650804900301.

31. Phillip T. Marucha, Janice K. Kiecolt-Glaser, and Mehrdad Favagehi, "Mucosal Wound Healing Is Impaired by Examination Stress," *Psychosomatic Medicine* 60, no. 3 (1998): 362–365, DOI: 10.1097/00006842-199805000-00025.

32. Janice K. Kiecolt-Glaser, Jean-Philippe Gouin, and Liisa Hantsoo, "Close Relationships, Inflammation, and Health," *Neuroscience & Biobehavioral Reviews* 35, no. 1 (2010): 33–38, DOI: 10.1016/j.neubiorev.2009.09.003.

33. Sara Konrath et al., "Motives for Volunteering Are Associated with Mortality Risk in Older Adults," *Health Psychology* 31, no. 1 (2012): 87, DOI: 10.1037/a0025226.

34. Michael J. Poulin et al., "Giving to Others and the Association Between Stress and Mortality," *American Journal of Public Health* 103, no. 9 (2013): 1649–1655, DOI: 10.2105/ajph.2012.300876.

35. Andrew Steptoe and Jane Wardle, "Positive Affect Measured Using Ecological Momentary Assessment and Survival in Older Men and Women," *Proceedings of the National Academy of Sciences* 108, no. 45 (2011): 18244–18248, DOI: 10.1073/pnas.1110892108.

36. Sara H. Konrath, Edward H. O'Brien, and Courtney Hsing, "Changes in Dispositional Empathy in American College Students over Time: A Meta-Analysis," *Personality and Social Psychology Review* 15, no. 2 (2011): 180–198, DOI: 10.1177/1088868310377395.

37. Vanessa Vega, "Social and Emotional Learning Research Review: Evidence-Based Programs," Edutopia, November 7, 2012, edutopia. org/sel-research-evidence-based-programs.

38. Joseph A. Durlak et al., "The Impact of Enhancing Students' Social and Emotional Learning: A Meta-Analysis of School-Based Universal Interventions," *Child Development* 82, no. 1 (2011): 405–432, DOI: 10.1111/j.1467-8624.2010.01564.x.

39. T. Darlene Bonner and David N. Aspy, "A Study of the Relationship Between Student Empathy and GPA," *Journal of Humanistic Counseling* 22, no. 4 (1984): 149–154, DOI: 10.1002/j.2164-4683.1984.tb00252.x.

40. Norma Deitch Feshbach and Seymour Feshbach, "Empathy and Education," in *The Social Neuroscience of Empathy*, ed. Jean Decety and William Ickes (Cambridge, MA: The MIT Press, 2011), 85–98.

41. Delores Gallo, "Educating for Empathy, Reason and Imagination," *Journal of Creative Behavior* 23, no. 2 (1989): 98–115, DOI: 10.1002/j.2162-6057.1989.tb00680.x.

42. William T. Harbaugh, Ulrich Mayr, and Daniel R. Burghart, "Neural Responses to Taxation and Voluntary Giving Reveal Motives for Charitable Donations," *Science* 316, no. 5831 (2007): 1622–1625, DOI: 10.1126/science.1140738.

43. Terrie E. Moffitt et al., "A Gradient of Childhood Self-Control Predicts Health, Wealth, and Public Safety," *Proceedings of the National Academy of Sciences* 108, no. 7 (2011): 2693–2698, DOI: 10.1073/pnas.1010076108.

44. Angela L. Duckworth and Martin E. P. Seligman, "Self-Discipline Outdoes IQ in Predicting Academic Performance of Adolescents," *Psychological Science* 16, no. 12 (2005): 939–944, DOI: 10.1111/j.1467-9280.2005.01641.x.

45. June P. Tangney, Roy F. Baumeister, and Angie Luzio Boone, "High Self-Control Predicts Good Adjustment, Less Pathology, Better Grades, and Interpersonal Success," *Journal of Personality* 72, no. 2 (2004): 271–324, DOI: 10.1111/j.0022-3506.2004.00263.x.

46. Sally Pearce Cox, "Leader Character: A Model of Personality and Moral Development" (PhD diss., University of Tulsa, 2000).

47. Wilhelm Hofmann et al., "Yes, but Are They Happy? Effects of Trait Self-Control on Affective Well-Being and Life Satisfaction," *Journal of Personality* 82, no. 4 (2014): 265–277, DOI: 10.1111/jopy.12050.

48. Terrie E. Moffitt et al., "A Gradient of Childhood Self-Control," 2693–2698.

49. Mark Muraven, Dikla Shmueli, and Edward Burkley, "Conserving Self-Control Strength," *Journal of Personality and Social Psychology* 91, no. 3 (2006): 524.

50. Kathleen D. Vohs and Natalie J. Ciarocco, "Interpersonal Functioning Requires Self-Regulation," in *Handbook of Self-Regulation: Research, Theory, and Applications*, ed. Roy. F. Baumeister and Kathleen. D. Vohs (New York: Guilford Press, 2004), 392–407.

51. Kevin M. Beaver et al., "Genetic and Environmental Influences on Levels of Self-Control and Delinquent Peer Affiliation: Results from a Longitudinal Sample of Adolescent Twins," *Criminal Justice and Behavior* 36, no. 1 (2009): 41–60, DOI: 10.1177/0093854808326992.

52. Sheldon Wagner et al., "'Metaphorical' Mapping in Human Infants," *Child Development* 52, no. 2 (1981): 728–731, DOI: 10.1111/j.1467-8624.1981.tb03106.x.

53. Howard Gardner, "Metaphors and Modalities: How Children Project Polar Adjectives onto Diverse Domains," *Child Development* 45, no.1 (1974): 84–91.

54. William James, "Attention," chap. 11 in *The Principles of Psychology* (New York: Henry Holt and Company, 1890).

CHAPTER 2: PRACTICAL NEUROSCIENCE FOR PARENTS

1. Timothy G. Moore et al., "Early Childhood Development and the Social Determinants of Health Inequities," *Health Promotion International* 30, no. S2 (2015): ii102–ii115, DOI: 10.1093/heapro/dav031.

2. Jack P. Shonkoff and Deborah A. Phillips, eds., "The Developing Brain," in *From Neurons to Neighborhoods: The Science of Early Childhood Development* (Washington, DC: National Academies Press, 2000), 183–219.

3. David A. Drachman, "Do We Have Brain to Spare?," *Neurology* 64, no. 12 (2005): 2004–2005, DOI: 10.1212/01.wnl.0000166914.38327.bb.

4. Drachman, "Do We Have Brain to Spare?," 2004–2005.

5. Peter R. Huttenlocher, "Synaptic Density in Human Frontal Cortex—Developmental Changes and Effects of Aging," *Brain Research* 163, no. 2 (1979): 195–205, DOI: 10.1016/0006-8993(79)90349-4.

6. Todd F. Roberts et al., "Rapid Spine Stabilization and Synaptic Enhancement at the Onset of Behavioural Learning," *Nature* 463, no. 7283 (2010): 948, DOI: 10.1038/nature08759.

7. Tonghui Xu et al., "Rapid Formation and Selective Stabilization of Synapses for Enduring Motor Memories," *Nature* 462, no. 7275 (2009): 915, DOI: 10.1038/nature08389.

8. Michael A. Sutton and Erin M. Schuman, "Dendritic Protein Synthesis, Synaptic Plasticity, and Memory," *Cell* 127, no. 1 (2006): 49–58, DOI: 10.1016/j.cell.2006.09.014.

9. James D. Fix, *High-Yield Neuroanatomy*, Board Review Series (Philadelphia: Williams & Wilkins, 1995).

10. Bernard Zalc, Daniel Goujet, and David Colman, "The Origin of the Myelination Program in Vertebrates," *Current Biology* 18, no. 12 (2008): R511–R512, DOI: 10.1016/j.cub.2008.04.010.

11. Daniel K. Hartline, "What Is Myelin?" *Neuron Glia Biology* 4, no. 2 (2008): 153–163, DOI: 10.1017/s1740925x09990263.

12. Gregory Z. Tau and Bradley S. Peterson, "Normal Development of Brain Circuits," *Neuropsychopharmacology* 35, no. 1 (2009): 147, DOI: 10.1038/npp.2009.115.

13. Nicole Baumann and Danielle Pham-Dinh, "Biology of Oligodendrocyte and Myelin in the Mammalian Central Nervous System," *Physiological Reviews* 81, no. 2 (2001): 871–927, DOI: 10.1152/physrev.2001.81.2.871.

14. Catherine Lebel et al., "Microstructural Maturation of the Human Brain from Childhood to Adulthood," *NeuroImage* 40, no. 3 (2008): 1044–1055, DOI: 10.1016/j.neuroimage.2007.12.053.

15. Catherine Lebel and Christian Beaulieu, "Longitudinal Development of Human Brain Wiring Continues from Childhood into Adulthood," *Journal of Neuroscience* 31, no. 30 (2011): 10937–10947, DOI: 10.1523/jneurosci.5302-10.2011.

16. R. Douglas Fields, "A New Mechanism of Nervous System Plasticity: Activity-Dependent Myelination," *Nature Reviews Neuroscience* 16, no. 12 (2015): 756, DOI: 10.1038/nrn4023.

17. Sara L. Bengtsson, "Extensive Piano Practicing Has Regionally Specific Effects on White Matter Development," *Nature Neuroscience* 8, no. 9 (2005): 1148, DOI: 10.1038/nn1516.

18. Manuel Carreiras et al., "An Anatomical Signature for Literacy," *Nature* 461, no. 7266 (2009): 983, DOI: 10.1038/nature08461.

19. Jan Scholz et al., "Training Induces Changes in White-Matter Architecture," *Nature Neuroscience* 12, no. 11 (2009): 1370, DOI: 10.1038/nn.2412.

20. Erin M. Gibson et al., "Neuronal Activity Promotes Oligodendrogenesis and Adaptive Myelination in the Mammalian Brain," *Science* 344, no. 6183 (2014): 1252304, DOI: 10.1126/science.1252304.

21. Fields, "Nervous System Plasticity," 756.

22. James E. Swain et al., "Parenting and Beyond: Common Neurocircuits Underlying Parental and Altruistic Caregiving," *Parenting* 12, no. 2–3 (2012): 115–123, DOI: 10.1080/15295192.2012.680409.

23. Malcolm Gladwell, *Outliers: The Story of Success* (New York: Little, Brown & Co., 2008).

24. Brooke N. Macnamara, David Z. Hambrick, and Frederick L. Oswald, "Deliberate Practice and Performance in Music, Games, Sports, Education, and Professions: A Meta-Analysis," *Psychological Science* 25, no. 8 (2014): 1608–1618, DOI: 10.1177/0956797614535810.

25. Adapted from BrainU: The Neuroscience Teacher Institute. Available at http://brainu.org/sites/brainu.org/files/movies/synapseschange_pc.html.

26. Denis Larrivee and Adriana Gini, "Is the Philosophical Construct of 'Habitus Operativus Bonus' Compatible with the Modern Neuroscience Concept of Human Flourishing Through Neuroplasticity? A Consideration of Prudence as a Multidimensional Regulator of Virtue," *Frontiers in Human Neuroscience* 8 (2014): 731, DOI: 10.3389/fnhum.2014.00731.

27. Javier Bernacer and Jose Ignacio Murillo, "The Aristotelian Conception of Habit and Its Contribution to Human Neuroscience," *Frontiers in Human Neuroscience* 10 (2014): 883, DOI: 10.3389/fnhum.2014.00590.

28. Catherine L'Ecuyer, "The Wonder Approach to Learning," *Frontiers in Human Neuroscience* 8 (2014): 764, DOI: 10.3389 /fnhum.2014.00764.

29. Michael C. Corballis, "Left Brain, Right Brain: Facts and Fantasies," *PLOS Biology* 12, no. 1 (2014): e1001767, DOI: 10.1371/journal .pbio.1001767.

30. Jared A. Nielsen et al., "An Evaluation of the Left-Brain vs. Right-Brain Hypothesis with Resting State Functional Connectivity Magnetic Resonance Imaging," *PLOS One* 8, no. 8 (2013): e71275, DOI: 10.1371/journal.pone.0071275.

CHAPTER 3: SECOND NATURE PARENTING

1. D. Tranel, S. W. Anderson, and A. Benton, "Development of the Concept of Executive Function and Its Relationship to the Frontal Lobes," in *Handbook of Neuropsychology*, vol. 8, ed. F. Boller and J. Grafman (Amsterdam: Elsevier, 1994), 125–48.

2. Fabio Del Missier, Timo Mäntylä, and Wändi Bruine de Bruin, "Executive Functions in Decision Making: An Individual Differences Approach," *Thinking & Reasoning* 16, no. 2 (2010): 69–97, DOI: 10.1080/13546781003630117.

3. Dietsje Jolles and Eveline A. Crone, "Training the Developing Brain: A Neurocognitive Perspective," *Frontiers in Human Neuroscience* 6 (2012): 76, DOI: 10.3389/fnhum.2012.00076.

4. Dietsje D. Jolles et al., "Practice Effects in the Developing Brain: A Pilot Study," *Developmental Cognitive Neuroscience* 2, S1 (2012): S180–S191, DOI: 10.1016/j.dcn.2011.09.001.

5. Joni Holmes, Susan E. Gathercole, and Darren L. Dunning, "Adaptive Training Leads to Sustained Enhancement of Poor Working Memory in Children," *Developmental Science* 12, no. 4 (2009): F9–15, DOI: 10.1111/j.1467-7687.2009.00848.x.

6. Mariët J. van der Molen et al., "Effectiveness of a Computerised Working Memory Training in Adolescents with Mild to Borderline Intellectual Disabilities," *Journal of Intellectual Disability Research* 54, no. 5 (2010): 433–447, DOI: 10.1111/j.1365-2788.2010.01285.x.

7. Max Owens, Ernst H. W. Koster, and Nazanin Derakshan, "Improving Attention Control in Dysphoria Through Cognitive Training: Transfer Effects on Working Memory Capacity and Filtering Efficiency," *Psychophysiology* 50, no. 3 (2013): 297–307, DOI: 10.1111/psyp.12010.

8. Adam D. Galinsky, Deborah H. Gruenfeld, and Joe C. Magee, "From Power to Action," *Journal of Personality and Social Psychology* 85, no. 3 (2003): 453.

9. Yi-Yuan Tang, Britta K. Hölzel, and Michael I. Posner, "The Neuroscience of Mindfulness Meditation," *Nature Reviews Neuroscience* 16, no. 4 (2015): 213, DOI: 10.1038/nrn3916.

10. Ivana Buric et al., "What Is the Molecular Signature of Mind–Body Interventions? A Systematic Review of Gene Expression Changes Induced by Meditation and Related Practices," *Frontiers in Immunology* 8 (2017): 670, DOI: 10.3389/fimmu.2017.00670.

11. Center for Wellness and Achievement in Education, "Research," cwae.org/research_intro.php (accessed March 17, 2018).

12. Catherine A. Haden, Rachel A. Haine, and Robyn Fivush, "Developing Narrative Structure in Parent-Child Reminiscing Across the Preschool Years," *Developmental Psychology* 33, no. 2 (1997): 295, DOI: 10.1037/0012-1649.33.2.295.

13. Amy M. Boland, Catherine A. Haden, and Peter A. Ornstein, "Boosting Children's Memory by Training Mothers in the Use of an Elaborative Conversational Style as an Event Unfolds," *Journal of Cognition and Development* 4, no. 1 (2003): 39–65, DOI: 10.1080/15248372.2003.9669682.

14. Larry R. Squire, "The Legacy of Patient H.M. for Neuroscience," *Neuron* 61, no. 1 (2009): 6–9, DOI: 10.1016/j.neuron.2008.12.023.

15. David A. Drachman, "Do We Have Brain to Spare?" *Neurology* 64, no. 12 (2005): 2004–2005, DOI: 10.1212/01.WNL.0000166914.38327.BB.

16. Karen Chan Barrett et al., "Art and Science: How Musical Training Shapes the Brain," *Frontiers in Psychology* 4 (2013): 713, DOI: 10.3389/fpsyg.2013.00713.

17. Ana Luísa Pinho et al., "Connecting to Create: Expertise in Musical Improvisation Is Associated with Increased Functional Connectivity Between Premotor and Prefrontal Areas," *Journal of Neuroscience* 34, no. 18 (2014): 6156–6163, DOI: 10.1523/JNEUROSCI.4769-13.2014.

18. Francisco J. Novo, "Habit Acquisition in the Context of Neuronal Genomic and Epigenomic Mosaicism," *Frontiers in Human Neuroscience* 8 (2014): 255, DOI: 10.3389/fnhum.2014.00255.

19. St. Thomas Aquinas, *Truth: Questions X–XX*, vol.2, trans. James V. McGlynn (Indianapolis, IN: Hackett Publishing, 1995), 82.

CHAPTER 4: THE NEUROSCIENCE OF CREATIVITY

1. Graham Wallas, *The Art of Thought* (London: Jonathan Cape, 1926), 10.
2. Annukka K. Lindell and Evan Kidd, "Why Right-Brain Teaching Is Half-Witted: A Critique of the Misapplication of Neuroscience to Education," *Mind, Brain, and Education* 5, no. 3 (2011): 121–127, DOI: 10.1111/j.1751-228X.2011.01120.x.
3. Dahlia W. Zaidel, "Creativity, Brain, and Art: Biological and Neurological Considerations," *Frontiers in Human Neuroscience* 8 (2014): 389, DOI: 10.3389/fnhum.2014.00389.
4. Maddalena Boccia et al., "Where Do Bright Ideas Occur in Our Brain? Meta-Analytic Evidence from Neuroimaging Studies of Domain-Specific Creativity," *Frontiers in Psychology* 6 (2015): 1195, DOI: 10.3389/fpsyg.2015.01195.
5. Ambar Chakravarty. "The Creative Brain–Revisiting Concepts." *Medical hypotheses* 74, no. 3 (2010): 606-612.
6. R. A. Chavez et al., "Neurobiology of Creativity: Preliminary Results from a Brain Activation Study," *Salud Mental* 27, no. 3 (2004): 38–46.
7. Suddendorf, Thomas, and Claire M. Fletcher-Flinn. "Theory of Mind and the Origin of Divergent Thinking." *The Journal of Creative Behavior* 31, no. 3 (1997): 169-179.
8. Hikaru Takeuchi et al., "White Matter Structures Associated with Creativity: Evidence from Diffusion Tensor Imaging," *NeuroImage* 51, no. 1 (2010): 11–18, DOI: 10.1016/j.neuroimage.2010.02.035.
9. Erin M. Gibson et al., "Neuronal Activity Promotes Oligodendrogenesis and Adaptive Myelination in the Mammalian Brain," *Science* 344, no. 6183 (2014): 1252304, DOI: 10.1126/science.1252304.
10. Hikaru Takeuchi et al., "White Matter Structures Associated with Creativity: Evidence from Diffusion Tensor Imaging," *NeuroImage* 51, no.1 (2010): 11–18, DOI: 10.1016/j.neuroimage.2010.02.035.
11. Robin J. M. Franklin and Charles Ffrench-Constant, "Remyelination in the CNS: From Biology to Therapy," *Nature Reviews Neuroscience* 9, no. 11 (2008): 839, DOI: 10.1038/nrn2480.
12. Robin J. M. Franklin and Charles Ffrench-Constant, "Remyelination in the CNS," 839.
13. Heidrun Karlic and Pia Baurek, "Epigenetics and the Power of Art," *Clinical Epigenetics* 2, no. 2 (2011): 279, DOI: 10.1007/s13148-011-0033-7.

14. Allison B. Kaufman et al., "Towards a Neurobiology of Creativity in Nonhuman Animals," *Journal of Comparative Psychology* 125, no. 3 (2011): 255, DOI: 10.1037/a0023147.
15. Kaufman et al., "Neurobiology of Creativity in Nonhuman Animals," 255.
16. Martin Reuter et al., "Identification of First Candidate Genes for Creativity: A Pilot Study," *Brain Research* 1069, no. 1 (2006): 190–197, DOI: 10.1016/j.brainres.2005.11.046.
17. Elena Shumay, Joanna S. Fowler, and Nora D. Volkow, "Genomic Features of the Human Dopamine Transporter Gene and Its Potential Epigenetic States: Implications for Phenotypic Diversity," *PLOS One* 5, no. 6 (2010): e11067, DOI: 10.1371/journal.pone.0011067.
18. Brad E. Sheese et al., "Parenting Quality Interacts with Genetic Variation in Dopamine Receptor DRD4 to Influence Temperament in Early Childhood," *Development and Psychopathology* 19, no. 4 (2007): 1039–1046, DOI: 10.1017/S0954579407000521.
19. Drake Morgan et al., "Social Dominance in Monkeys: Dopamine D2 Receptors and Cocaine Self-Administration," *Nature Neuroscience* 5, no. 2 (2002): 169–174, DOI: 10.1038/nn798.
20. Ambar Chakravarty, "The Creative Brain–Revisiting Concepts," *Medical Hypotheses* 74, no. 3 (2009): 606–612, DOI: 10.1016/j. mehy.2009.10.014.
21. Mathias Benedek and Aljoscha C. Neubauer, "Revisiting Mednick's Model on Creativity-Related Differences in Associative Hierarchies: Evidence for a Common Path to Uncommon Thought," *Journal of Creative Behavior* 47, no. 4 (2013): 273–289, DOI: 10.1002/jocb.35.
22. Benedek and Neubauer, "Revisiting Mednick's Model," 273–289.
23. E.P. Torrance, *Torrance Tests of Creative Thinking: Directions Manual and Scoring Guide* (Bensenville, IL: Scholastic Testing Service, 1990).
24. Torrance, *Torrance Tests*.
25. Gil Gonen-Yaacovi et al., "Rostral and Caudal Prefrontal Contribution to Creativity: A Meta-Analysis of Functional Imaging Data," *Frontiers in Human Neuroscience* 7 (2013): 465, DOI: 10.3389/fnhum.2013.00465.
26. James C. Kaufman, *Creativity 101* (New York: Springer, 2016).
27. Benedek and Neubauer, "Revisiting Mednick's Model," 273–289.
28. Society for Laboratory Automation and Screening, "Think About It: Nobel Prize Winner Sir Harold Kroto Throws Down the Gauntlet," *SLAS Electronic Laboratory Neighborhood*, September 7, 2012, eln.slas.org/story/1/74-think-about-it-nobel-prize-winner-sir-harold -kroto-throws-down-the-gauntlet-/.

29. Mathilda Marie Joubert, "The Art of Creative Teaching: NACCCE and Beyond," in *Creativity in Education*, ed. Anna Craft, Bob Jeffrey, and Mike Liebling (London: Continuum, 2001), 17–34.

30. Milica Cerovic et al., "Molecular and Cellular Mechanisms of Dopamine-Mediated Behavioral Plasticity in the Striatum," *Neurobiology of Learning and Memory* 105 (2013): 63–80, DOI: 10.1016/j.nlm.2013.06.013.

CHAPTER 5: HOW TO RAISE A CREATIVE CHILD

1. Zuyeon Kim, "The Creativity Crisis: The Decrease in Creative Thinking Scores on the Torrance Tests of Creative Thinking," *Creativity Research Journal* 23, no. 4 (2011): 285–295, DOI: 10.1080/10400419.2011.627805.

2. Yasuyuki Kowatari et al., "Neural Networks Involved in Artistic Creativity," *Human Brain Mapping* 30, no. 5 (2009): 1678–1690, DOI: 10.1002/hbm.20633.

3. Balder Onarheim and Morten Friis-Olivarius, "Applying the Neuroscience of Creativity to Creativity Training," *Frontiers in Human Neuroscience* 7 (2013): 656, DOI: 10.3389/fnhum.2013.00656.

4. Ronald A. Beghetto and James C. Kaufman, "Do We All Have Multicreative Potential?" *ZDM* 41, no. 1–2 (2009): 39–44, DOI: 10.1007/s11858-008-0143-7.

5. Ambar Chakravarty, "The Creative Brain—Revisiting Concepts," *Medical Hypotheses* 74, no. 3 (2009): 606–612, DOI: 10.1016/j.mehy.2009.10.014.

6. Alice W. Flaherty, "Frontotemporal and Dopaminergic Control of Idea Generation and Creative Drive," *Journal of Comparative Neurology* 493, no. 1 (2005): 147–153, DOI: 10.1002/cne.20768.

7. Lev S. Vygotsky, *Mind in Society: The Development of Higher Psychological Processes*, rev. ed. (1930; repr., Cambridge, MA: Harvard University Press, 1978).

8. M. C. Chesimet, B. N. Githua, and J. K. Ng'eno, "Effects of Experiential Learning Approach on Students' Mathematical Creativity among Secondary School Students of Kericho East Sub-County, Kenya," *Journal of Education and Practice* 7, no. 23 (2016): 51–57.

9. Christine Charyton and John A. Merrill, "Assessing General Creativity and Creative Engineering Design in First Year Engineering Students," *Journal of Engineering Education* 98, no. 2 (2009): 145–156, DOI: 10.1002/j.2168-9830.2009.tb01013.x.

10. Afida Ayob et al., "Assessment of Creativity in Electrical Engineering," *Procedia—Social and Behavioral Sciences* 60 (2012): 463–467, DOI: 10.1016/j.sbspro.2012.09.407.

11. Mark Leikin, "The Effect of Bilingualism on Creativity: Developmental and Educational Perspectives," *International Journal of Bilingualism* 17, no. 4 (2013): 431–447, DOI: 10.1177/1367006912438300.

12. Anatoliy V. Kharkhurin, *Multilingualism and Creativity* (Bristol, UK: Multilingual Matters, 2012).

13. Angela Ka-yee Leung, "Multicultural Experience Enhances Creativity: The When and How," *American Psychologist* 63, no. 3 (2008): 169, DOI: 10.1037/0003-066X.63.3.169.

14. William W. Maddux and Adam D. Galinsky, "Cultural Borders and Mental Barriers: The Relationship Between Living Abroad and Creativity," *Journal of Personality and Social Psychology* 96, no. 5 (2009): 1047, DOI: 10.1037/a0014861.

15. Carmit T. Tadmor, Adam D. Galinsky, and William W. Maddux, "Getting the Most Out of Living Abroad: Biculturalism and Integrative Complexity as Key Drivers of Creative and Professional Success," *Journal of Personality and Social Psychology* 103, no. 3 (2012): 520, DOI: 10.1037/a0029360.

16. Karl Duncker, "On Problem-Solving," trans. Lynne S. Lees, *Psychological Monographs* 58, no. 5 (1945): i–113.

17. Terence L. Belcher, "Modeling Original Divergent Responses: An Initial Investigation," *Journal of Educational Psychology* 67, no. 3 (1975): 351.

18. Chinmay Kulkarni, Steven P. Dow, and Scott R. Klemmer, "Early and Repeated Exposure to Examples Improves Creative Work," in *Design Thinking Research* (Berlin: Springer International Publishing, 2014): 49–62, DOI: 10.1007/978-3-319-01303-9_4.

19. Ursula Debarnot et al., "Experts Bodies, Experts Minds: How Physical and Mental Training Shape the Brain," *Frontiers in Human Neuroscience* 8 (2014): 280, DOI: 10.3389/fnhum.2014.00280.

20. S. Akbari Chermahini and Bernhard Hommel, "More Creative Through Positive Mood? Not Everyone!" *Frontiers in Human Neuroscience* 6 (2012): 319, DOI: 10.3389/fnhum.2012.00319.

21. Kenneth R. Ginsburg et al., "The Importance of Play in Promoting Healthy Child Development and Maintaining Strong Parent-Child Bonds," *Pediatrics* 119, no. 1 (2007): 182–191, DOI: 10.1542/peds.2006-2697.

22. Maite Garaigordobil and Laura Berrueco, "Effects of a Play Program on Creative Thinking of Preschool Children," *Spanish Journal of Psychology* 14, no. 2 (2011): 608–618.

23. Deena Skolnick Weisberg, "Talking It Up: Play, Language Development, and the Role of Adult Support," *American Journal of Play* 6, no. 1 (2013): 39.

24. Kaomi Goetz, "How 3M Gave Everyone Days Off and Created an Innovation Dynamo," *Fast Company*, February 1, 2011, fastcodesign.com/1663137/how-3m-gave-everyone-days-off -and-created-an-innovation-dynamo.

25. Lampros Perogamvros et al., "Sleep and Dreaming Are for Important Matters," *Frontiers in Psychology* 4 (July 25, 2013): 474, DOI: 10.3389/fpsyg.2013.00474.

26. Denise J. Cai et al., "REM, Not Incubation, Improves Creativity by Priming Associative Networks," *Proceedings of the National Academy of Sciences* 106, no. 25 (2009): 10130–10134, DOI: 10.1073 /pnas.0900271106.

27. Charles J. Limb and Allen R. Braun, "Neural Substrates of Spontaneous Musical Performance: An fMRI Study of Jazz Improvisation," *PLOS One* 3, no. 2 (2008), DOI: 10.1371/journal .pone.0001679.

28. Pierre Maquet et al., "Functional Neuroanatomy of Human Rapid-Eye-Movement Sleep and Dreaming," *Nature* 383, no. 6596 (1996): 163, DOI: 10.1038/383163a0.

29. Ruth Ann Atchley, David L. Strayer, and Paul Atchley, "Creativity in the Wild: Improving Creative Reasoning through Immersion in Natural Settings," *PLOS One* 7, no. 12 (2012): DOI: 10.1371/journal.pone.051474.

30. Francesca Gino and Dan Ariely, "The Dark Side of Creativity: Original Thinkers Can Be More Dishonest," *Journal of Personality and Social Psychology* 102, no. 3 (2011): 445, DOI: 10.1037/a0026406.

CHAPTER 6: THE NEUROSCIENCE OF EMPATHY

1. Sara H. Konrath, Edward H. O'Brien, and Courtney Hsing, "Changes in Dispositional Empathy in American College Students Over Time: A Meta-Analysis," *Personality and Social Psychology Review* 15, no. 2 (2011): 180–198, DOI: 10.1177/1088868310377395.

2. Ariel Knafo-Noam et al., "The Developmental Origins of a Disposition Toward Empathy: Genetic and Environmental Contributions," *Emotion* 8, no. 6 (2008): 737, DOI: 10.1037/a0014179.

3. Ronald J. Iannotti, "Effect of Role-Taking Experiences on Role Taking, Empathy, Altruism, and Aggression," *Developmental Psychology* 14, no. 2 (1978): 119, DOI: 10.1037/0012-1649.14.2.119.

4. Mirja Kalliopuska, "Empathy in School Students" (Department of Psychology, University of Helsinki, 1983), files.eric.ed.gov/fulltext/ED240423.pdf.

5. Nancy Eisenberg-Berg and Paul Mussen, "Empathy and Moral Development in Adolescence," *Developmental Psychology* 14, no. 2 (1978): 185, DOI: 10.1037/0012-1649.14.2.185.

6. Lynda A. Haynes and Arthur W. Avery, "Training Adolescents in Self-Disclosure and Empathy Skills," *Journal of Counseling Psychology* 26, no. 6 (1979): 526, DOI: 10.1037/0022-0167.26.6.526.

7. Penney Clarke, "What Kind of Discipline Is Most Likely to Lead to Empathic Behaviour in Classrooms?" *History and Social Science Teacher* 19, no. 4 (1984): 240–241.

8. Mohammadreza Hojat et al., "Physicians' Empathy and Clinical Outcomes for Diabetic Patients," *Academic Medicine* 86, no. 3 (2011): 359–364, DOI: 10.1097/ACM.0b013e3182086fe1.

9. David P. Rakel et al., "Practitioner Empathy and the Duration of the Common Cold," *Family Medicine* 41, no. 7 (2009): 494.

10. Stefano Del Canale et al., "The Relationship Between Physician Empathy and Disease Complications: An Empirical Study of Primary Care Physicians and Their Diabetic Patients in Parma, Italy," *Academic Medicine* 87, no. 9 (2012): 1243–1249, DOI: 10.1097/ACM.0b013e3182628fbf.

11. John M. Kelley et al., "The Influence of the Patient-Clinician Relationship on Healthcare Outcomes: A Systematic Review and Meta-Analysis of Randomized Controlled Trials," *PLOS One* 9, no. 4 (2014): DOI: 10.1371/journal.pone.0094207.

12. Samantha A. Batt-Rawden et al., "Teaching Empathy to Medical Students: An Updated, Systematic Review," *Academic Medicine* 88, no. 8 (2013): 1171–1177, DOI: 10.1097/ACM.0b013e318299f3e3.

13. Heather Marie Higgins, "Empathy Training and Stress: Their Role in Medical Students' Responses to Emotional Patients" (PhD diss., University of British Columbia, 1990).

14. Jamil Zaki and Kevin N. Ochsner, "The Neuroscience of Empathy: Progress, Pitfalls and Promise," *Nature Neuroscience* 15, no. 5 (2012): 675, DOI: 10.1038/nn.3085.

15. Carolien Rieffe, Lizet Ketelaar, and Carin H. Wiefferink, "Assessing Empathy in Young Children: Construction and Validation of an Empathy Questionnaire (EmQue)," *Personality and Individual Differences* 49, no. 5 (2010): 362–367, DOI: 10.1016/j .paid.2010.03.046.

16. Carolyn Zahn-Waxler, Marian Radke-Yarrow, and Robert A. King, "Child Rearing and Children's Prosocial Initiations Toward Victims of Distress," *Child Development* 50, no. 2 (1979): 319–330, DOI: 10.1111/j.1467-8624.1979.tb04112.x.

17. Carolyn Zahn-Waxler et al., "Development of Concern for Others," *Developmental Psychology* 28, no. 1 (1992): 126, DOI: 10.1037/0012-1649.28.1.126.

18. Carolyn Zahn-Waxler, JoAnn L. Robinson, and Robert N. Emde, "The Development of Empathy in Twins," *Developmental Psychology* 28, no. 6 (1992): 1038, DOI: 10.1037/0012-1649.28.6.1038.

19. Matthew Aney, "'Babywise' Advice Linked to Dehydration, Failure to Thrive," *AAP News* 14, no. 4 (1998): 21.

20. David Elliman and Margaret A. Lynch, "The Physical Punishment of Children," *Archives of Disease in Childhood* 83, no. 3 (2000): 196–198, DOI: 10.1136/adc.83.3.196.

21. Barbara A. Hotelling, "Styles of Parenting," *The Journal of Perinatal Education* 13, no. 1 (2005): 42, DOI: 10.1624/105812404826423.

22. Gianluca Esposito et al., "Infant Calming Responses During Maternal Carrying in Humans and Mice," *Current Biology* 23, no. 9 (2013): 739–745, DOI: 10.1016/j.cub.2013.03.041.

23. Ian C. G. Weaver et al., "Epigenetic Programming by Maternal Behavior," *Nature Neuroscience* 7, no. 8 (2004): 847, DOI: 10.1038 /nn1276.

24. Andrea Guzzetta et al., "Massage Accelerates Brain Development and the Maturation of Visual Function," *Journal of Neuroscience* 29, no. 18 (2009): 6042–6051, DOI: 10.1523/JNEUROSCI.5548-08.2009.

25. Patrick O. McGowan, "Epigenetic Regulation of the Glucocorticoid Receptor in Human Brain Associates with Childhood Abuse," *Nature Neuroscience* 12, no. 3 (2009): 342, DOI: 10.1038/nn.2270.

26. Kathleen C. Light, Karen M. Grewen, and Janet A. Amico, "More Frequent Partner Hugs and Higher Oxytocin Levels Are Linked to Lower Blood Pressure and Heart Rate in Premenopausal Women," *Biological Psychology* 69, no. 1 (2005), 5–21, DOI: 10.1016/j .biopsycho.2004.11.002.

27. Sheldon Cohen et al., "Does Hugging Provide Stress-Buffering Social Support? A Study of Susceptibility to Upper Respiratory Infection and Illness," *Psychological Science* 26, no. 2 (2015): 135–147, DOI: 10.1177/0956797614559284.

28. Alberto Gallace and Charles Spence, "The Science of Interpersonal Touch: An Overview," *Neuroscience & Biobehavioral Reviews* 34, no. 2 (2008): 246–259, DOI: 10.1016/j.neubiorev.2008.10.004.

29. Ronald J. Iannotti, "Effect of Role-Taking Experiences on Role Taking, Empathy, Altruism, and Aggression," *Developmental Psychology* 14, no. 2 (1978): 119, DOI: 10.1037/0012-1649.14.2.119.

30. Craig K. Ewart et al., "High Blood Pressure and Marital Discord: Not Being Nasty Matters More Than Being Nice," *Health Psychology* 10, no. 3 (1991): 155, DOI: 10.1037//0278-6133.10.3.155.

31. Simon Baron-Cohen, Alan M. Leslie, and Uta Frith, "Does the Autistic Child Have a 'Theory of Mind'?" *Cognition* 21, no. 1 (1985): 37–46, DOI: 10.1016/0010-0277(85)90022-8.

32. Danielle Bons et al., "Motor, Emotional, and Cognitive Empathy in Children and Adolescents with Autism Spectrum Disorder and Conduct Disorder," *Journal of Abnormal Child Psychology* 41, no. 3 (2013): 425–443, DOI: 10.1007/s10802-012-9689-5.

33. Sidney L. Hahn, "Let's Try a Positive Approach," *Foreign Language Annals* 13, no. 5 (1980): 415–417, DOI: 10.1111/j.1944-9720.1980.tb01368.x.

34. Hedda Black and Shelley Phillips, "An Intervention Program for the Development of Empathy in Student Teachers," *Journal of Psychology* 112, no. 2 (1982): 159–168, DOI: 10.1080/00223980.1982.9915373.

35. Lynda A. Haynes and Arthur W. Avery, "Training Adolescents in Self-Disclosure and Empathy Skills," *Journal of Counseling Psychology* 26, no. 6 (1979): 526, DOI: 10.1037/0022-0167.26.6.526.

36. Mirja Kalliopuska, "Empathy in School Students" (Department of Psychology, University of Helsinki, 1983), eric.ed.gov/?id=ED240423.

37. John F. Kremer and Laura L. Dietzen, "Two Approaches to Teaching Accurate Empathy to Undergraduates: Teacher-Intensive and Self-Directed," *Journal of College Student Development* 32, no. 1 (1991), 69–75.

38. Edward V. Pecukonis, "A Cognitive/Affective Empathy Training Program as a Function of Ego Development in Aggressive Adolescent Females," *Adolescence* 25, no. 97 (1990): 59.

39. Claude M. Steele and Joshua Aronson, "Stereotype Threat and the Intellectual Test Performance of African Americans," *Journal of Personality and Social Psychology* 69, no. 5 (1995): 797.

40. Steven J. Spencer, Claude M. Steele, and Diane M. Quinn, "Stereotype Threat and Women's Math Performance," *Journal of Experimental Social Psychology* 35, no. 1 (1999): 4–28, DOI: 10.1006/jesp.1998.1373.

41. P. Matthijs Bal and Martijn Veltkamp, "How Does Fiction Reading Influence Empathy? An Experimental Investigation on the Role of Emotional Transportation," *PLOS One* 8, no. 1 (2013): DOI: 10.1371/journal.pone.0055341.

42. David Comer Kidd and Emanuele Castano, "Reading Literary Fiction Improves Theory of Mind," *Science* 342, no. 6156 (2013): 377–380, DOI: 10.1126/science.1239918.

43. Raymond A. Mar, Jennifer L. Tackett, and Chris Moore, "Exposure to Media and Theory-of-Mind Development in Preschoolers," *Cognitive Development* 25, no. 1 (2010): 69–78, DOI: 10.1016/j.cogdev.2009.11.002.

44. Helen Riess et al., "Empathy Training for Resident Physicians: A Randomized Controlled Trial of a Neuroscience-Informed Curriculum," *Journal of General Internal Medicine* 27, no. 10 (2012): 1280–1286, DOI: 10.1007/s11606-012-2063-z.

45. Laura L. Brock et al., "Children's Perceptions of the Classroom Environment and Social and Academic Performance: A Longitudinal Analysis of the Contribution of the *Responsive Classroom* Approach," *Journal of School Psychology* 46, no. 2 (2008): 129–149, DOI: 10.1016/j.jsp.2007.02.004.

46. L. Brook E. Sawyer and Sara E. Rimm-Kaufman, "Teacher Collaboration in the Context of the *Responsive Classroom* Approach," *Teachers and Teaching: Theory and Practice* 13, no. 3 (2007): 211–245, DOI: 10.1080/13540600701299767.

47. Sara E. Rimm-Kaufman and Yu-Jen I. Chiu, "Promoting Social and Academic Competence in the Classroom: An Intervention Study Examining the Contribution of the *Responsive Classroom* Approach," *Psychology in the Schools* 44, no. 4 (2007): 397–413, DOI: 10.1002/pits.20231.

48. Sara E. Rimm-Kaufman et al., "The Contribution of the *Responsive Classroom* Approach on Children's Academic Achievement: Results from a Three Year Longitudinal Study," *Journal of School Psychology* 45, no. 4 (2007): 401–421.

CHAPTER 7: APPLIED EMPATHY IS COMPASSION

1. Willa Litvack-Miller, Daniel McDougall, and David M. Romney, "The Structure of Empathy during Middle Childhood and Its Relationship to Prosocial Behavior," *Genetic, Social, and General Psychology Monographs* 123, no. 3 (1997): 303–325.

2. P. L. Lockwood, A. Seara-Cardoso, and E. Viding, "Emotion Regulation Moderates the Association Between Empathy and Prosocial Behavior," *PLOS One* 9, no. 5 (2014): DOI: 10.1371/journal.pone.0096555.

3. Harvard University Graduate School of Education, "Making Caring Common Project," mcc.gse.harvard.edu/ (accessed March 17, 2018).

4. Alfie Kohn, "Caring Kids: The Role of the Schools," *Phi Delta Kappan* 72, no. 7 (1991): 496–506.

5. Rosemary S. L. Mills and Joan E. Grusec, "Cognitive, Affective, and Behavioral Consequences of Praising Altruism," *Merrill-Palmer Quarterly* 35, no. 3 (1989): 299–326.

6. David G. Perry, Kay Bussey, and Kathryn Freiberg, "Impact of Adults' Appeals for Sharing on the Development of Altruistic Dispositions in Children," *Journal of Experimental Child Psychology* 32, no. 1 (1981): 127–138, DOI: 10.1016/0022-0965(81)90098-9.

7. Bill Underwood and Bert Moore, "Perspective-Taking and Altruism," *Psychological Bulletin* 91, no. 1 (1982): 143, DOI: 10.1037/0033-2909.91.1.143.

8. James H. Fowler and Nicholas A. Christakis, "Cooperative Behavior Cascades in Human Social Networks," *Proceedings of the National Academy of Sciences* 107, no. 12 (2010): 5334–5338, DOI: 10.1073/pnas.0913149107.

9. Louisa Pavey, Tobias Greitemeyer, and Paul Sparks, "Highlighting Relatedness Promotes Prosocial Motives and Behavior," *Personality and Social Psychology Bulletin* 37, no. 7 (2011): 905–917, DOI: 10.1177/0146167211405994.

10. Lara B. Aknin, J. Kiley Hamlin, and Elizabeth W. Dunn, "Giving Leads to Happiness in Young Children," *PLOS One* 7, no. 6 (2012): DOI: 10.1371/journal.pone.0039211.

11. Netta Weinstein and Richard M. Ryan, "When Helping Helps: Autonomous Motivation for Prosocial Behavior and Its Influence on Well-Being for the Helper and Recipient," *Journal of Personality and Social Psychology* 98, no. 2 (2010): 222, DOI: 10.1037/a0016984.

12. Elizabeth W. Dunn, Lara B. Aknin, and Michael I. Norton, "Prosocial Spending and Happiness: Using Money to Benefit Others Pays Off," *Current Directions in Psychological Science* 23, no. 1 (2014): 41–47, DOI: 10.1177/0963721413512503.

13. Lawrence W. Sherman et al., "Restorative Justice: The Evidence," The Smith Institute, 2007, iirp.edu/pdf/RJ_full_report.pdf.

14. Marguerite La Caze, "The Asymmetry Between Apology and Forgiveness," *Contemporary Political Theory* 5, no. 4 (2006): 447–468, DOI: 10.1057/palgrave.cpt.9300259.

15. Bernard Weiner et al., "Public Confession and Forgiveness," *Journal of Personality* 59, no. 2 (1991): 281–312, DOI: 10.1111 /j.1467-6494.1991.tb00777.x.

16. Institute of Education Sciences National Center for Education Statistics, "Student Reports of Bullying and Cyber-Bullying: Results from the 2013 School Crime Supplement to the National Crime Victimization Survey," 2015, nces.ed.gov/pubs2015/2015056.pdf.

17. Jeff Latimer, Craig Dowden, and Danielle Muise, "The Effectiveness of Restorative Justice Practices: A Meta-Analysis," *Prison Journal* 85, no. 2 (2005): 127–144, DOI: 10.1177/0032885505276969.

18. ABC News, "Woman Ordered to Spend Night in Woods for Abandoning Kittens," November 23, 2005, abcnews.go.com/GMA /LegalCenter/story?id=1322751.

19. Jeremy Hogeveen, Michael Inzlicht, and Sukhvinder S. Obhi, "Power Changes How the Brain Responds to Others," *Journal of Experimental Psychology: General* 143, no. 2 (2013): 755, DOI: 10.1037/a0033477.

20. Emory-Tibet Partnership, "CBCT Compassion Training," Emory University, tibet.emory.edu/cognitively-based-compassion-training/ (accessed March 17, 2018).

CHAPTER 8: THE NEUROSCIENCE OF SELF-CONTROL

1. Richard H. Thaler and H. M. Shefrin, "An Economic Theory of Self-Control," *Journal of Political Economy* 89, no. 2 (1981): 392–406, DOI: 10.1086/260971.

2. Vicki Anderson, "Assessing Executive Functions in Children: Biological, Psychological, and Developmental Considerations," *Pediatric Rehabilitation* 4, no. 3 (1998): 119–136, DOI: 10.1080/713755568.

3. Walter Mischel, Yuichi Shoda, and Monica I. Rodriguez, "Delay of Gratification in Children," *Science* 244, no. 4907 (1989): 933–938, DOI: 10.1126/science.2658056.

4. Walter Mischel and Ebbe B. Ebbesen, "Attention in Delay of Gratification," *Journal of Personality and Social Psychology* 16, no. 2 (1970): 329, DOI: 10.1037/h0029815.

5. B. J. Casey et al., "Behavioral and Neural Correlates of Delay of Gratification 40 Years Later," *Proceedings of the National Academy of Sciences* 108, no. 36 (2011): 14998–15003, DOI: 10.1073 /pnas.1108561108.

6. Clancy Blair, "School Readiness: Integrating Cognition and Emotion in a Neurobiological Conceptualization of Children's Functioning at School Entry," *American Psychologist* 57, no. 2 (2002): 111, DOI: 10.1037/0003-066X.57.2.111.

7. Clancy Blair and Rachel Peters Razza, "Relating Effortful Control, Executive Function, and False Belief Understanding to Emerging Math and Literacy Ability in Kindergarten," *Child Development* 78, no. 2 (2007): 647–663, DOI: 10.1111/j.1467-8624.2007.01019.x.

8. C. Cybele Raver and Jane Knitzer, "Ready to Enter: What Research Tells Policymakers about Strategies to Promote Social and Emotional School Readiness Among Three- and Four-Year-Old Children," (policy paper no. 0205, Columbia University Academic Commons, 2002), DOI: 10.7916/d82v2qvx.

9. Sara E. Rimm-Kaufman, Robert C. Pianta, and Martha J. Cox, "Teachers' Judgments of Problems in the Transition to Kindergarten," *Early Childhood Research Quarterly* 15, no. 2 (2000): 147–166, DOI: 10.1016/s0885-2006(00)00049-1.

10. Alix Spiegel, "Old Fashioned Play Builds Serious Skills," Morning Edition, National Public Radio, February 21, 2008, npr.org/templates/story/story.php?storyId=19212514.

11. Bettina Lamm et al., "Waiting for the Second Treat: Developing Culture-Specific Modes of Self-Regulation," *Child Development* 89, no. 3 (2017): e261–e277, DOI: 10.111/cdev.12847.

12. Adam Fine, Laurence Steinberg, Paul J. Frick, and Elizabeth Cauffman, "Self-Control Assessments and Implications for Predicting Adolescent Offending," *Journal of Youth and Adolescence* 45, no. 4 (2016): 701–712, DOI: 10.1007/s10964-016-0425-2.

13. Adam Fine et al., "Does the Effect of Self-Regulation on Adolescent Recidivism Vary by Youths' Attitudes?" *Criminal Justice and Behavior* 45, no. 2 (2017): 214–233, DOI: 10.1177/0093854817739046.

14. Daniel A. Weinberger and Gary E. Schwartz, "Distress and Restraint as Superordinate Dimensions of Self-Reported Adjustment: A Typological Perspective," *Journal of Personality* 58, no. 2 (1990): 381–417, DOI: 10.1111/j.1467-6494.1990.tb00235.x.

15. Adam Fine et al., "Predicting Adolescent Offending," 701–712.

16. Brady Reynolds et al., "Dimensions of Impulsive Behavior: Personality and Behavioral Measures," *Personality and Individual Differences* 40, no. 2 (2006): 305–315, DOI: 10.1016/j.paid.2005.03.024.

17. Grant L. Iverson, "Go/No-Go Testing," in *Encyclopedia of Clinical Neuropsychology*, ed. Jeffrey Kreutzer, John DeLuca, and Bruce Caplan (New York: Springer, 2011): 1162–1163.

18. Adam Fine et al., "Predicting Adolescent Offending," 701–712.

19. Alexander T. Vazsonyi and Gabriela Ksinan Jiskrova, "On the Development of Self-Control and Deviance from Preschool to

Middle Adolescence," *Journal of Criminal Justice* 56 (2018): 60–69, DOI: 10.1016/j.jcrimjus.2017.08.005.

20. Tyler W. Watts, Greg J. Duncan, and Haonan Quan, "Revisiting the Marshmallow Test: A Conceptual Replication Investigating Links Between Early Delay of Gratification and Later Outcomes," *Psychological Science* 29, no. 7 (2018): 1159-1177, DOI: 10.1177/0956797618761661.

21. Katya Rubia, "Functional Brain Imaging Across Development," *European Child & Adolescent Psychiatry* 22, no. 12 (2013): 719–731, DOI: 10.1007/s00787-012-0291-8.

22. Allison C. Waters and Don M. Tucker, "Positive and Negative Affect in Adolescent Self-Evaluation: Psychometric Information in Single Trials Used to Generate Dimension-Specific ERPs and Neural Source Models," *Psychophysiology* 50, no. 6 (2013): 538–549, DOI: 10.1111/psyp.12035.

23. Koji Jimura, Maria S. Chushak, and Todd S. Braver, "Impulsivity and Self-Control During Intertemporal Decision Making Linked to the Neural Dynamics of Reward Value Representation," *Journal of Neuroscience* 33, no. 1 (2013): 344–357, DOI: 10.1523/JNEUROSCI.0919-12.2013.

24. Todd A. Hare, Colin F. Camerer, and Antonio Rangel, "Self-Control in Decision-Making Involves Modulation of the vmPFC Valuation System," *Science* 324, no. 5927 (2009): 646–648, DOI: 10.1126/science.1168450.

25. Hare et al., "Self-Control in Decision-Making," 646–648.

CHAPTER 9: HOW TO HELP KIDS DEVELOP SELF-CONTROL

1. Mark Muraven and Roy F. Baumeister, "Self-Regulation and Depletion of Limited Resources: Does Self-Control Resemble a Muscle?" *Psychological Bulletin* 126, no. 2 (2000): 247, DOI: 10.1037/0033-2909.126.2.247.

2. Roy F. Baumeister et al., "Ego Depletion: Is the Active Self a Limited Resource?" *Journal of Personality and Social Psychology* 74, no. 5 (1998): 1252.

3. Roy F. Baumeister et al., "Self-Regulation and Personality: How Interventions Increase Regulatory Success, and How Depletion Moderates the Effects of Traits on Behavior," *Journal of Personality* 74, no. 6 (2006): 1773–1802, DOI: 10.1111/j.1467-6494.2006.00428.x.

4. Mark Muraven, Roy F. Baumeister, and Dianne M. Tice, "Longitudinal Improvement of Self-Regulation Through Practice: Building Self-Control Strength Through Repeated Exercise," *Journal of Social Psychology* 139, no. 4 (1999): 446–457, DOI: 10.1080/00224549909598404.

5. Megan Oaten and Ken Cheng, "Improvements in Self-Control from Financial Monitoring," *Journal of Economic Psychology* 28, no. 4 (2007): 487–501, DOI: 10.1016/j.joep.2006.11.003.

6. Annie Bernier, Stephanie M. Carlson, and Natasha Whipple, "From External Regulation to Self-Regulation: Early Parenting Precursors of Young Children's Executive Functioning," *Child Development* 81, no. 1 (2010): 326–339, DOI: 10.1111/j.1467-8624.2009.01397.x.

7. Matthew T. Gailliot et al., "Self-Control Relies on Glucose as a Limited Energy Source: Willpower Is More Than a Metaphor," *Journal of Personality and Social Psychology* 92, no. 2 (2007): 325, DOI: 10.1037/0022-3514.92.2.325.

8. Holly C. Miller et al., "Self-Control Without a 'Self'? Common Self-Control Processes in Humans and Dogs," *Psychological Science* 21, no. 4 (2010): 534–538, DOI: 10.1177/0956797610364968.

9. Emer J. Masicampo and Roy F. Baumeister, "Toward a Physiology of Dual-Process Reasoning and Judgment: Lemonade, Willpower, and Expensive Rule-Based Analysis," *Psychological Science* 19, no. 3 (2008): 255–260, DOI: 10.1111/j.1467-9280.2008.02077.x.

10. Joshua J. Clarkson et al., "When Perception Is More Than Reality: The Effects of Perceived Versus Actual Resource Depletion on Self-Regulatory Behavior," *Journal of Personality and Social Psychology* 98, no. 1 (2010): 29, DOI: 10.1037/a0017539.

11. Katharina Bernecker et al., "Implicit Theories About Willpower Predict Subjective Well-Being," *Journal of Personality* 85, no. 2 (2017): 136–150, DOI: 10.1111/jopy.12225.

12. David Tod, James Hardy, and Emily Oliver, "Effects of Self-Talk: A Systematic Review," *Journal of Sport and Exercise Psychology* 33, no. 5 (2011): 666–687, DOI: 10.1123/jsep.33.5.666.

13. Adele Diamond et al., "Preschool Program Improves Cognitive Control," *Science* 318, no. 5855 (2007): 1387, DOI: 10.1126/science.1151148.

14. Dianne M. Tice et al., "Restoring the Self: Positive Affect Helps Improve Self-Regulation Following Ego Depletion," *Journal of Experimental Social Psychology* 43, no. 3 (2007): 379–384, DOI: 10.1016/j.jesp.2006.05.007.

15. Mark Muraven, Dianne M. Tice, and Roy F. Baumeister, "Self-Control as a Limited Resource: Regulatory Depletion Patterns," *Journal of Personality and Social Psychology* 74, no. 3 (1998): 774.

16. Diamond et al., "Preschool Program Improves Cognitive Control," 1387.

17. Diamond et al., "Preschool Program Improves Cognitive Control," 1387.

18. Kevin Rounding et al., "Religion Replenishes Self-Control," *Psychological Science* 23, no. 6 (2012): 635–642, DOI: 10.1177/0956797611431987.

19. Malte Friese and Michaela Wänke, "Personal Prayer Buffers Self-Control Depletion," *Journal of Experimental Social Psychology* 51 (2014): 56–59, DOI: 10.1016/j.jesp.2013.11.006.

20. Paul Karoly, "Mechanisms of Self-Regulation: A Systems View," *Annual Review of Psychology* 44 (1993): 23–52, DOI: 10.1146/annurev.ps.44.020193.000323.

CHAPTER 10: WHAT IS SELF-REGULATION?

1. Michel Audiffren and Nathalie André, "The Strength Model of Self-Control Revisited: Linking Acute and Chronic Effects of Exercise on Executive Functions," *Journal of Sport and Health Science* 4, no. 1 (2015): 30–46, DOI: 10.1016/j.jshs.2014.09.002.

2. Dale H. Schunk, and Barry J. Zimmerman, eds., *Self-Regulated Learning: From Teaching to Self-Reflective Practice* (New York: Guilford Press, 1998).

3. Daphna Bassock, Scott Latham, and Anna Rorem, "Is Kindergarten the New First Grade?" *AERA Open* 2, no. 1 (2016): DOI:10.1177/23328584156166358.

4. Thomas S. Dee and Hans Henrik Sievertsen, "The Gift of Time? School Starting Age and Mental Health," *Health Economics* 27, no. 5 (2018): 781–802, DOI: 10.3386/w21610.

5. Louisa Diffey and Sarah Steffes, "Age Requirements for Free and Compulsory Education," Education Commission of the States, November 7, 2017, ecs.org/age-requirements-for-free-and-compulsory-education/.

6. Adele Diamond and Kathleen Lee, "Interventions Shown to Aid Executive Function Development in Children 4 to 12 Years Old," *Science* 333, no. 6045 (2011): 959–964, DOI: 10.1126/science.1204529.

7. Lev S. Vygotsky, "The Role of Play in Development," in *Mind in Society*, trans. M. Cole (Cambridge, MA: Harvard University Press, 1978), 92–104.

8. D. J. Leong and E. Bodrova, "Self-Regulation in the Early Childhood Classroom," *Early Childhood Today* 18, no. 1 (2003): 16–19.

9. Victoria J. Molfese et al., "Executive Function Skills of 6–8 Year Olds: Brain and Behavioral Evidence and Implications for School Achievement," *Contemporary Educational Psychology* 35, no. 2 (2010): 116–125, DOI: 10.1016/j.cedpsych.2010.03.004.

10. Diamond et al., "Preschool Program Improves Cognitive Control," 1387.

11. Angeline Lillard and Nicole Else-Quest, "The Early Years: Evaluating Montessori," *Science* 313, no. 5795 (2006): 1893–1894, DOI: 10.1126/science.1132362.

12. Lillard and Else-Quest, "Evaluating Montessori," 1893–1894.

13. Rachel A. Razza, Dessa Bergen-Cico, and Kimberly Raymond, "Enhancing Preschoolers' Self-Regulation via Mindful Yoga," *Journal of Child and Family Studies* 24, no. 2 (2015): 372–385, DOI: 10.1007/s10826-013-9847-6.

14. Elena Bodrova, Carrie Germeroth, and Deborah J. Leong, "Play and Self-Regulation: Lessons from Vygotsky," *American Journal of Play* 6, no. 1 (2013): 111.

15. Diamond et al., "Preschool Program Improves Cognitive Control," 1387.

16. James E. Johnson, James F. Christie, and Francis Wardle, *Play, Development, and Early Education* (London: Pearson, 2004).

17. Yuriy V. Karpov, *The Neo-Vygotskian Approach to Child Development* (Cambridge University Press, 2005).

18. Sandra W. Russ and Jessica A. Dillon, "Changes in Children's Pretend Play over Two Decades," *Creativity Research Journal* 23, no. 4 (2011): 330–338, DOI: 10.1080/10400419.2011.621824.

19. Zinadia V. Manuilenko, "The Development of Voluntary Behavior in Preschool-Age Children," *Journal of Russian and East European Psychology* 13, no. 4 (1975): 65–116, DOI: 10.2753/RPO1061-0405130465.

20. Bodrova et al., "Play and Self-Regulation," 111.

21. Jerome L. Singer, "Imagination and Waiting Ability in Young Children," *Journal of Personality* 29, no. 4 (1961): 396–413, DOI: 10.1111/j.1467-6494.1961.tb01670.x.

22. Fa-Chung Chiu, "The Effects of Exercising Self-Control on Creativity," *Thinking Skills and Creativity* 14 (2014): 20–31, DOI: 10.1016/j.tsc.2014.06.003.

23. Brandon J. Schmeichel, Cindy Harmon-Jones, and Eddie Harmon-Jones, "Exercising Self-Control Increases Approach Motivation," *Journal of Personality and Social Psychology* 99, no. 1 (2010): 162, DOI: 10.1037/a0019797.

24. Clancy Blair, "School Readiness: Integrating Cognition and Emotion in a Neurobiological Conceptualization of Children's Functioning at School Entry," *American Psychologist* 57, no. 2 (2002): 111, DOI: 10.1037/0003-066X.57.2.111.

25. Blair, "School Readiness," 111.

26. Susanne A. Denham, "Social-Emotional Competence as Support for School Readiness: What Is It and How Do We Assess It?" *Early Education and Development* 17, no. 1 (2006): 57–89, DOI: 10.1207/s15566935eed1701_4.

27. Benjamin J. Levy and Michael C. Anderson, "Inhibitory Processes and the Control of Memory Retrieval," *Trends in Cognitive Sciences* 6, no. 7 (2002): 299–305, DOI: 10.1016/s1364-6613(02)01923-x.

28. B. Alan Wallace, *Genuine Happiness: Meditation as the Path to Fulfillment* (Hoboken, NJ: John Wiley & Sons, 2005).

29. Jon Kabat-Zinn, *Coming to Our Senses: Healing Ourselves and the World Through Mindfulness* (New York: Hyperion, 2005).

CHAPTER 11: HOW TO WIN AT PARENTING

1. Zoltán Dörnyei and Ema Ushioda, *Teaching and Researching: Motivation* (Abingdon, UK: Routledge, 2014).

2. Linda M. Anderson and Richard S. Prawat, "Responsibility in the Classroom: A Synthesis of Research on Teaching Self-Control," *Educational Leadership* 40, no. 7 (1983): 62–66.

3. Jon L. Pierce, Michael P. O'Driscoll, and Anne-Marie Coghlan, "Work Environment Structure and Psychological Ownership: The Mediating Effects of Control," *Journal of Social Psychology* 144, no. 5 (2004): 507–534, DOI: 10.3200/socp.144.5.507-534.

4. Chantal Olckers and Yvonne Du Plessis, "The Role of Psychological Ownership in Retaining Talent: A Systematic Literature Review," *SA Journal of Human Resource Management* 10, no. 2 (2012): DOI: 10.4102/sajhrm.v10i2.415.

5. Ilona Buchem, "Psychological Ownership and Personal Learning Environments: Do Sense of Ownership and Control Really Matter?" *PLE Conference Proceedings* 1, no. 1 (2012).

6. Sheila J. Cunningham et al., "Yours or Mine? Ownership and Memory," *Consciousness and Cognition* 17, no. 1 (2008): 312–318, DOI: 10.1016/j.concog.2007.04.003.

7. Selen Turkay, "Setting Goals: Who, Why, How," (manuscript, Harvard University, 2014), hilt.harvard.edu/files/hilt/files/settinggoals.pdf.

8. Gary P. Latham and Edwin A. Locke, "New Developments in and Directions for Goal-Setting Research," *European Psychologist* 12, no. 4 (2007): 290–300, DOI: 10.1027/1016-9040.12.4.290.

9. Edwin A. Locke and Judith F. Bryan, "Cognitive Aspects of Psychomotor Performance: The Effects of Performance Goals on Level of Performance," *Journal of Applied Psychology* 50, no. 4 (1966): 286, DOI: 10.1037/h0023550.

10. Judith F. Bryan and Edwin A. Locke, "Goal Setting as a Means for Increasing Motivation," *Journal of Applied Psychology* 51, no. 3 (1967): 274, DOI: 10.1037/h0024566.

11. Edwin A. Locke and Gary P. Latham, "Building a Practically Useful Theory of Goal Setting and Task Motivation: A 35-Year Odyssey," *American Psychologist* 57, no. 9 (2002): 705, DOI: 10.1037/0003-066x.57.9.705.

12. Edwin A. Locke et al., "Goal Setting and Task Performance: 1969–1980," *Psychological Bulletin* 90, no. 1 (1981): 125, DOI: 10.1037//0033-2909.90.1.125.

13. Laura Michaelson et al., "Delaying Gratification Depends on Social Trust," *Frontiers in Psychology* 4 (2013): 355, DOI: 10.3389/fpsyg.2013.00355.

14. *Oxford English Dictionary*, s.v. "discipline (*v.*)," en.oxforddictionaries.com/definition/discipline (accessed March 17, 2018).

15. David J. DeWit et al., "Age at First Alcohol Use: A Risk Factor for the Development of Alcohol Disorders," *American Journal of Psychiatry* 157, no. 5 (2000): 745–750, DOI: 10.1176/appi.ajp.157.5.745.

16. Harris Cooper, Jorgianne Civey Robinson, and Erika A. Patall, "Does Homework Improve Academic Achievement? A Synthesis of Research, 1987–2003," *Review of Educational Research* 76, no. 1 (2006): 1–62, DOI: 10.3102/00346543076001001.

17. Darshanand Ramdass and Barry J. Zimmerman, "Developing Self-Regulation Skills: The Important Role of Homework," *Journal of Advanced Academics* 22, no. 2 (2011): 194–218, DOI: 10.1177/1932202x1102200202.

18. Colin F. Camerer, "Behavioral Game Theory and the Neural Basis of Strategic Choice," in *Neuroeconomics: Decision Making and the Brain* (London: Elsevier, 2009): 193–206, DOI: 10.1016/b978-0-12-374176-9.00013-0.

19. Daeyeol Lee, "Game Theory and Neural Basis of Social Decision Making," *Nature Neuroscience* 11, no. 4 (2008): 404, DOI: 10.1038/nn2065.

20. Chris D. Frith and Tania Singer, "The Role of Social Cognition in Decision Making." *Philosophical Transactions of the Royal Society of London B: Biological Sciences* 363, no. 1511 (2008): 3875–3886.

21. Krueger, Frank, Jordan Grafman, and Kevin McCabe, "Neural Correlates of Economic Game Playing," *Philosophical Transactions of the Royal Society B: Biological Sciences* (2008): 3859-3874. DOI: 10.1098/rstb.2008.0165.

22. Kristin Hansen Lagattuta, Larry Nucci, and Sandra Leanne Bosacki, "Bridging Theory of Mind and the Personal Domain: Children's Reasoning about Resistance to Parental Control," *Child Development* 81, no. 2 (2010): 616–635, DOI: 10.1111/j.1467-8624.2009.01419.x.

23. Kathleen H. Corriveau et al., "To the Letter: Early Readers Trust Print-Based over Oral Instructions to Guide Their Actions," *British Journal of Developmental Psychology* 32, no. 3 (2014): 345–358, DOI: 10.1111/bjdp.12046.

CONCLUSION: PARENTS SHAPE FUTURE FREE WILL

1. Kimberly D. Tanner, "Promoting Student Metacognition," *CBE-Life Sciences Education* 11, no. 2 (2012): 113–120, DOI: 10.1187/cbe.12-03-0033.

2. Manita van der Stel, "Development of Metacognitive Skills in Young Adolescents: A Bumpy Ride to the High Road" (thesis, Developmental and Educational Psychology, Faculty of Social and Behavioural Sciences, Leiden University, 2011), openaccess .leidenuniv.nl/bitstream/handle/1887/17910/07.pdf?sequence=8.

3. Robert O. Doyle, "Free Will: It's a Normal Biological Property, Not a Gift or a Mystery," *Nature* 459, no. 7250 (2009): 1052, DOI: 10.1038/4591052c.

4. Roy F. Baumeister, E. J. Masicampo, and C. Nathan DeWall, "Prosocial Benefits of Feeling Free: Disbelief in Free Will Increases Aggression and Reduces Helpfulness," *Personality and Social Psychology Bulletin* 35, no. 2 (2009): 260–268, DOI: 10.1177/0146167208327217.

5. Gilad Feldman, Subramanya Prasad Chandrashekar, and Kin Fai Ellick Wong, "The Freedom to Excel: Belief in Free Will Predicts Better Academic Performance," *Personality and Individual Differences* 90 (2016): 377–383, DOI: 10.1016/j.paid.2015.11.043.

6. John Piper, "What Is Freedom? Filling Out the Passion," *Desiring God*, January 7, 2012, desiringgod.org/articles /what-is-freedom-filling-out-the-passion-2012-message.

APPENDIX 1: COMMONSENSE NEUROANATOMY

1. Philipp Mergenthaler et al., "Sugar for the Brain: The Role of Glucose in Physiological and Pathological Brain Function," *Trends in Neurosciences* 36, no. 10 (2013): 587–597, DOI: 10.1016/j.tins.2013.07.001.

2. Dheeraj S. Roy et al., "Distinct Neural Circuits for the Formation and Retrieval of Episodic Memories," *Cell* 170, no. 5 (2017): 1000–1012, DOI: 10.1016/j.cell.2017.07.013.

3. Jeremy D. Schmahmann and David Caplan, "Cognition, Emotion and the Cerebellum," *Brain* 129, no. 2 (2006): 290–292, DOI: 10.1093/brain/awh729.

4. American Association for Advancement in Science, "Selections from Science: The Nobel Prize in Physiology or Medicine," *Science*, sciencemag.org/site/feature/data/nobelprize/ (accessed March 17, 2018).

5. Michael Davis and Paul J. Whalen, "The Amygdala: Vigilance and Emotion," *Molecular Psychiatry* 6, no. 1 (2001): 13, DOI: 10.1038/sj.mp.4000812.

APPENDIX 2: EPIGENETICS

1. Francis Galton, *Hereditary Genius: An Inquiry into Its Laws and Consequences* (London: Macmillan, 1869), 14, galton.org/books/hereditary-genius/text/pdf/galton-1869-genius-v3.pdf.

2. John Broadus Watson, *Behaviorism*, rev. ed. (Chicago: University of Chicago Press, 1930), 104.

3. Avijit Hazra and Santanu Kumar Tripathi, "Folic Acid Revisited," *Indian Journal of Pharmacology* 33, no. 5 (2001): 322–342.

4. Nicholas D. E. Greene, Philip Stanier, and Andrew J. Copp, "Genetics of Human Neural Tube Defects," *Human Molecular Genetics* 18, no. R2 (2009): R113–R129, DOI: 10.1093/hmg/ddp347.

5. National Institutes of Health Office of Dietary Supplements, "Folate: Dietary Supplement Fact Sheet," March 2, 2018, ods.od.nih.gov/factsheets/Folate-HealthProfessional/.

6. Aisling A. Geraghty et al., "Nutrition During Pregnancy Impacts Offspring's Epigenetic Status: Evidence from Human and Animal Studies," supplement, *Nutrition and Metabolic Insights* 8, no. S1 (2015): 41–47, DOI: 10.4137/nmi.s29527.

7. Keith M. Godfrey et al., "Epigenetic Gene Promoter Methylation at Birth Is Associated with Child's Later Adiposity," *Diabetes* 60, no. 5 (2011): 1528–1534, DOI: 10.2337/db10-0979.

8. Frederica Perera and Julie Herbstman, "Prenatal Environmental Exposures, Epigenetics, and Disease," *Reproductive Toxicology* 31, no. 3 (2011): 363–373, DOI: 10.1016/j.reprotox.2010.12.055.

9. Qingying Meng et al., "Systems Nutrigenomics Reveals Brain Gene Networks Linking Metabolic and Brain Disorders," *EBioMedicine* 7 (2016): 157–166, DOI: 10.1016/j.ebiom.2016.04.008.

10. Jennifer T. Wolstenholme, Emilie F. Rissman, and Jessica J. Connelly, "The Role of Bisphenol A in Shaping the Brain, Epigenome and Behavior," *Hormones and Behavior* 59, no. 3 (2011): 296–305, DOI: 10.1016/j.yhbeh.2010.10.001.

11. Antonia M. Calafat et al., "Urinary Concentrations of Bisphenol A and 4-Nonylphenol in a Human Reference Population," *Environmental Health Perspectives* 113, no. 4 (2005): 391, DOI: 10.1289/ehp.7534.

12. Danielle Simmons, "Epigenetic Influence and Disease," *Nature Education* 1, no. 1 (2008): 6.

APPENDIX 3: NEUROMYTHS VERSUS NEUROFACTS

1. Frances H. Rauscher, Gordon L. Shaw, and Catherine N. Ky, "Music and Spatial Task Performance," *Nature* 365, no. 6447 (1993): 611, DOI: 10.1038/365611a0.

2. Frances H. Rauscher and Sean C. Hinton, "The Mozart Effect: Music Listening Is Not Music Instruction," *Educational Psychologist* 41, no. 4 (2006): 233–238, DOI: 10.1207/s15326985ep4104_3.

3. Deena Skolnick Weisberg et al., "The Seductive Allure of Neuroscience Explanations," *Journal of Cognitive Neuroscience* 20, no. 3 (2008): 470–477, DOI: 10.1162/jocn.2008.20040.

4. Google Scholar (database), scholar.google.com/.

5. What Works Clearinghouse (database), National Center for Education Evaluation and Regional Assistance, ies.ed.gov/ncee/wwc/.

6. PubMed (database), US National Library of Medicine and the National Institutes of Health, ncbi.nlm.nih.gov/pubmed/.

7. APA PsycNET (database), American Psychological Association, psycnet.apa.org/search.

8. Online Mendelian Inheritance in Man (database), National Center for Biotechnology Information, www.omim.org/.

Acknowledgments

THANK YOU to Brandi Bowles and Amy Rost for your expert help getting this science out in the world and making this book a reality.

Thank you to my peer reviewers for your time and neuroscience expertise: Dr. Jessica Couch, Dr. Amy Ryan, Dr. Catherine Croft, and Dr. Carlita Favero, as well as Dr. Shannon Hardie and Dr. Jessica Janiczek.

Mom and Dad, thanks for your support throughout this project.

Seth, thank you for my children and for loving them so much. When we sit back down in Aberystwyth in 20 years, we'll know we did the absolute best we could do for these kids.

Index

About the Author

ERIN CLABOUGH is a mother of four who holds a PhD in neuroscience. Her parenting style has been highly influenced by her neuroscience background.

An assistant professor at a small liberal arts college in Virginia, she teaches biology and neuroscience, and she heads an active research program that investigates how we can alter neuronal synaptic plasticity, how the brain functions over development including fetal alcohol spectrum disorders, and neurodegnerative disease. She is also interested in experiential learning as a way to reflect neuroscience principles in the classroom.

Erin received her bachelor of arts degree in psychology and English literature from Randolph-Macon College in 1997. She worked as a neuropsychological technician for a year before attending a developmental cognitive neuroscience program at the University of Denver, where she was involved in Down syndrome, autism, and schizophrenia research. She received her doctorate in neuroscience from the University of Virginia in 2006, specializing in Huntington's disease and the molecular genetics of neurodegeneration. Afterward, she held a 3-year postdoctoral research position at the University of Virginia in neuroscience and biomedical engineering. Erin's scientific research has resulted in many peer-reviewed journal articles.

She writes for such outlets as *Psychology Today* and the websites mindbodygreen and Today Parenting.

About Sounds True

SOUNDS TRUE is a multimedia publisher whose mission is to inspire and support personal transformation and spiritual awakening. Founded in 1985 and located in Boulder, Colorado, we work with many of the leading spiritual teachers, thinkers, healers, and visionary artists of our time. We strive with every title to preserve the essential "living wisdom" of the author or artist. It is our goal to create products that not only provide information to a reader or listener, but that also embody the quality of a wisdom transmission.

For those seeking genuine transformation, Sounds True is your trusted partner. At SoundsTrue.com you will find a wealth of free resources to support your journey, including exclusive weekly audio interviews, free downloads, interactive learning tools, and other special savings on all our titles.

To learn more, please visit SoundsTrue.com/freegifts or call us toll-free at 800.333.9185.